THIEF

THIEF

The Bizarre Story of Fugitive Financier Martin Frankel

J. A. Johnson, Jr.

LEBHAR-FRIEDMAN BOOKS

New York • Chicago • Los Angeles • London • Paris • Tokyo

Lebhar-Friedman Books
425 Park Avenue
New York, NY 10022

Published by Lebhar-Friedman Books
Lebhar-Friedman Books is a company of Lebhar-Friedman, Inc.

Printed in the United States of America

Library of Congress Cataloging-in-Publication Data

Johnson, J. A., Jr.
    Thief : the bizarre story of fugitive financier Martin Frankel / J.A.
Johnson, Jr.
        p. cm.
    ISBN 0-86730-811-7 (alk. paper)
    1. Frankel, Martin. 2. Embezzlement—United States.   I. Title.

HV6679.J64 2000
364.16'2—dc21
[B]   00-035218

Visit our Web site at lfbooks.com

Thank you, Loredana,
for your love and support.

Acknowledgments

Most of the information in this book comes from my reporting of the Martin Frankel story for *Greenwich Time* as well as additional research I later conducted specifically for this project. I did, however, rely on the news gathering by others for some information, and I therefore wish to acknowledge the fine work of reporters from *The Wall Street Journal, The New York Times, Franklin Review-Appeal, The Blade, The Hartford Courant, CNN,* and *Fortune,* among others.

I talked with many people who knew Frankel either as acquaintances or associates, and most are identified in these pages. But there were several who would speak with me only on the condition of anonymity, and who therefore are not named in the book.

TJ, I am much indebted to you for your help.

Others who provided valuable assistance include Chris Huntington, Peter Robbins, James Walters, Richard Greenburg, Philip Russell, and Steven Cohen.

Thank you Tim Dumas for urging me to write something longer than a fifteen-inch column, and thank you Joe Pisani and Bruce Hunter for allowing me out of the stable.

Lori, *molto grazie* for your Italian translations.

Finally, I want to thank my agent, Peter Sawyer, my publisher, Geoff Golson and my editor, Frank Scatoni, for taking a chance.

Preface

The beginning of the end of the Martin Frankel story began on a typical early-spring day in Greenwich on May 5, 1999. In other words, there wasn't a heck of a lot happening.

Things were no different for me, the police reporter for the town's only daily newspaper. I had returned to the newsroom from making my rounds at the police station with no serious crime to report, my notebook containing just the usual petty larcenies, vandalism, and other odds and ends that took me no time to write up for the daily police blotter.

With most of the day left to kill, I was open for general assignment.

After writing a story about a Greenwich volunteer who was heading west to aid Oklahoma tornado victims, my 8:30-A.M.-to-4:30-P.M. shift ended as uneventfully as it began, and I headed for my home in New York.

Two hours later, the tinny words of a fire department dispatcher came through the scanner at my vacated desk: "Station 1, Station 5. Respond. 889 Lake Avenue. Automatic fire alarm. Repeat: Station 1, Station 5. Respond. 889 Lake Avenue. Automatic fire alarm."

The scratchy broadcast seemed no different from countless others that are heard throughout the newsroom every day. Automatic fire alarm activations barely register as a blip on a reporter's radar screen, for they nearly all end up the same way: "Alarm set off in error, all engines returning." It's usually only when a second alarm goes out that ears perk up.

Assistant city editor Katie Mulvaney's ears perked up when she heard over the scanner a fire officer ordering subordinates to be careful with the contents of a file cabinet. Mulvaney directed one of the night reporters, Eric Rimbert, to shoot a call to the fire department to find out what was happening. When he did, Rimbert was told surprisingly little.

When I arrived at the paper the next day I picked up a copy of *Greenwich Time* and began reading. On the bottom of page four I saw the headline above the two-inch blurb Rimbert had written about the previous evening's incident: "Fire at Lake Ave. Home Investigated."

Judging from the story's length and placement, I didn't think it was anything significant. But when I began reading I knew I would be following up, because it looked like a case of arson—a police story.

"Fire officials are investigating what they label a suspicious fire that occurred last night at a Lake Avenue home," the story said.

When I read where the fire had been, the address jumped off the page— 889 Lake Avenue. It was the same property that had been implicated two years earlier in the strange death of Frances Burge. Even though the death had officially been declared a suicide, I recalled how the detectives who investigated the incident had murmured about bizarre goings-on at the Lake Avenue address.

I sensed this would be more than a routine follow-up when I read the last of the story's three short paragraphs:

"Two fire trucks responded, and when they arrived, firefighters found smoke in the building and a small fire burning in a file cabinet. No one was home when firefighters arrived."

I immediately went rummaging through my file cabinets looking for the notes I had taken two years before when Frances Burge's suicide was a local news story.

Knowing at least a tiny bit of the history at 889 Lake Avenue, I of course was brimming with questions upon arriving at the police station the morning of May 6.

A press release that the police department had prepared held none of the answers.

The Greenwich Police Department is actively investigating the fire, which occurred at 889 Lake Avenue on May 5, 1999. Numerous leads have been received and followed up. Many avenues of investigation are currently open and active. It would be inappropriate for the Department to comment further on the nature of these leads at this time. Progress is being made and a successful conclusion to this investigation is anticipated.

Every cop I approached—even my most reliable sources—seemed to be reading from the same script.

"Sorry, Joe, I have to refer you to the chief on this one" was the common refrain.

So I went to see the town's top cop, Chief Peter Robbins.

"I'm sorry, Joe, but I can't talk about it," Robbins said with grave earnestness.

"C'mon, Chief, what's really happening?" I entreated him. "Can't you even give me an idea *off* the record? I mean, what the hell are you doing up there, pulling bodies from crawl spaces or something?"

Robbins shot me a look and replied, "Look, Joe, when this is all over, you'll understand why I can't say anything."

I then told him that I had heard about a file cabinet that had been set on fire. Robbins finally offered a partial explanation saying that, among other scenarios, his detectives were looking into the possibility that the fire might have been intentionally set to destroy evidence of a crime. Evidence of what, though, he would not say.

Two days later I found out the extreme to which the police chief was attempting to keep things under wraps. I was shown a copy of a memorandum he had issued:

FROM: Chief Peter J. Robbins
DATE: May 8, 1999
SUBJECT: Police Investigation, 889 Lake Ave., Greenwich, Conn.

As most are aware a police investigation is ongoing at the aforementioned address, as a result of the report of a fire at that location. As a matter of standard procedure during a police investigation, NO POLICE PERSONNEL OR OTHER POLICE DEPARTMENT EMPLOYEES ARE TO MAKE ANY COMMENTS TO ANYONE CONCERNING THEIR KNOWLEDGE OF THE INVESTIGATION.

Should inquiries be made by anyone they are to be directed to the Captain of Detectives or the Chief of Police.

You should understand that this is a DIRECT ORDER!

Going through my old notes, I refreshed my memory about how in 1997 a man named Mike King was renting 889 Lake Avenue, as well as the adjacent estate at 881 Lake Avenue where Frances Burge's body was found. The notes showed that several neighbors harbored strong doubts about the official suicide designation and shared a keen uneasiness about their reclusive neighbor.

They said that after King moved into 881 Lake Avenue he had taken extraordinary security measures, including the installation of a six-foot fence around the six-acre property's perimeter, high-intensity lighting, motion detectors, and surveillance cameras. But what had really made the neighbors uneasy was that they regularly saw many young women coming and going from King's houses. One rumor going around said King was either running a prostitution ring or making skin flicks. Others thought King might be a major narcotics trafficker. One neighbor believed King's security guards not only carried firearms but had access to a missile launcher.

In the days following the suicide I attempted to learn more about Mike King and what was really going on at his two estates. Looking through land records in the basement of Greenwich Town Hall, I found that King owned neither 881 Lake Avenue nor 889. I searched the Internet for references about Mike King, Michael King, and M. King, but found none.

I had also spoken with Greenwich police detectives Scott McConnell and Ed Zack, who were assigned to investigate Frances Burge's death. They had told me that while interviewing King for their report, they learned that the man's name was actually Martin Frankel, and that he was using an alias because he was convinced a man from his hometown in Ohio wanted him dead for having stolen his wife and sent him to prison.

The detectives further told me that they had learned Frankel had been accused of fraud by the United States Securities and Exchange Commission (SEC) and in 1992 was banned for life from investing other people's money. My notes also showed that the detectives' interview had taken place in a room guarded by a cipher lock and filled with at least thirty computers, and that Frankel had boasted that he did all the investing for "a major Swiss bank."

On top of that, the detectives told me of having seen evidence that either Frankel or a person living with him was possibly engaged in serious sadomasochistic activities. The evidence consisted of S&M videotapes, handcuffs, and a riding crop. The dead girl's father had told police that one of his daughter's duties at the Greenwich compound was to accept UPS deliveries of packages of money.

Believing that whatever business Frankel was practicing might have been in violation of the SEC ban, the detectives passed on their information to federal authorities. They never heard back.

At that time I had definitely smelled a story, but I was handcuffed by the fact that after the Burge death investigation was closed, I could not confirm that any law enforcement agencies were actively investigating Frankel. *Greenwich Time* could not in good conscience publish a story about how a man who had a run-in with the government years ago was renting the property where a suicide had occurred.

I had driven out to Frankel's house to try to see for myself what was going on there but was chased away by someone who appeared to be a plainclothes security guard packing a handgun. I made occasional inquiries after that, but for all intents and purposes the story was dead.

The May 5 fire suddenly changed all that.

After a day or two of intense investigation, *Greenwich Time* uncovered enough information about Frankel's empire to justify publishing what had been learned from police sources two years ago—that the investigation involved a property owned by the shell company of a disgraced former securities dealer from Toledo named Martin Frankel.

Although a roadblock manned by uniformed Greenwich police officers blocked the entrance to Frankel's cul-de-sac, I got onto the property anyway. Borrowing a horse from one of Frankel's neighbors, as well as a riding hat and boots, I must have looked like a backcountry Greenwich gentleman as I rode by the checkpoint unchallenged. Upon riding up the driveway of 889 Lake Avenue, I was confronted by two FBI agents. As one of the agents led me back down the driveway, she pointed to the house across the street and said, "And stay away from that property as well."

The mounted excursion gave *Greenwich Time* another story: "The minor but suspicious fire involving a file cabinet in a house that had been connected with a young woman's suicide under unusual circumstances was now being investigated by the U.S. Justice Department."

Not only that, the investigation encompassed a second property.

Word of what was being reported in the Greenwich newspaper had somehow made its way down to Jackson, Mississippi, where state insurance regulators had been conducting an investigation of their own. Eventually

Mississippi Department of Insurance special projects director Shepard G. Montgomery called the newsroom asking for copies of the follow-ups to the fire investigation. I asked Montgomery to explain why his department was interested in a fire hundreds of miles away in Greenwich, Connecticut. He reluctantly said that the fire coincided with his department's inquiry into certain "fiscal irregularities" involving investments three Mississippi insurance companies had made through Liberty National Securities, a brokerage that listed 889 Lake Avenue as its address.

In exchange for the articles, Montgomery sent a copy of a document filed May 10 in Mississippi's Hinds County chancery court in which state insurance commissioner George Dale sought authority to take over the three insurance companies. The petition stated: "During the course of administrative supervision, the commissioner or his representatives have attempted to obtain confirmation as to the amount, value, location and form of the insurance company assets invested through its securities broker, Liberty National Securities Inc." After noting the insurance company officers were unable to provide the requested information, Dale's petition concluded, "There is reasonable cause to believe there may have been embezzlement from the insurer, wrongful sequestration or diversion of the insurer's assets, forgery or fraud affecting the insurer, or other illegal conduct that if established would endanger assets in an amount threatening the solvency of the insurer."

The amount of money that the three insurance companies had entrusted to the Greenwich brokerage and were now unable to account for totaled $171 million. But that was not all.

I soon learned that the Mississippi companies were only a few of about a dozen firms in five states owned by Thunor Trust, an entity that had been established in 1991 in Tennessee, and that all of those firms had invested huge sums of money with the Greenwich brokerage. I then found out that Thunor had been formed by a group of silent investors with direct links to Frankel.

I spent most of May 20 on the telephone with officials in Mississippi, Missouri, Arkansas, Tennessee, and Oklahoma, finding out how much money their insurance companies were missing. Hundreds of pages of court documents were faxed to the newsroom from all five states. When I got off the phone with the final official, Oklahoma insurance commissioner Carroll Fisher, the magnitude of the burgeoning scandal finally set in.

The next day's *Greenwich Time* ran the banner headline "Estate May Be

Linked to $1 Billion Loss." The story that followed mapped out what appeared to be a massive fraudulent enterprise that had been masterminded from Frankel's Greenwich mansion. The story also contained the Oklahoma insurance official's description of the apparent embezzlement scheme's scope, which turned out to be the understatement of the year: "We are very concerned about the missing money," Fisher said. "This is potentially a very large problem. Nine hundred fifty million dollars isn't the kind of money that just disappears."

Through several interviews with friends, business consultants, employees, and other associates of Frankel over the next few weeks, an unbelievable portrait of Frankel emerged. Martin R. Frankel, a skinny, timid man from the Midwest, had transformed a Greenwich mansion into his own version of *Citizen Kane*'s Xanadu—a palace where he used millions of embezzled dollars to live out a twisted version of the American dream.

INTRODUCTION

*"The point is, ladies and gentlemen, that greed, for lack of
a better word, is good.
Greed is right. Greed works.
Greed cuts through, clarifies, and captures the essence
of the evolutionary spirit."*

—Gordon Gekko (Michael Douglas)
in the movie *Wall Street*

One humid afternoon in August 1997 a woman's shrill scream pierced the
smug silence in the backcountry of Greenwich, Connecticut, one of the
richest communities in America.

The shriek had not come from a victim who was being murdered, as
one neighbor who heard it had thought; it came from the mouth of a panicked young woman who had just found a lifeless body dangling from a
rope beneath the rear deck of a secluded mansion. Authorities concluded
that twenty-two-year-old Frances Burge had committed suicide, but the
strange circumstances surrounding her life and death would trouble both
police and neighbors for many months to come.

Burge had been one of several devoted female followers of Martin R.
Frankel, a self-taught investment guru who claimed to have earned hundreds of millions of dollars through a unique market analysis formula he
had developed years ago. Those women formed what might be described as
a money-worshiping cult—a cadre of materialistic women that Frankel surrounded himself with inside the fortified compound he created out of adjacent estates he owned in Greenwich.

None of his well-heeled neighbors knew Frankel; he had always lived as
a recluse. For many months after Burge's death there were whispers of possible narcotics trafficking and a prostitution ring as the neighbors tried
explaining the steady flow of limousines and young women they saw going
in and out of Frankel's Lake Avenue compound.

All rumors were put to rest in early 1999, when a seemingly small incident revealed a reality that was in some respects stranger than fiction. Smoke from a small fire had activated an alarm, bringing firefighters and police to the Frankel compound. When the authorities got there, they found that the house had been mysteriously ransacked and abandoned. The cause of the fire: the combustion of massive quantities of paper and files. Mounds of paperwork were deliberately being burned in a fireplace, and the ensuing fire had raged out of control.

As they picked through the looted mansion, police found such tantalizing clues as a to-do list that noted some necessary chores such as "launder money." They also found a few astrological charts that had been created to answer such questions as "Will I go to prison?"

Other documents seemed to indicate that Frankel—from within his lavish cocoon—had masterminded one of the largest, most bizarre embezzlement schemes in American history, one that rocked the insurance and investment industries and spanned the globe from the unassuming town of Toledo, Ohio, to the gilded dome of the Vatican.

It was a massive pyramid scheme in which Frankel used money he stole from investment clients to buy one insurance company after another. Each time he bought a new company for a few million dollars, he instantly had access to cash reserves worth many millions more—money that he quickly siphoned to a Swiss bank account. From that account, Frankel would launder his money by making such large purchases as luxury automobiles and real estate. He would also have the Swiss bank send regular shipments of traveler's checks, usually in bundles of $50,000.

So what had begun as a local arson investigation quickly turned into an international manhunt for one of the FBI's most wanted fugitives. But Martin Richard Frankel, the self-anointed investment guru, was in the end nothing more than a con man, a fast-talking purveyor of snake oil. He had used deceit and keen manipulative powers to create a false persona that was removed as far as possible from the reality of the insecure little boy from Ohio. Though he had often bragged of being a genius, Frankel was only a slick salesman who spent his whole life convincing others that he was a genius.

He was James Gatz incarnate, the small-town midwestern boy of F. Scott Fitzgerald's imagination who moved east to reinvent himself in mythological proportions as the mysterious Jay Gatsby. Like Gatz, Frankel needed to adopt a new identity to make his metamorphosis complete. Actually, he opted for quite a few identities—David Rosse, Mike King, and Eric Stevens, to name just some.

Whatever name they knew him by, a collection of rich and powerful people had become so enamored with Frankel and his apparent knack for creating great wealth that they left themselves wide open to being bamboozled. Others had simply ignored their suspicions and turned a blind eye to wrongdoing just to be near Frankel, so that they too could profit from Frankel's myriad schemes.

Despite the many red flags that should have indicated that something was terribly amiss, several influential people were taken in by Frankel's goofy charm. Among the marks were a former federal prosecutor and policy adviser to President Reagan, and a onetime ambassador to the Soviet Union who remained an influential Beltway lawyer. Several top officials within Vatican City were also duped by the wayward investor.

And then there were the lawyers, accountants, business consultants, and other professionals who should have been able to smell a scam a mile away but instead found themselves on Frankel's growing list of suckers or accomplices.

Demonstrating a total disregard for the law, Frankel was on the prowl for more embezzlement opportunities right up until the day his house of cards collapsed around him. It took the fire at the Greenwich mansion to pull aside the curtain and reveal the wizard for what he really was—an emotionally frail and disturbed man who used fraudulent claims and ruthless cunning to live luxuriously at the expense of others.

THIEF

Chapter One

The Frankel saga began in a place not dissimilar to the North Dakota of James Gatz.

The birthplace of Martin Richard Frankel came into existence out of a bloodless, five-day conflict in 1836 between the state of Ohio and the Michigan Territory. To the victors went 468 acres of swampy lowlands called the Toledo Strip, where the Maumee River and Swan Creek converge before emptying into Lake Erie.

After claiming the swamps from the amphibious denizens from which the city earned the nickname "Frog Town," Toledo steadily grew to become one of the nation's most important industrial centers. Oil refineries sprang up like mushrooms along the Maumee, and Toledo was the end of the line for mile-long trains hauling grain from the Great Plains states. The Port of Toledo became one of the world's busiest freshwater ports, and from it a steady stream of grain-laden barges and oil tankers made sail across Lake Erie and headed for destinations in the Northeast and overseas. Another of Toledo's nicknames, "Glass City," derives from the Corning glass factory, which had made the city one of the world's largest glass-producing centers and today remains an integral part of the city's economy.

Despite its prosperity, the city had to continually overcome negative images. One image in particular came about during Prohibition. The Toledo Strip was given its name by the author Washington Irving after he had served as ambassador to Spain and became familiar with that country's

Toledo, an early center of Catholic culture. "Unholy Toledo," as the Ohio city came to be called in mocking allusion to its European namesake, was widely known as a haven for bootleggers, gangsters, corrupt politicians, and other scoundrels. As a main railroad terminus for trains hauling grain from the Midwest, and with its close proximity to the Canadian border, it was very easy for criminals to slip in and out of Toledo unnoticed, and made for a convenient entry point for illegal hooch from up north.

After World War II Toledo's economy flourished as a beneficiary of the robust automobile industry that was headquartered in nearby Detroit. Unemployment was negligible, as many plants for assembling vehicles and producing related components had sprung up in Toledo and the surrounding areas, supplying work for all who wanted it. But after several decades of prosperity Toledo found itself smack dab in the middle of the "Rust Belt," as the northern industrial regions came to be known during the great industrial meltdown of the late 1970s and early 1980s.

Thousands of blue-collar workers were thrown out of work and the doors of their factories were chained for good. The unemployment rate nearly tripled to 12.6 percent in only a few years. Mass emigration of laid-off workers looking for jobs caused the city's population to dwindle by more than 70,000.

Amid this decline, the best this gritty city of boarded-up factories and warehouses seemed able to offer the rest of the world was that it was the hometown of a television character popularized by actor Jamie Farr. In the hit television series M*A*S*H, Corporal Klinger was a cross-dressing soldier desperately seeking a Section 8 discharge out of the Korean War. Toledo was also the home of Corporal Klinger's favorite team, the Mud Hens, a professional minor-league baseball organization.

But brighter days seemed to be in the offing, and as the end of the twentieth century neared, Toledo began undergoing a rebirth of sorts. Owens-Corning built a new $100 million headquarters on the banks of the Maumee, becoming the crown jewel of a downtown revitalization project. The city's economy received tremendous boosts when DaimlerChrysler sank $164 million into its Jeep assembly plant in Toledo for retooling and modernization, and Alcoa built a new aluminum auto parts factory nearby. Not far from there, Northstar Steel began construction of a $400 million plant. To attract tourist dollars, the landmark Valentine Theatre was given a face-lift and new attractions were installed at the Toledo Zoo, adding to a cultural life that already featured the world-class Toledo Museum of Art. At this point in its history, Toledo—a resurgent city—certainly did not need the black eye it would soon receive from its native son Martin Frankel.

A thriving textile trade had made Cleveland the nation's largest garment industry center outside of New York City, and it was in nearby Toledo that David Frankel relocated from Harlem to found the Toledo Hosiery and Underwear Company. All five of David's brothers—Artie, Joe, Hillel, Sam, and Leon—also left New York behind, and each at one time or another went to work for David's company as they studied to become lawyers, dentists, and members of other respected professions.

Leon Frankel had earned a law degree at St. John's University and worked as an attorney in New York for sixteen years before joining his brothers in Ohio. Upon relocating to Toledo, Leon boned up on his new state's laws while working for David. After passing the Ohio state bar examination, he went on to have a distinguished career with the Lucas County domestic relations court, where he handled over five thousand cases each year. It has been reported that not a single of Leon Frankel's rulings had ever been overturned before he retired from the court in 1965 as chief referee.

Leon Frankel and his wife, Tillie, a city clerk, first lived in what is known as Old West Toledo, where they had three children, Robert, Martin, and Amy. Martin, the middle child, was born on November 21, 1954.

If the astrological indicators Martin Frankel so trusted are to be believed, Frankel, a Scorpio, would grow up to be an intense, obsessive, and manipulative adult harboring an overwhelming fear of abandonment and annihilation. Scorpios, astrologers say, are good at handling other people's money, and therefore tend to become bankers and money managers. They are attracted to taboos and spend their lives in the gray area between right and wrong. When Scorpios turn criminal, they do so big time.

By all accounts, Martin Frankel was an intensely bright, inquisitive, and even precocious child. He was entirely comfortable being around adults, who were often impressed by the skinny miniature man with black thick-rimmed eyeglasses who talked so seriously about subjects well beyond his years. But when it came to kids his own age, young Frankel was socially awkward and very shy.

"I never remember him having a lot of friends," recalled an elementary school classmate. "He was somewhat of a loner and somewhat different."

Not much is known about the relationships the young Frankel had with his parents and siblings while growing up, but it is clear that Frankel had an unhappy childhood. He would later tell acquaintances that he had been subjected to constant emotional and sometimes physical abuse. One of those acquaintances, Ted Bitter, recalled how Frankel once told of an incident in which his mother had chased him around the house while holding a kitchen knife.

Frankel appeared to have been closer emotionally to his father than his domineering mother, whom he resented because of his inability to please her and live up to her expectations.

"Most of the time, Marty liked to portray his father as a loser, although it was clear he loved his father," said Mona Kim, a woman who later worked for Frankel. "But then, Marty always liked to paint his background as pathetically as possible so that his rise to stardom would seem that much more spectacular."

For most of his life Frankel would suffer from a host of phobias and psychological problems, and in the late 1980s was hospitalized after a nervous breakdown. He later confided to others how he, Robert, and Amy shared a similar "chemical imbalance" of the brain.

Whatever was unique or unusual about Frankel was glimpsed early on by Fulton Elementary School teacher Susan Ochs. In 1964, while teaching her fifth-grade class, Ochs noticed Frankel reading a college-level astronomy textbook.

"I don't want to call him a nerd," the schoolteacher would later reminisce. "But he was in his own little world. Sometimes the really bright kids are all by themselves and thinking about what they're going to do next."

Ochs was the type of teacher who took pride in her students and closely followed their development. She maintained albums containing their class photographs along with newspaper clippings of their activities and accomplishments. One such picture was of Frankel's fifth-grade class dressed in costumes for a school Halloween party. There was young Martin, dressed as Uncle Sam and carrying a poster promoting his candidates for political office: Joe Nice, John Good, and George Citizen. They were all running on a platform of world peace and equal rights.

That Frankel was exhibiting liberal tendencies at such a young age may or may not have been remarkable for blue-collar Toledo. While other classmates learned the ways of the world from the dinner-table grousing of fathers cursing the "commies"—who were trying to take over the world through military might abroad and under the guise of the civil rights movement at home—Frankel and his siblings were exposed to much more reasoned thinking.

Leon Frankel was an ardent Democrat who involved himself in charitable work for much of his adult life. He was an active member of the Old Newsboys of Toledo, a foundation that assisted the city's underprivileged, and a respected member of his synagogue. When young Martin heard discussion in his home about the assassinations of Medgar Evers and Martin Luther King Jr., he did not hear a father applauding the murder of a rabble-rousing "nigger," but listened to a man lamenting the death of leaders in the struggle for equal rights.

Learning at such a young age in this manner to empathize with the oppressed and less fortunate and sympathize with noble causes, Frankel already began to be set apart from his peers in his overwhelmingly white, conservative, and Christian community.

When Frankel was thirteen years old his family moved into a modest ranch house in a post–World War II development in West Toledo called Lincolnshire. The neighborhood was then and is still today called "Little Israel" by Toledo gentiles because of its dense Jewish population.

In the eighth grade Frankel attended Jefferson Junior High School, where it appeared the ethic of civic responsibility within Leon Frankel's progeny was beginning to sprout. Marty Frankel ran for the student council and got elected on the strength of a platform promising that he would work hard on behalf of fellow students to secure them the best possible programs and activities. Although still on the shy side, he also started to become more involved socially, joining school organizations such as the French and chess clubs.

Frankel next attended Whitmer High School. In the shadow of a nearby Chevrolet assembly plant, Frankel continued down a path that was uniquely his own. Just to look at him—an intense, lanky youth who bounced with purpose down the hallways in an easily recognizable rubbery gait—one would sense that this was no ordinary adolescent. His fellow students might have thought Frankel strange, but adults often found his quirky behavior disarming, especially when he punctuated a clever remark or observation with his wry, crooked, gap-toothed grin.

"When he came to my class I found him to be refreshing," recalled one of his teachers, John Weglian, now chief prosecutor with the Special Units Division at the Lucas County Courthouse in Toledo. "He was a very intelligent, extremely well spoken young man, and he participated in class a great deal. He was full of this intellectual energy at all times, and when he wanted to say something in class he would get so excited about what he was saying, but usually in a very charming way. I enjoyed having him in my class."

By the age of sixteen, Frankel had surpassed nearly all of his peers academically, and he was constantly impressing teachers with writings that appeared to be more like postgraduate than high-school-level work.

"He was a lot smarter than I was, and I had seven, eight years on him at the time—maybe even nine years," Weglian said. "To me, Marty Frankel was the most intelligent student I ever taught."

The depth of Frankel's intelligence was starkly illustrated for Weglian when he had his class read the play *The Caine Mutiny Court-martial*. Based on the classic novel by Herman Wouk, the play is about the trial of a group of navy officers charged with mutiny during World War II for taking over their ship after concluding that their captain had gone insane. Their navy lawyer proves the mutineers had acted justifiably under military law but questions whether they had behaved in a morally responsible way against a career officer who had dedicated himself to peacetime defense and the approaching war in Europe while they were enjoying the freedoms of civilian life.

"Marty was the only student in the class who understood the paradox of the defense attorney's final scene," Weglian said.

The former teacher said that he most clearly remembered the reading of *The Caine Mutiny Court-martial* because of Frankel's boundless enthusiasm.

"Marty loved it. He would have liked to have read every role in the play out loud, and he had the opportunity to do so," Weglian said. "Most of the other students gave a very flat reading, but Marty understood what the lines meant and understood how they should be said. Many times a student would read a line improperly, or with not the right inflection, and Marty not only knew what the line meant, he knew how it should sound. He would butt in and say, 'You didn't read that right—it should sound like this,' even though it wasn't his part."

Not only did Frankel "get it" when it came to the story's plot, he might also have closely identified with Captain Queeg as the misunderstood and unappreciated loner. Such an association with a fictional character would become a leitmotif of Frankel's life.

Also by this time, Frankel was giving voice to a set of moral convictions that seemed to be taking firm root.

"I can't remember a specific thing he wrote, but I do know that what he wrote was well written, well thought out, and carried with it a biased liberal sentiment. And it was extremely persuasive," Weglian said. "You have to look at the times—it was the early 1970s, it's after the Chicago riots outside the Democratic convention, the National Guardsmen shooting the students at Kent State, the civil rights movement and the antiwar protesting. All of those things were causes célèbres of the liberals of the time, and Marty Frankel was a true believer. He believed in the sanctity of the individual and championed those causes. He expressed those things sometimes in class, and that was not a viewpoint that was commonly shared by most of the students at that time."

The prosecutor reminisced about how he would sometimes wonder what became of Martin Frankel after high school, and pictured him as having become a politician or a college philosophy professor. "I saw Marty as a liberal do-gooder crusader, and that's what I expected would become of his life," Weglian said.

By his junior year, it wasn't just Frankel's good grades and breadth of knowledge that set him apart from the other students. His appearance loudly proclaimed that he was different, a nonconformist. When he first arrived at Whitmer High, he had dressed the part of a conventional liberal—button-down shirt beneath a corduroy sports jacket with patched elbows. That style gradually gave way to the battle garb of the radical liberal—olive green army jacket, T-shirt, and blue jeans.

With hair that had grown down to his shoulders, Frankel was now rebelling against authority, just like many other antiestablishment youths who were united in their opposition to the Vietnam War, the military draft, segregation, and the many other issues that were dividing the nation.

It was also a time when many youths like Frankel began to ponder the most fundamental of questions: "What is right and wrong? Who am I? Is there a God?" Drug use, which had become an important social ritual for many youths, only fueled the search for truth by seeming to reveal new realities that could not be explained through organized religion and other traditional means. Some looked toward Eastern cultures for spiritual guidance, leading to a surge of interest in meditation, yoga, and astrology. The groundwork was being laid for what is now known as the New Age movement, of which Frankel would become an ardent member.

Frankel became further estranged from his peers when he was placed into Whitmer's fast-track program for advanced students, which involved independent study. He had already seemed a misfit among the high school's three thousand students and did not belong with either of the two major cliques, the "jocks" and the "socials." That he was in the "smart kids" program, which allowed him to come and go pretty much as he pleased, only made those who already didn't like him despise him that much more.

But such snobbishness went both ways. In his dealings with students who were not as smart as he, Frankel would behave condescendingly and even arrogantly. And coming upon people his own age who were brighter than he was, Frankel would either ignore them or become intensely competitive. That is probably why Frankel never befriended, and hardly even spoke with, any of the three highly intelligent boys who lived near him on Stanhope Drive.

"His next-door neighbor, Lee Rosenbaum, was one of the smartest guys I ever knew in my life," said a mutual friend of Frankel's and Rosenbaum's. "Lee had two older brothers, Greg and Gary, and all three were genius material. Lee became a big entertainment industry attorney, and his two older brothers are both successful entrepreneurs. I spoke to Lee after the story about Marty broke, and he told me he and Marty never really spoke, that for some reason Marty never liked him."

Eventually Frankel found camaraderie in an emerging subclique of youths he could relate to—the "heads," a refuge for dispossessed school-age youths who found commonality through rock music, drug use, and anti-establishment attitudes.

Since a large part of Whitmer's student body consisted of children who adhered to or mimicked their parents' staunch patriotism and conservative values, many of the heads were either dropouts or enrolled at other schools. Frankel spent less and less time at Whitmer, and when he stopped showing up altogether, some of the students thought he had moved in with a commune of hippies on the city's Old West End. It was also rumored that Frankel had gotten busted for selling pot and used his father's courthouse connections to have the charges dropped.

While Frankel was still attending Whitmer High, some of the debilitating psychological tics that would dog him the rest of his life began to manifest themselves. Although he managed to finish high school with a grade point average of nearly 4.0, Frankel was notorious among teachers for failing to hand in assignments. For some reason, despite all his intelligence, he was unable to finish what he had started. And he exhibited an intense phobia of test taking, which in essence was really a fear of performing under pressure that would haunt Frankel the rest of his life. Weglian, who taught one of Frankel's independent-study classes, had to ask Leon and Tillie to his house in order to discuss why their son had stopped attending class.

"I explained to them that even though Marty was in an independent program, I would like to see him in class just to verify his existence," Weglian said.

The Frankels sought counseling for their son, and both they and school officials agreed on a psychologist's recommendation that Marty be placed with the high school's home study program. Such an arrangement agreed with the young Frankel. He thrived intellectually within the safe confines of his parents' house, spending countless hours not just on coursework but devouring the contents of books on a wide range of subjects. In this way he was able to earn his Whitmer diploma in what would have been his junior year, in 1971.

That summer Frankel got a job as a busboy at a local restaurant, but it wasn't long before he tired of cleaning up after the remains of meals left by the diners and quit. Besides, it just wasn't dignified for someone with his superior intelligence to be engaged in such demeaning work.

In the fall of 1971 he enrolled at the University of Toledo, a school that, interestingly enough, can boast of an alumnus who became an infamous con artist of an altogether different sort. It was there that Janet Cooke earned a master's degree before going to work as a reporter for the *Washington Post*. In 1981 she won a Pulitzer prize for "Jimmy's World," a riveting story she wrote for the *Post* about an eight-year-old heroin addict. The only problem was the story was fabricated, and Cooke was forced to return the coveted award.

Frankel's college experience could hardly be described as typical. He didn't belong to a fraternity, didn't go chugging beer with buddies at the campus pub, and didn't root on the UT Rockets football and basketball teams. In fact, he hardly socialized at all with other students, and most days after classes he hurried back into the safety of his room, where he preferred to learn about the ways of the world by reading about them.

Academically, college for Frankel was a dismal failure. His test anxiety, which had begun in grade school, had grown worse than ever, and before dropping out after two years, Frankel had racked up nearly two hundred hours of uncompleted coursework. Upon leaving the University of Toledo, Frankel ordered the registrar to seal his record. Some people now believe he did that in order to protect the myth of genius he worked so hard to create.

But one of the courses that Frankel did complete and excelled in was twentieth-century American fiction, in which he would fervently engage in debate over the merits and meanings of a particular piece of literature with the professor, Clarence Lindsay, and the other students.

He took particular interest in Hemingway's *The Sun Also Rises* and repeatedly sparred with Lindsay over the role of one of the novel's characters, Robert Cohn. While Lindsay adhered to the generally accepted view that Cohn was but a foil to the story's protagonist, Jake Barnes, Frankel would argue that Cohn was in fact the hero. The professor sensed that Frankel identified with Cohn's outsider status. As narrator of the story, Barnes makes continual casual but pointed anti-Semitic barbs, commenting on Cohn's prominent nose and "Jewish stubbornness."

But perhaps more important, Frankel disputed the notion that Cohn embodied all the qualities that were despised by Hemingway, the manliest of manly American writers. In fact, none of the four men in the novel represents Hemingway's ideal, although each has certain traits that enable the author to explore what it truly means to be a man. Cohn is the least sympathetic of the characters. He is whiny and morally weak, and has little understanding of others and himself.

According to Lindsay, Frankel overlooked those character flaws and saw Cohn as a romantic figure, a knight in shining armor. Cohn is enamored of a highly promiscuous woman, Brett Ashley, and when Barnes plainly identifies her for what she is, Cohn refuses to see it because he is blinded by his own romantic notion of what his affair with Brett means.

"What Marty Frankel did not see is that Robert Cohn is in love with his role in that romantic fiction he created," the professor said. "American fiction is filled with these stories of men who cannot see women because they have these fables that they want to inhabit. And Marty Frankel, in a sense, in his criticism, repeats Robert Cohn. He doesn't see what Robert

Cohn doesn't see. The reason he doesn't see is by not seeing, he occupies a story. He's at the center of a story that he prefers. It's a question of identity, and by not seeing the reality, then he has a reality that suits him."

After completing Lindsay's course, and even after dropping out of the university, Frankel repeatedly returned to the professor's classroom to continue arguing on Cohn's behalf.

"Over the next five or six years, he would somehow find out when I was teaching (the course), and at the beginning of our discussion there would be a knock on the classroom door, and it would open, and it would be Marty," Lindsay recalled. "He would always be very polite and diffident, and would say, 'Professor Lindsay, would you mind if I sat in on the discussion?'"

Lindsay came to expect Frankel's visit as he would the change in the seasons, and each year he readily welcomed him into his class because of how Frankel, with his peculiar points of view, never failed to stimulate debate among the students.

"It was a great way for my class to have someone stake out a very clearly conceptual argument that way," the professor said. "Marty would always be very patient. He'd let me go through whatever rhetorical strategies I would have for introducing these ideas, and then he would make his point and the other people would argue against him. It really helped with the class discussions. Marty was alone in his point of view, but it was obviously very important to him, or he wouldn't have come back year after year."

After leaving the university, the only job Frankel considered for a while was selling real estate. In 1976 he obtained a broker's license and affiliated himself with a local firm, Brogham Realty. He didn't sell a single property, however.

It was also about then that Frankel first took an interest in business, especially the world of high finance. While in college he had taken some business-related courses, none of which he completed, and audited virtually every economics and political science course the University of Toledo had to offer.

As a result of that exposure, something inside Frankel had clicked. He had begun to understand the dynamic interrelationships between world events and the behavior of financial markets. He realized how those who understood the former could predict the latter. It dawned on him like an epiphany that if he could learn to divine which stocks, bonds, and commodities would benefit from events in the news, he would be an extremely successful and wealthy man.

From that moment on, all things financial became a consuming preoccupation. Although Leon Frankel, who had devoted his life to the law and earned respect from colleagues in domestic relations court, worked hard to support a family of five and admirably serve the community at large, Frankel looked down on his father as a "loser." Marty was not going to keep his nose to the grindstone only to come up with a much shorter nose, trapped for life in a cookie-cutter housing tract. With mere phone calls and taps of his computer keyboard, he was going to use his brain to make more money in a single day than his father earned in a year.

"Marty was kind of a jack of all trades, master of none," said George Windau, one of Frankel's very few college friends. "And then he became a master of one: the stock market, commodities, and currencies."

Frankel decided that what he needed to know could not be found in classrooms. His real education began in earnest when he swapped his textbooks for *The Wall Street Journal, Business Week, Investors Business Daily,* and similar publications that the power brokers of Wall Street relied upon in the same way serious horse race bettors needed the *Daily Racing Form.*

"I spent an enormous amount of time—many thousands, if not tens [of thousands of hours]—devoted to studying all of the financial press," Frankel would later recall at an SEC hearing.

The wiry young man who was a bundle of nervous energy and brimming with intense curiosity had become a fixture at Paine Webber, E. G. Edwards, Merrill Lynch, and other offices in downtown Toledo, looking over the shoulders of securities dealers and asking lots of questions. "I was spending as much time as I could at brokerages, learning how to use the machines and learning from people at brokerages who traded," Frankel said. "If there was a firm with a quote machine where they would let you use it, I was there."

Frankel followed this routine for several years until he felt sufficiently confident in his self-taught knowledge to be no longer just a passive observer in the exciting world of buying and selling. He had decided he wanted to be a player. After all, Ronald Reagan was now president of the United States. Under Reagan's leadership, boardroom visionaries and financial alchemists were going to cleanse the nation of the malaise, stagnation, and defeatism that had set in during the Carter administration—years marked by OPEC oil embargoes, the Iranian hostage crisis, and an invasion of fuel-efficient Japanese automobiles.

The conservative Republican's election in 1980 imbued the nation with its "supply-side economics" ethic that claimed when the rich get richer, everyone benefited. When the bounty overflowed from goblets of the ruling class, it would trickle down to quench the working class and underclass. This sent a powerful "anything goes" message to the financial markets, and once again America's business had become business.

Corporate takeovers appeared to become the new national pastime. Ivan Boesky, Michael Milken, and other arbitrageurs who seemed to make millions between the time they brushed their teeth and ate breakfast became household names on Wall Street. Stories about brokers at Merrill Lynch and Solomon Brothers becoming multimillionaires before their thirtieth birthday were not uncommon.

The sentiment of the era was brilliantly captured by director Oliver Stone in his 1987 film *Wall Street*. Perhaps Frankel saw himself as the movie's Bud Fox, a broker for a second-tier Wall Street firm who idolized Gordon Gekko, a ruthless corporate raider who contemptuously viewed small investors as mere dupes on whom empires are built.

It was also at about this time that Frankel began his fascination with and admiration of some of the nation's most infamous white-collar criminals. Foremost in Frankel's pantheon of swindlers was Robert Vesco.

In 1972, along with forty-one others, Vesco was charged by the U.S. Securities and Exchange Commission with the misappropriation of $224 million from four Switzerland-based mutual funds. At the time, it was the largest financial fraud in history. Vesco was also accused of making an illegal $200,000 contribution to President Richard Nixon's 1972 reelection campaign.

Vesco fled the United States to avoid prosecution, and he moved with his family from country to country to avoid extradition—Costa Rica, Nicaragua, the Bahamas, Antigua, and finally Cuba. He was arrested by Cuban authorities for bilking investors with an unproven cancer-fighting drug. He was sentenced in 1996 and is now serving a thirteen-year prison sentence in Cuba.

So in the mid-1980s Frankel saw the time as being ripe for him to jump into the fray. But first he would need to dip his toes in the water. He slowly began to put his knowledge of the financial markets to the test among some of the clients and traders he got to know at his brokerage firm haunts.

"I told people what would happen, and it happened, and after a while some of the people began to listen to me and, I am certain, take some of my advice," Frankel later recalled. "I didn't do it for monetary gain; I did it with the aim of becoming a broker and eventually having these people as clients."

He would make his first foray into the real world of business in 1985, at John F. Schulte Inc. The small brokerage firm in Oregon, a rural community on Toledo's outskirts, was where Frankel had been spending most of his time as an observer. But it was also at Schulte that he would become enmeshed in a real-life soap opera that would be played out on the front page of the local newspaper. It was a drama that would have a significant impact on the rest of Frankel's life.

Chapter Two

In 1985 Martin Frankel was thirty years old and still living with his parents. He had not known the love of a woman other than the one who gave him birth. And when he finally did fall in love it would be with the wife of his first and only boss in the securities industry. As the third factor in an extremely volatile equation, Frankel came to be blamed by his boss for wrecking his family, destroying his career, and sending him to prison. As a result, Frankel would live in constant fear, thinking that deadly retribution lay just around every corner.

The first factor in the above-mentioned equation was John Schulte, born in 1955 to Wayne and Joanne Schulte of Stony Ridge, Ohio. Wayne Schulte was a respected member of the tiny community of about 350 residents, and had served as township trustee and executive vice president of the local Farmers Savings Bank. John, born in between two sisters, was a serious young man who seemed destined to follow his father into banking and public service.

Upon graduating from the University of Toledo in 1977, the same year his father retired, John immediately went to work at Farmers Savings Bank. He was intent on picking up where the old man left off, and of one day owning his own bank.

The equation's second factor came from Elmore, a small farming community with a population of about six hundred, located several miles east of Toledo in Ottawa County. It was here that a Florida high school student named Preston Howe had gained employment as a farmhand one summer long ago. Working in the golden grain fields that stretched all the way north to Lake Erie was agreeable with young Preston Howe. So was a young woman named Delphine, who still lived in the farmhouse at 32 South Nessen Street where she was born. Howe had found two good reasons to want to remain in Elmore.

Preston and Delphine married and settled on the eighty acres of farmland Delphine's father gave to them, and there he built the house in which Delphine gave birth to four girls. The second oldest of the Howe daughters was Sonia, who, except for Tillie Frankel, would become the most important woman in Martin Frankel's life.

Born December 28, 1959, Sonia grew up to become a pretty, vivacious, and popular teenager. She was head majorette for the Woodmore High School marching band and once recalled that her most memorable moment was "twirling my baton down the football field to 'Baby Face' in the pouring rain and still smiling!" By the time Sonia graduated from high school, the only time she had ventured outside of Elmore was when she attended a band sleep-away camp. But soon after leaving Woodmore High, an adventurous streak emerged that led Sonia to Hawaii, Las Vegas, and then to Europe, where she went backpacking at a time when such an activity would have been unheard-of behavior for a young Ohio farm girl.

After her brief exploration of the outside world, Sonia returned to Elmore and enrolled at the University of Toledo, where she majored in business. On top of her studies she worked as a teller at Farmers Savings Bank, and by the time she graduated from college in 1981 she had risen to become the bank's vice president for marketing. By that time she had begun dating another of the bank's vice presidents, John Schulte. Originally paired with different partners on a blind double date, Sonia and John were attracted to each other after discovering that, among other things, they shared a love of business and a passion for making money.

John and Sonia began to date steadily toward the end of 1980, and during the several months of their courtship they frequently discussed how as a team they could set the business world on fire. They both wanted to raise a family but also agreed that the immediate priority was to create the Toledo area's first discount securities brokerage. Less than a month after tying the knot on October 17, 1981, the couple affiliated with the Dominick and Dominick securities clearinghouse on Wall Street and opened the doors of John F. Schulte Inc.

On the surface, the Schultes seemed to be a happy and dynamic couple, intent on making a mark in both the business world and civic arena. Sonia gave birth to two daughters, Leslie Michele in 1984 and Elizabeth in 1986.

In 1988 John declared his candidacy for the Ohio state senate and finished a strong second in the Republican primary. Following the loss, he and Sonia sent voters postcards thanking them for their support. On the front was a color portrait of domestic bliss: a smiling John and Sonia Schulte with their daughters seated on their laps. Sonia also sent her husband's supporters copies of a handwritten note she had written, which read: "John is not only my marriage partner, he is also my business partner, and a very special person," whom she called "a fighter and a leader." John Schulte, in other words, would be back to fight again.

Sonia was a very capable securities broker, and she and John always seemed to be in competition to be their firm's lead producer. Many of Sonia's clients were elderly men and women who found themselves more at ease with the bright-faced country girl's down-home style than they would be with a more aggressive male. Not in small part due to Sonia, who in addition to managing investment accounts also did the firm's bookkeeping, business at John F. Schulte Inc. was steadily growing. In June 1986, when the Schultes' client list had grown to more than five hundred investors, they relocated their firm from its strip-mall storefront and into a building at 2427 Woodville Road in Oregon, Ohio, that they bought for $170,000.

But there had been serious trouble brewing behind the Schultes' happy facade. On April 14, 1989, Sonia packed her bags and left with her daughters to move back to the Elmore homestead. Her parents bought a used trailer and parked it next to their house for Sonia and the children to live in. Three months later Sonia filed for divorce, alleging that John was an alcoholic and that he physically abused her. Sonia also stated that she and her husband had long ago ceased being intimate and that John sexually abused both daughters, then ages three and five, while taking baths with them.

Two days after Sonia filed for divorce, John retaliated with a lawsuit of his own. Seeking $1.4 million in damages, he alleged that his estranged wife had stolen client lists and other "trade secrets" from John F. Schulte Inc., and accused Sonia of "conversion of [clients'] money for her own use."

The rancor only grew worse after Sonia opened a competing Toledo-area brokerage. Before the couple separated, allegations of check kiting and other irregularities at Schulte Inc. had caused Dominick and Dominick to sever ties with them, at which time the Schultes found themselves a new securities clearinghouse, Thomas F. White and Co. in San Francisco. A new round of insinuations and allegations began in March 1990 when Sonia mailed copies of a letter to current and former Thomas F. White clients that warned them "to use extreme caution in dealing with the former representatives at the Oregon office."

In another letter Sonia advised investors that John Schulte "has been fired by our company *for your own protection*. Please sign the enclosed form to prevent John Schulte from attempting to act as a broker."

Thomas White personally intervened in the dispute and suspended both of the Schultes while he investigated the matter. John, meanwhile, had become affiliated with Great Lakes Equities in Detroit. Thomas White lifted Sonia's suspension and sought to allay investors' concerns in a letter of his own in which he disavowed the letter that Sonia had sent.

White's letter, which acknowledged the Schultes' pending divorce, stated: "We are embarrassed by and apologize for any misunderstanding [Sonia's letters] may have caused. We are sorry to have involved you in this unpleasant episode. I assure you it will not happen again."

On March 29, 1990, *The Blade* ran a front-page story titled "Brokers' Bitter Divorce Splits Business," and then all of Toledo knew about the "unusually messy separation" of John and Sonia Schulte. The story recounted the bitter tug-of-war over the former couple's four thousand clients and made public the sexual abuse allegations against John Schulte.

Immediately after the allegations were made public, most clients of John F. Schulte Inc. closed down their accounts, not wanting to be affiliated with an accused child molester. Monthly earnings for the company plummeted from $70,000 to $7,000.

John was arrested on three counts of sexual assault of a minor, but he claimed exoneration after a judge threw out his case at the end of a six-day trial in April 1993 on the basis that there hadn't been enough probable cause for an arrest. The judge noted, however, that it had been highly improper for John to have bathed with his two young girls.

Later that same year, as John arrived for work the morning of November 11, 1993, he found a dozen federal agents patiently waiting for him in the parking lot. They invited themselves into his offices with a search-and-seizure warrant and carted away box loads of records and documents. The

U.S. attorney for Ohio accused John Schulte of having dipped into clients' accounts for his own use. Schulte admitted to wrongdoing but explained it away by saying he had to in order to pay the mountain of legal bills that had piled up in the three years since the molestation charges were leveled against him. John Schulte was later indicted on one count of wire fraud and two counts of income tax fraud, and in September 1994 he pleaded guilty.

John Schulte was given the maximum penalty of fifteen months in prison, but he served less than half that time. But all the while he was locked up in the federal penitentiary in Bradford, Pennsylvania, he dwelled on what had landed him there and laid the blame for all of his woes squarely at the feet of Martin Frankel.

"Frankel was behind the whole thing—the master manipulator from day one," Schulte later insisted. "No one got in the way of him if he set his course on a target for seek and destruction. And he destroyed me, not just by taking my wife and children, but by making accusations that just weren't true. Frankel was the devil incarnate. He spent his entire day plotting a strategy on how he could destroy me."

Frankel had entered Schulte's life nearly a decade earlier when, in the summer of 1985, the then-thirty-year-old walked into the offices of John F. Schulte Inc. and announced he wanted to open an account. Although he never funded the account, Frankel expressed a keen interest in the markets and asked if he could hang around the office to watch the Schultes' brokers in action.

When introduced to Sonia, Frankel was immediately struck by the pretty young woman's warmth and intelligence. He told Sonia he wanted her to be his personal broker. From that day on, Frankel was a daily visitor to the small brokerage firm, spending hours on end watching the financial monitors and discussing investment strategies with the brokers, especially Sonia. He impressed Sonia with his own knowledge of the dynamics of the various markets, explaining how events such as extreme weather dictated the prices of commodity futures and how certain business developments, including mergers and acquisitions and announcements of large corporate earnings, caused upward swings in the stock market.

Sonia was intrigued by her new client, who had also quickly become a friend and confidant. She told John about Frankel's ideas for investment strategies and of his desire to become a broker, and she urged her husband to hire Frankel. John said he would think about it. When he asked Frankel into his office to discuss a possible position with the firm, Frankel was unable to furnish a proper resume, as he lacked any real experience in the securities field. But he falsely claimed to be still enrolled at the University of Toledo, where he was taking business courses, and said that he was a serious student of the markets. He told of having an IQ of 160, and of how he used that intelligence to develop a sophisticated trading system for picking sure-fire winners that would help to place John F. Schulte Inc. on the Toledo business map.

John was sufficiently impressed by what he heard that he was willing to take a chance on Frankel, and so he hired him as an analyst in January 1986. Frankel was not yet a licensed broker, however, and it took him three tries to pass the Series 7 General Securities Sales Examination to become officially sanctioned to transact trades.

A storage closet at the rear of John F. Schulte Inc. was cleaned out and made into an office for Frankel. The new broker insisted that in order for him to implement his trading strategies he needed all the latest in financial information monitoring equipment, and so he filled his cramped quarters with quote terminals, news wire machines, and television sets.

As days and weeks passed, John Schulte began wondering whether he had made a mistake by hiring the new broker. This guy who professed to have the inside line on the markets talked a great game and had all of the necessary tools, but he had yet to make a single trade.

"Frankel didn't know how to trade—he couldn't trade," John Schulte recalled years later. "He could tell you why the market did everything that it did, but he would only do that in hindsight. Telling someone what the market had done is a lot easier than predicting what it's going to do in the future, and Frankel could not do that.

"Frankel had this air about him that he was so conservative with the clients' money that he was fearful of taking even the most minute step forward for fear that he might lose some of the clients' money. Of course, in the securities industry, principal going up is far better than principal going down when you're transacting. But in the real world, obviously your batting average is not much better than .500. But Frankel, of course, was telling everyone that he was going to trade the markets in a special way, that he was never going to have a losing month, and would never make a transaction that didn't have a greater percentage chance of winning.

"And so he was afraid to trade. He was afraid of defeat, and of the inability of the market to do what he hoped it would do. He didn't have any forecasting abilities."

But perhaps most irritating for John Schulte—a compulsively neat dresser who was concerned about always projecting the proper image to clients and the public—was the fact that Frankel flatly refused to obey the company's dress code. Frankel could not bear to relinquish his baggy blue jeans and flannel shirt for a restrictive jacket and tie. It was an issue over which boss and employee would clash time and time again.

John Schulte also noticed that Frankel seemed to be spending an inordinate amount of time with Sonia. Without Schulte realizing, Sonia and Frankel had found themselves to be kindred spirits, united by their growing dislike of Schulte himself.

In Frankel, Sonia had found a sympathetic listener. She was comforted by being able to confide in this unusually sympathetic man about how her husband was developing a drinking problem and would become violent whenever he drank too much.

Sonia's domestic problems only confirmed for Frankel his belief that John Schulte was a no-good bastard, for he already despised his boss and looked down on Schulte as his intellectual inferior. And he hated Schulte's constant harping on the way he dressed for work. He considered his boss's tirades simply as the ravings of a small and insignificant man using the company's dress code as a means of asserting control.

The two men continually locked horns, but John Schulte found himself unable to get rid of his nonproductive and insubordinate employee as long as Sonia remained a staunch Frankel advocate.

"Every night when we'd go home I'd discuss what a bum and no-good person Frankel was, but Sonia, of course, had a different opinion of that," John recalled. "I'd like to think that Sonia felt sorry for the guy because he was totally inept. She believed in him, and was very insistent on my not letting him go because eventually Marty would lead us to this pot of gold at the end of the rainbow."

Frankel finally had the opportunity to demonstrate his greatness through an unlikely partnership with a tool-and-die worker from nearby Millbury named Ted Bitter. Bitter had accumulated a nest egg of $68,000 and as he neared retirement age was hoping to invest all of it in order to ensure a sufficient income that would support him and his wife, Sharon, into their old age. Bitter knew John Schulte from St. John's Lutheran Church in Stony Ridge, of which they were both members, and Schulte persuaded Bitter to open an account with his firm. One Sunday after church in January 1986, John suggested to Bitter that he drop by the office to meet a promising new broker whom he had recently hired. Bitter made the fateful decision to accept the invitation.

A simple, hardworking, and God-fearing man, Bitter was easily impressed with Frankel's confident, staccato patter as the broker explained in highly technical terms how the markets behaved and why. As he looked around Frankel's cramped office at the rear of the small brokerage firm, he saw all the trappings of a successful trader—video terminals directly linked to the New York Stock Exchange, which gave up-to-the-minute stock quotes and bond prices, other machines that quoted foreign currency exchange rates, and a news wire terminal that flashed constant business news updates. Bitter noticed that Frankel was the only one at John F. Schulte Inc. with such an elaborate array of machines.

Bitter also took note of the many high stacks of newspapers and magazines that cluttered Frankel's office, periodicals with such prestigious names as *The Wall Street Journal, Business Week, Forbes,* and *Investors Business Daily.*

"Those are the kinds of publications Marty studied, and of course that impressed me very much," Bitter recalled. "What also impressed me about Marty was that he tended toward a discipline of trading that concentrated on news. He studied the news and used the news to his best advantage by beating other investors to the punch. He believed very strongly that when a news story broke and you knew how to play that, that gave you an advantage."

Frankel's theoretical approach toward playing the markets in the mid-1980s has since become widely known as day trading. Frankel called it "informational analysis."

In fact, Frankel credited himself with developing the day trading system in the biography/resume he would later distribute to prospective investors. In the five-page document, in which Frankel refers to himself in the third person throughout, the section on Frankel's trading "secret" reads as follows:

Marty Frankel began his active studies of the financial markets in the spring of 1978. Since then he has spent tens of thousands of hours studying the financial markets in an attempt to discover if the short-term swings of financial instruments in our markets can be predicted through scientific methods. Marty Frankel has unearthed a method he uses to predict the movement of financial instruments, a method of prediction he calls "informational analysis."

This method of prediction, which is based on using news events, has yielded between a 92% and 96% rate of accuracy. When the system gives a signal to buy or sell a particular investment instrument, the probability of success in investing is very high. In the construction of this system of financial analysis, Marty Frankel employed the scientific method, i.e., he observed similarities in discrete phenomena, and then he postulated hypotheses to explain the phenomena. He of course also devised obvious methods to take advantage of his knowledge.

With all this supposed knowledge, however, Frankel still was not conducting any business. He lamented to Bitter about his inability to "pull the trigger" on the investment strategies he devised. The phobia that had manifested itself in the test anxiety that crippled Frankel's academic career had reemerged to hamper him professionally in the form of trader's block.

Bitter would constantly plead with his broker, "Marty, make the trade."

The extent to which trader's block flustered Frankel was evident in the way he stumbled over his words in a feeble attempt to explain this affliction during a deposition taken in connection with a later U.S. Securities and Exchange Commission investigation: "It is a very unusual thing for a person who, if a person is very skilled at the markets and, say, a trader's block is if a person devotes, in my case, describes the real thing—a person devotes all their time to an enterprise and is by everyone else's objective evaluation—his clients and other people—is extremely good at predicting what will happen in the markets. If he then doesn't have the guts, or the nerve, or whatever it is to pull the trigger and bet, place the actual, put the money on the line on what he believes, that is a trader's block."

Whether due to trader's block or just plain incompetence, Frankel wasn't pulling his weight, and John Schulte was growing impatient with the young broker's lack of performance. The so-called genius was not earning the company a nickel in commissions. John had also grown tired of admonishing Frankel for not dressing properly in the office. And the uneasiness he harbored concerning his wife's friendship with their employee grew.

When Frankel finally did conduct one transaction on Bitter's behalf, he managed to nearly double his client's investment. John Schulte considered Frankel's success a fluke. But for Bitter, it only bolstered his faith that the eccentric financial whiz was going to make him lots and lots of money.

The final straw for John Schulte came in April 1986 when he was summoned to Dominick and Dominick's headquarters in New York to explain certain irregularities, including the fact that someone with his firm had made misrepresentations when entering into contracts for Dow Jones Telerate machines and a Reuters wire service terminal.

In the mid-1980s, the only way to gain electronic access to the New York Stock Exchange was to lease electronic financial data monitors with the backing of a member of the exchange. Frankel was not going to allow Schulte's refusal to get the equipment stand in his way of getting the tools he needed to master his trade. So he went ahead anyway, falsely identifying himself as an authorized representative of Dominick and Dominick when signing two- and three-year contracts for the financial monitoring devices.

Officers with Dominick and Dominick concluded that because of Frankel's actions—in addition to allegations that the Toledo brokerage was kiting checks from client accounts—John F. Schulte Inc. had become a liability. They gave Schulte ninety days to phase out his affiliation with the New York firm.

Although devastated by the news, John Schulte rejoiced because he now had an ironclad excuse for getting rid of Frankel, one that Sonia could not possibly argue against. The first thing John did upon returning to Toledo was to relieve himself of the thorn that had caused him so much grief.

Frankel did not go quietly, however, and he created a loud and ugly scene in the office. Pointing a bony finger in accusation, he told John Schulte he had brought his problems on himself because he had reneged on an agreement he made to begin paying for Frankel's monitoring equipment after Frankel had been with the firm for a few months.

Schulte said he vividly recalled Frankel's departure because Frankel used "the most vulgar language I had ever heard." Among his parting words, according to Schulte, were: "You'll be sorry for this, John, I promise. I'm going to get you!"

Accompanied by his father, Frankel returned to John F. Schulte Inc. later that day to pack up his monitors and bring them home to Stanhope Drive. There were no further confrontations between boss and former employee, and when Frankel left with his treasured equipment, John Schulte thought he had seen and heard the last of the highly strung man whom he considered to be an obnoxious and insubordinate geek.

A little more than two years later, the night after losing the Republican state senate primary, the telephone rang in the Schulte residence. When John answered, he was surprised to hear Frankel's excited voice on the other end of the line.

"What the hell are you doing calling here?" he demanded.

"I'm calling to speak with Sonia," Frankel said.

"Well, what do you want?"

"John, I've got the ability to buy the bank that you've always wanted to own!"

Schulte ignored Frankel's provocative proclamation.

"Frankel, I wouldn't do any business with you even if you were the last person on earth," he said, and then slammed down the phone's receiver.

John stormed upstairs to the bedroom and demanded an explanation from Sonia as to why Frankel was calling their house.

"Oh, he checks on me often," Sonia responded. "We're friends."

That night John Schulte learned that his wife had been seeing their former employee behind his back since the day he gave Frankel the boot.

"Frankel and I had been at odds, totally, all of the time, but Sonia had a soft spot for him," John Schulte later said. "I mean, she actually felt sorry for him because he certainly wasn't a normal person, a normal man. He was very frail in stature, and when he first came in he acted somewhat wimpish. He had the ability to draw on those emotions of the people who were around him, and Sonia was around him a lot more than I. And, obviously, that relationship was building unbeknownst to me at the time."

The Schultes separated several months later, and John Schulte would come to blame Frankel for everything that went wrong in his life over the next decade and a half. According to Schulte, it was Frankel who convinced Sonia to leave him and then file for divorce. When Sonia went into business on her own, it was Frankel's idea to mail out letters to investors discrediting her estranged husband. When that didn't work, it was Frankel's scheme to break John Schulte by leveling allegations he had sexually molested his own two children. To give credence to the allegations, Frankel bought and paid for a psychologist's report concluding that Leslie and Elizabeth had indeed been sexually abused. And when local authorities refused to prosecute

Schulte on the allegations, it was Frankel who used his father's court connections to bring in a special prosecutor to make a child molestation case. When Sonia moved out of the trailer on her parents' property, it was Frankel who paid for Sonia's apartment in fashionable Ottawa Hills. And, finally, it was Frankel who dropped a dime to the feds, blowing the whistle on illegal business practices that landed John Schulte in prison.

When Schulte fired Frankel, he lost not only an employee but also a good client. At the beginning of 1987 Ted Bitter closed his account at John F. Schulte Inc. He had made a decision to stick with Frankel because, as he later explained, "I believed Marty was going to lead me to that pot of gold on the other side of the rainbow." So on March 30, 1987, Bitter turned over $32,701 to Frankel. The following month he gave Frankel another $41,152, and in so doing effectively relinquished control of his entire life savings.

With Bitter as his sole account, Frankel set up his own brokerage in his bedroom at his parents' house. The tool-and-die worker believed so much in his broker's potential that he chipped in a couple thousand dollars so that Frankel could keep making payments on his leased monitors, and Frankel lined his treasured machines against the wall opposite his bed.

Frankel's next step was to call LaSalle Street Securities in Chicago. He was able to convince the brokerage house over the telephone to let him be its "Toledo branch manager." An agreement was reached without anyone from LaSalle Street ever meeting Frankel or investigating his claims or looking over his track record as a broker. All Frankel had to do was fill out a questionnaire the firm had mailed to him.

Until this point, the only crime of which Frankel may have been guilty was that he had deluded himself and conned others into believing he was some sort of investment guru. But now, as his own boss, Frankel committed his first actual criminal act. He established a company called Winthrop Capital, which he would use to assume the debts on the expensive leased financial monitoring equipment should he go into bankruptcy. On the incorporation document, Frankel listed as Winthrop Capital's president a former friend of his, James Spencer. There was just one small problem, and that was that Spencer hadn't heard from Frankel in years and had no idea his name was being used to commit fraud.

The deceit went further than that. Frankel took the tax identification number assigned to his new company and used it as James Spencer's social security number. On a line that asked for Spencer's net worth, Frankel invented a figure of $1.5 million.

"It was a joke," he would feebly explain years later.

Frankel then opened an account for Winthrop Capital with Mesirow Financial Holdings in Chicago, giving as Winthrop Capital's mailing address not the Frankel residence on Stanhope Drive but a rented private mailbox in Sylvania, Ohio.

"I wanted to hold the option opened [sic] of trading in an account where Mesirow would not know it was me who was doing the trading," Frankel later explained. "And so, I opened it up, which I shouldn't have done."

His reason for renting the private mailbox?

"I was using that address so they wouldn't see that it was my home address," Frankel said.

To attract clients to the Toledo bedroom branch of LaSalle Street, Frankel took out an advertisement in the local yellow pages. It was a display ad larger than those of E. F. Hutton and Merrill Lynch. Coincidentally, the ad was placed side by side with the slightly smaller ad for the Thomas F. White and Co. branch headed by Sonia Schulte.

John Herlihy, who lived in the Toledo suburb of Sylvania, had just retired as a Sears Roebuck salesman and decided to invest his savings in a safe, conservatively managed stock portfolio. Realizing he needed a broker to do so, he began flipping through the phone book and came across the LaSalle Street Toledo branch's advertisement. He was impressed that the brokerage advertised itself as the only firm that "insured" its accounts.

He called the listed phone number and spoke with a man who identified himself as Marty Frankel, the branch manager. Herlihy liked what Frankel had to say, especially when he likened the management of other people's money to a "sacred trust," one that should never be jeopardized through risky and speculative trades.

Listening to Frankel as he authoritatively and reassuringly explained how he would safeguard his money and make only the safest investments, Herlihy surely did not envision the person at the other end of the telephone line sitting on the edge of his bed in his parents' house. The image he likely conjured was that of a man wearing a starched white shirt with tie and seated at his desk in a properly appointed office complete with a receptionist, secretaries, and rows of brokers likewise seated at desks of their own.

Herlihy said he would consider opening an account with LaSalle Street Securities, and Frankel mailed the requisite company brochures, including one he made on his personal computer that touted his alleged credentials as a broker. On March 30, 1987, Herlihy decided to sign over to Frankel all 4,538 shares of his Sears stock, which had a total value of $231,178.28. He apparently did not think it was strange that the receipt Frankel gave him was handwritten on notepaper in Frankel's nearly illegible scrawl. Three months later Herlihy closed out his savings account and handed Frankel all the money that had been in it, $63,363.72.

Now Frankel had two clients. But Ted Bitter turned out to be much more than that. As he had done at John F. Schulte Inc., Bitter spent many hours at Frankel's house discussing investment strategies, giving the two men time to forge an unlikely friendship. As many others had thought, Bitter found Frankel to be a bit weird and not a little neurotic. But he forgave Frankel his foibles because not only did he think Frankel was a brilliant financial analyst, he also found him fascinating.

"As much as he annoyed me, I tolerated a lot because, I figured, that's just Marty," Bitter said. "He's eccentric, and he's kind of odd, but I knew that's what I was dealing with, so I just rolled most of that off."

Despite Frankel's purported investing prowess, Bitter never saw his broker execute a single trade. What Frankel was doing the entire time of their relationship was what both men referred to as "paper trading."

"Marty was capable of serious analysis of a wide array of investments," according to Bitter. "And in this way, he would tantalize you with thoughts of great wealth."

An example of Frankel's paper trading provided by Bitter went like this: "Marty would be watching orange juice futures and then notice that the National Weather Service was predicting an early freeze. As a result of that forecast he would expect the price of the orange juice futures to rise sharply, and then tell you how much he could have made if the trade had actually been made."

But Bitter was growing impatient as well as frustrated that after having made just one successful transaction, this "genius" was not doing a thing to make him any more money. All of his pleadings for Frankel to make trades seemed to be falling on deaf ears. So Bitter decided to see what he could do to perhaps kick-start his personal money manager.

"One of the things I tried was to do research that I could use to reinforce

Marty's views and hopefully give him enough encouragement and enough confidence to execute the trades," Bitter said. "There were several months when I would get up early in the morning and run to the store to get my *Wall Street Journal* and then beat it back to the shop and spend fifteen to twenty-five minutes studying the *Journal* for ideas. And he would do the same thing. Then I would call him up so we could compare notes. But that didn't work, so after a couple of months I gave up. I was wasting my energy."

His mounting frustration with the trader's block problem notwithstanding, Bitter stuck with Frankel.

"Early on, Marty and I just seemed to hit it off," Bitter recalled. "Marty was interesting because he was born into a Jewish family, and I was born into a German Lutheran family, so it was an unusual mix. Marty was the only Jewish person I ever knew, so I had a lot of questions. We'd talk about his Jewish heritage, and I found that fascinating.

"And he was very intelligent. He would express a lot of views about things, and his perspective would change my own perspective in some ways. For example, he used to talk about people who were addicted to drugs, and where I'd always been a hard-line conservative, he took a more liberal attitude, saying that drugs should be treated like a medical problem. He's the first person that I'd ever heard express that point of view, that instead of arresting people they should be given medical treatment. The more I thought about it the more reasonable that became to me. If I had not known Marty, I'd likely not have that perspective now."

Bitter frequently queried his friend about the Holocaust, a subject on which Frankel was extremely well versed. At these times Frankel would spew venom at Catholics.

"He was very critical of the Catholic Church because he felt the Church was responsible for much of the suffering by the Jewish people," Bitter said. "He was definitely sensitive about the suffering that the Jews had tolerated through the years, especially when the Holocaust occurred. And he blamed not only Germany—Hitler and the Nazis—he also blamed Christians for not resisting those crimes."

Although he did not practice the Hebrew faith, Frankel told Bitter that he had written a comprehensive history of the Jews and that the unpublished manuscript was in a box in his parents' garage.

In addition to the many lofty subjects the two men conversed about, Frankel spent a good deal of his time grousing about his parents. Leon and

Tillie Frankel had grown impatient with having to support a thirty-one-year-old son who still lived at home, and they were constantly on his back about getting a steady job.

"Most of the time when he spoke about his parents, he expressed great anger, and he would frequently curse and call them nasty, nasty names," Bitter said. "They aggravated him, and sometimes it seemed they would say things just to egg him on. They would suggest that he get some menial job, and that would always rankle Marty, who always considered himself intellectually powerful."

Although Frankel would occasionally talk about an attractive cashier at the store where he bought his newspapers, he rarely gave Bitter any indication that he had even a remote interest in women. So one day, when Frankel began pouring his heart out about how he felt about Sonia, Bitter was flabbergasted.

"Part of the reason I was so stunned was because I looked at Marty and couldn't imagine anyone being attracted to him," Bitter said. "My first reaction was, 'What did you say?' And Marty answered in this real soft voice, 'Ted, I'm in love with Sonia.' So I said, 'Does she feel the same way about you?' And he said, 'Yeah,' very softly—as if he didn't want to admit it."

After revealing his secret, Frankel continued to confide in Bitter about the big plans he had in store for him and Sonia.

"He was talking about how they were going to be collaborators, how they were going to be this team and that they were going to go places together," recalled Bitter, who had to wonder what was motivating his eccentric money manager.

"All during this time, Marty had this grudge against John Schulte, and who knows to what extent his attraction to Sonia was kind of a way of getting back at John," Bitter mused. "I think you almost have to factor that in, because the dynamics at work here were very complicated. John always had it in for Marty, and Marty always had it in for John, and that grudge just permeated every aspect of their business relationship and every interaction between the two no matter how indirect it might have been. If there was ever a way that Marty could get even with John, he would do it. And the other way around. It was a mutual contempt."

And so the two men would talk this way each Saturday afternoon, when Bitter would pick up Frankel at his house and drive to Barry's Bagels or the Hungry Eye for lunch. It was during these weekly encounters that Bitter began noticing his companion's strange behavior, which he attributed to Frankel's eccentric genius. At times Frankel seemed paranoid. He would suddenly lower his voice in the belief that other diners were listening in on him. His eyes would continually dart about the restaurant to see if he was being watched.

Bitter recalled how after lunch one Saturday afternoon, they returned to Frankel's house to continue their discussion on the front lawn: "While we were talking, Marty suddenly stood up. He kept on talking, and I just kept looking at him, not really listening to him. I did a lot of that because Marty was always jabbering, and a lot of it went in one ear and out the other. And Marty started unbuckling his pants and lowering his zipper, and I looked at him and said, 'Marty, if you have to go to the bathroom, go in the house and go to the bathroom and I'll wait here.' He said, 'Oh, you know me. I just get so wrapped up in my thoughts. You'll wait here?'"

Bitter put up with such antics because he considered it all to be the behavior of an eccentric genius. But he was a little bit unsettled by what he was coming to know as Frankel's "squishy ethics."

Bitter recalled, "Marty did not have a clear right-and-wrong attitude toward morality. He tended to have a situation-ethics approach. Right and wrong depended on the circumstances. He also had made quite a study of Robert Vesco and similar swindlers. We had numerous conversations about these international con artists. I couldn't say that he admired them, but he certainly was very fascinated by them. He could give you chapter and verse on what they did, how they did it, where they went so they couldn't be caught, and how they got away with it."

But even that kind of talk from the man controlling his money did not overly concern the small investor. "I never thought that he was dangerous," Bitter would later lament.

Little did the trusting tool-and-die maker know that Frankel was about to put his theoretical knowledge of investment fraud into practice.

Chapter Three

If Frankel had taken his baby steps on the path of white-collar crime when forging his friend's name to open the Mesirow account, he would soon be taking giant strides down that road while serving a sort of swindler's apprenticeship under a more experienced and savvy businessman.

When he was still working with the Schultes in 1986, Frankel had struck up a telephone relationship with broker Manny Green, who was with Gateway Commodities in Chicago. Because John Schulte had rightly believed his firm's relationship with Dominick and Dominick was nearing the end, he had asked Frankel to help scout around for another clearinghouse that John F. Schulte Inc. could affiliate itself with. Although Green agreed in principle to hook up the Toledo brokerage with Gateway, the alliance never happened.

By the time Frankel had been fired by John Schulte, Green had moved on to become Chicago branch manager of a commodities firm called International Futures Strategists, owned by Douglas I. Maxwell III, a businessman from Nashville, Tennessee. One day in early 1986 Maxwell called Green to tell him that one of his relatives, a wealthy retired Texas oil executive named John Leo Burns, was unhappy with the performance of his IRA account, managed by American Capital Government Securities Fund and worth over a half million dollars. Maxwell told Green he had promised Burns that he would look around for other money managers who might be able to perform better. Green suggested that he try the Toledo man he knew who had developed an "informational analysis" approach toward investing that had produced amazing results.

Maxwell called Frankel at his parents' home in April 1987, introducing himself as the owner of both International Futures Strategists and PDS Securities International, a stock brokerage with offices in Chicago, West Palm Beach, and Dallas. Maxwell told Frankel he had heard about his ability to pick winning stocks, and Frankel—as was now a deeply ingrained habit of his—stretched the truth when telling Maxwell about himself. He embellished his resume by saying he was managing millions of dollars' worth of accounts as a stockbroker with LaSalle Street Securities and as a commodities broker with Stottler and Co.

It was a deception he could easily justify.

"Well, when I hooked up with Doug Maxwell I told him, as many other salesmen do when they hook up with firms, that they are much bigger producers than they actually are," Frankel later explained. "I don't know many salesmen at all in this business that would get a job starting fresh with a firm without exaggerating their potential."

In turn, Maxwell got Frankel's undivided attention by telling him about his rich relative in Texas and other wealthy potential investors he knew, and how if they pooled their resources they could do very well indeed. Over the course of many such conversations, Maxwell and Frankel hatched the idea for the Frankel Fund, which would be made up of limited partnerships requiring minimum investments of $50,000.

If Frankel is to be believed, Maxwell already had larceny on his mind when the two partners teamed up, and the main targets were to be the wealthy Floridians Maxwell knew.

"He apparently has enough contacts in the circles of extremely wealthy individuals that you can go through a lot of very, very rich people," Frankel said in May 1988. "And if you rip 'em off, they don't scream, apparently, because it's too embarrassing."

The plan was simple. Maxwell would bait and set the hooks, Frankel would reel the fish in, and together they would fry them.

On Maxwell's end of the Frankel Fund, the initial major investor would be Burns. Burns and Maxwell had met five years earlier when Burns' son married a cousin of Maxwell's. Frankel would bring in his two clients, Bitter and Herlihy.

Burns was introduced to Frankel by Maxwell during a three-way conference call, after which Frankel mailed Burns promotional material that included his fabricated past performance record and resume. In it, he falsely took full credit for all $70,000 in monthly commissions John F. Schulte Inc. had earned during his brief time there, and he explained that he left Schulte "in order to concentrate more on money management than retail brokerage."

He further wrote, "Marty Frankel's prowess at investing is powerful. For five years Marty Frankel has placed in the top rank of money managers in the United States. Unlike most other professional money managers, Marty Frankel requires no minimum amount from his clients. He is honored to serve all who seek his services. Frankel believes the job of money management is a sacred profession, like that of a doctor, and he approaches his clients with the same degree of care."

Burns liked what he read and eagerly signed over to Frankel his entire IRA, worth $568,000. He went a step further by orally giving Frankel authorization to invest the money however he saw fit—without Burns' prior approval. The Texan would be unaware that the following month Frankel would forge the name of John L. Burns on a Frankel Fund limited partnership agreement that formalized the oral agreement.

When in May 1988 Frankel was questioned by an SEC official about why he had forged Burns' name, Frankel opted for his own version of the Nuremberg defense: "Because Doug was pressuring me that we had to get this account opened and we had to trade it, and we had to do it, and we had to do it now, and this was the only way to do it. And the rest of it would be made legal, and it didn't, and Mr. Burns was giving his approval to do anything and to send it to him and then have Mr. Burns sign it. But Mr. Burns couldn't sign that document because it didn't look legal or whatever—I am trying to think—at the time when I signed that it wasn't, it didn't look legal. It was just, 'Do it now, do it fast,' or whatever. And I did it."

"So you are saying that Maxwell instructed you to sign Burns' name?"

"Yes, he instructed me to sign."

"Was Maxwell there when you signed the name?"

"No, we hadn't met at all. We didn't meet at all for months and months."

"Maxwell, not Burns?"

"Yes. I was assuming. Also, that Mr. Burns was—obviously Mr. Burns tells you—Mr. Burns said everything was okay any way I wanted to do it.

Anything in a fund or a limited partnership, anywhere that I wanted to do it was fine. And Mr. Burns just wanted to get going and get trading. He was champing at the bit, according to Doug.

"And you know, there didn't seem to me to be anything at all at that time that we were going—I was not—and I was not doing anything against the clients' wishes. What I wasn't doing was protecting myself from Doug and protecting the client. And protecting the client from Doug, also."

After the funds in Burns' IRA were transferred to PDS, Frankel needed a broker identification number for the accounts that would be under his control. Maxwell had told Frankel that Burns' net worth was $7 million—implying that his Texas relative would be looking to invest even more of his money down the road—and so he suggested that his partner use 777.

"Doug Maxwell picked the number," said Frankel. "I can see it now—the $7 million he promised, the $7 million Burns was worth, so he picked 777. That was to be a lucky number. I was broker number 777."

The number never proved to be a charm. In fact, while using it during his association with Maxwell, Frankel got himself into more trouble than he ever could have imagined. Yet, for some reason, he would hold on to that number for years to come. When in the 1990s he set up shop in Greenwich and had over a dozen phone lines installed for his operation, Frankel chose 777 as his extension number.

Maxwell was just as excited as Frankel about the new partnership, and it is doubtful his enthusiasm would have diminished even if Frankel had immediately told him about his trader's block. When Burns had his money in the Frankel Fund for several months and began inquiring as to why he was not receiving regular accounting statements from his account, Maxwell confronted Frankel about his inactivity. It was only then that Maxwell learned about his partner's debilitating mental affliction. As Frankel had become used to stating, he told Maxwell that despite all the meticulous analysis and planning, he simply could not bring himself to "pull the trigger" upon identifying favorable stocks to buy.

Knowledge of the trader's block did not seem to bother the Nashville businessman one bit, because Maxwell knew Frankel would still look good on paper to potential investors, and that many gullible well-to-do people would undoubtedly love to have a man of his purported genius handling their money. To satisfy his rich relative, Maxwell simply began making unauthorized trades for Burns on his own. And he began losing money—lots of it.

Frankel knew that Maxwell was phoning in buy orders to Mesirow Financial Holdings' trading desk on Burns' behalf, and although he later claimed to have been concerned about how his partner had taken matters into his own hands, he did nothing to stop it.

"I just was worried that this was the beginning of something bad because I didn't want him trading in this account—that wasn't our deal," Frankel told the SEC in 1988. "He was to keep his hands off, yet he was going to bring me huge amounts of rich people—just to fulfill my dream of managing money for people, and I didn't know how to stop him. If I stopped him, I thought, I don't know if he would yank the account. It's his account; he brought it to me. I mean, he could just take it away like he brought it."

Throughout the summer of 1987, Maxwell urged Frankel to move to Palm Beach in order to be closer to the wealthy individuals he knew so that they might be convinced to put their money into the Frankel Fund as well. Frankel was awestruck by the fact that Maxwell said he knew members of European royalty who lived there. He was intrigued with the prospect of being the manager for kings and queens.

Maxwell promised to make the transition as smooth as possible by setting up a $100,000 expense account for Frankel to help him with moving costs and get him established in Palm Beach. And so on October 31, 1987, Frankel packed his bags for sunny Florida, taking along his sister, Amy, who would be his secretary and personal assistant.

Frankel rented a house on Flagler Drive next to the Breakers, the swank resort hotel complex built in 1926 by heirs to Henry Flagler, John D. Rockefeller's Standard Oil partner. The house was owned by exiled King Michael and Queen Anne of Romania, who leased it to Frankel for $3,000 a month, and whenever the royals were in town they stayed in rooms they maintained upstairs.

As the new partnership set out to market itself, Maxwell and Frankel drew up promotional material for PDS International Wealth Management and Investment Services, filling it with false claims and glowing but hyperbolic descriptions of Frankel's remarkable talent.

In its brochure about the Frankel Fund, PDS showcased its money manager as follows:

The Fund's General Partner and Trading Expert is Marty Frankel.
He operates consistently on the premise that to be successful in the

market one must receive, analyze, and react to news about economic affairs before the general public and other traders. He has developed indicators that are proven action-triggering signals in his system of "informational analysis." These indicators have made it possible for him to speculate with outstanding success on relatively short-term movements.

Potential Frankel Fund investors were provided the "proof" of the money manager's fantastic success rate by being furnished a copy of "Marty Frankel's Composite Performance Record of All Discretionary Accounts." This so-called record tracked how from March 1983—three years before Frankel was even licensed as a broker—Frankel took a beginning equity in the amount of $850,000 and in four years made it mushroom to a whopping $4.3 million. This was accomplished by realizing astonishing annual rates of return of between 20.2 and 33.7 percent, and with the addition of less than $900,000 in new investments.

Queen Anne was one of those who decided to take advantage of this extraordinary financial opportunity, investing the minimum amount of $50,000 with the Frankel Fund.

As the beautiful people of Palm Beach frolicked in the surf and sun just outside his air-conditioned abode, Frankel's face still had that pasty white complexion it had always had in Toledo. By this time he had become such an ardent believer in astrology that he was now charting his own horoscopes. So when he wasn't "working"—that is, glued to his electronic monitors *but* not trading—Frankel was spending much of his time at his desk putting questions at the center of horoscope wheels.

Frankel's faith in astrology remained strong even though it never seemed to let him know when a fortuitous day for trading would be. It became curious, then, how in one section of PDS's profile of its vaunted money manager, Frankel seems to discredit astrology as he blasts away at Robert Prechter, chief proponent of the Elliot Wave Theory of market behavior. The theory, developed in the 1930s, was a logical extension of the Dow theory, which states that the stock market is in an upswing when either the Dow Jones Industrial Average or the Dow Jones Transportation Average advances above a previous important high, and is accompanied or followed by a similar advance in the other Dow average.

The Elliot Wave Theory holds that as with an ocean's tides, market activity ebbs and flows in repetitive cycles, with each cycle made up of upward "waves" of advance followed by three downward "waves," or corrections.

Perhaps seeking to overthrow the reigning market guru, Frankel lashed out at Prechter:

> It is accepted on the Street that if Robert Prechter ever issues a clear sell signal, then many would believe it imprudent to purchase stock index futures, on a short-term trading basis, on the opening after such a prediction is broadcast by Mr. Prechter over his telephone hotline. The "Elliot Wave" guru's power must not be underestimated at present; a wise traveler in any foreign culture takes heed of the local customs. When you are traveling in a foreign land it does not matter if the local superstition is unsound; you must observe the rules of the culture for the precise reason that everyone else in the foreign land is observing them.
>
> Thus the astute stock market player must assume he is a stranger in a strange land on Wall Street, a jungle where serious men invest millions based upon a theory whose epistemological underpinnings resemble I Ching. It should come as no surprise, then, that *such lunatics as avowed astrology* nuts can occasionally be found pontificating on popular television shows, informing us that, since there will be a solar eclipse on Friday, the stock market must swoon. These fruitcakes do not have much influence at present; but, if such anti-intellectual pseudo-scientists ever gain the influence of a Prechter, I shall reluctantly begin to take notice of their inanities.

Robert Prechter was an accepted expert on market behavior because he had gone to great lengths to support the reasons why he accepted the Elliot wave theory, as the numerous books he has written on the subject will attest. Not to be outdone, Frankel, in the PDS profile, referred readers to the definitive explanation of his revolutionary informational analysis system that is found in *How to Make Money on Wall Street*, by Marty Frankel. Frankel does not indicate who published his work, if such a work ever even existed. There are no records supporting his claims to be a published author.

In a later writing, Frankel would expand on his phantom publishing credentials, stating, "[My] work in this field [of informational analysis] has been confirmed, in part, by the work of leading economists and psychologists at Yale, Cornell, Stanford, and the University of California at Berkeley." He also referred potential clients to *An Introduction to Marty Frankel's Trading System* and *A Sociology of the Stock Market*, also by Marty Frankel.

During its brief existence the Frankel Fund amassed slightly over $1 million, nearly all of which belonged to Burns and Herlihy. In addition to Bitter and Queen Anne, the fund had been able to attract only a few other investors before it collapsed, including a Tennessee company called Sumner Anesthesia and some others Frankel knew from Ohio whom he convinced to contribute the minimum amount of $50,000. Each investor's account was supposed to have been segregated from the others, but in the end they were all intermingled as one big piggy bank for Frankel and Maxwell.

In addition to the approximately $130,000 it had lost due to bad trades Maxwell made, the Frankel Fund was frequently tapped in order to pay bills. And when the SEC in 1988 asked Frankel to explain why he used investor funds for his personal expenses, Frankel once again tried laying the blame on his business partner: "Doug Maxwell lied to me.... He said he was going to have a $100,000 fund set up, and he was going to pay expenses out of it. And he kept saying, 'Well, it is going to be next month when that fund is paying back all the damn expenses.' And when I got down there [to Florida] Doug said, you know, 'Write it out of this money and do it. You pay the rent out of this money and you do it.' And I did it."

Frankel's stay in Florida lasted only from November 1987 to March 1988. But in those four months, he used money from the Frankel Fund to pay $16,000 to Queen Anne for rent, and for one month's rental of office space in downtown Palm Beach, costing $3,250. One Frankel Fund check for $5,000 was made out to Leon Frankel, as partial reimbursement of a $20,000 loan Leon and Tillie Frankel had made to their son. Another for the amount of $4,294 was cut to Amy Frankel as compensation for whatever work she did for her brother. Frankel Fund checks totaling $12,500 were made out for moving expenses; others for a total of over $11,000 had paid for subscriptions to *The Wall Street Journal*, *Investors Daily*, and other publications, as well as for financial quote machine rentals. Frankel spent thousands more paying off telephone and insurance bills, brokerage fees, and the like, and $60,000 went toward what he called "miscellaneous expenses."

Meanwhile, Frankel was telling his Ohio investors that everything was just fine. Bitter had gotten regular oral reports from Frankel as they continued the relationship the two had begun in Toledo over the telephone. Frankel had been lying to Bitter all along during these conversations, and if the tool-and-die worker had listened carefully, he might have picked up on clues that something was terribly amiss.

"One of the primary concerns that I had when I would talk with him was, 'What are you doing with my money, Marty?' And he always said it was just sitting idly in an interest-bearing account," Bitter recalled. "He said there were trades being made and losses were mounting up, but it was somebody else's money. So I wasn't too concerned about somebody else's money."

At about the same time, Herlihy was growing concerned because he was not receiving regular accounting statements. When he called the number for LaSalle Street Securities' Toledo branch, he was stunned to find out it was for Frankel's parents' house. Herlihy told Leon Frankel about his predicament and was further jolted by the news that Frankel had moved to Florida.

When his father called to alert him about how upset Herlihy had been, and mentioned that he had even talked about wanting his money back, Frankel rushed back to Toledo.

"Marty tried to calm John down and convince him to not take his money out of the Frankel Fund," recalled one of Herlihy's attorneys, Terry Davis. "He told both John Herlihy and Ted Bitter that their money was safe and secure, and just like always, he told them their money was guaranteed to make a good return. And at that point he guaranteed them a 10 percent return and, coincidentally, the next thing they knew they got from Frankel were statements showing them that their money was invested in an account and that it had earned exactly 10 percent."

The attorney added, "As we later found out, Marty was just cranking these false account statements for them on his little Apple laptop computer."

Frankel's problems began to mount when Herlihy complained to LaSalle Street Securities, prompting the brokerage firm's compliance director, Grant Nelson, to fire off an urgent letter to Frankel.

"Since your registration with LaSalle covers only approval in the state of Ohio, we need to know why your Toledo telephone has been disconnected and your clients are unable to reach you," Nelson wrote on March 8, 1988. "Since you are not registered in the state of Florida, we need an explanation of what you are doing, and have been doing, from a business standpoint while in Florida. Since we are extremely concerned about your status and your activities, it is absolutely imperative that you respond in writing as soon as possible. Failure to do so will force us to take further action."

On March 17 Nelson mailed Frankel an "Indemnification and Hold Harmless Agreement," for the wayward broker to release LaSalle from any liability for his fraudulent behavior. The firm fired Frankel the following month.

Herlihy's lawyers would later accuse officers of LaSalle Street Securities of having known full well what Frankel had been up to in Florida, and filed an arbitration claim with the National Association of Securities Dealers on Herlihy's behalf. The claim sought over $1.6 million in damages from the Chicago brokerage house on charges of negligence for having employed Frankel.

"LaSalle Street hired Frankel by telephone. He never met in person anyone from LaSalle Street," Herlihy's arbitration claim stated. "Apparently, LaSalle Street did not bother to check beyond Frankel's brief tenure at Dominick & Dominick, the only other job he had held in the securities industry. In fact, had they bothered to check his background at all, they would have quickly determined that Frankel's tenure at Dominick & Dominick (where he had made only one non-directed trade for a customer before he was fired) was the first real job that Frankel had ever had since he graduated from high school nearly twelve years before." LaSalle eventually settled with Herlihy out of court.

At about the same time Frankel was fired by LaSalle, Burns had lost faith in the Frankel Fund and was demanding that all his money be returned. It was, but instead of being told that a huge chunk of his investment had been lost through bad trades, Burns was repaid with money from Bitter's and Herlihy's accounts. On April 4 Frankel wire-transferred $500,000 out of the Frankel Fund to John Burns' account at First Trust Bank of Denver. Bitter and Herlihy were virtually wiped out.

Frankel panicked. He sought the advice of a cousin of his who had a law practice in Toledo. Paul Frankel instantly realized that cousin Marty was in deep trouble and advised him that he needed to retain an attorney in Illinois, because that was the state where many of the banks and brokerages that handled Frankel Fund trades were located. And for that reason, that was the state in which any prosecution of wrongdoing would occur. Frankel hired Chicago attorney James Koch, to whom he told the story of a "disaster in Florida" that had been precipitated by Maxwell's theft of $500,000.

On Paul Frankel's advice, whatever money was left in the Frankel Fund was transferred to a Chicago bank and subsequently sequestered in a trust account in anticipation of forthcoming litigation.

Frankel moved back home from Palm Beach, now in a deep funk.

"He was really depressed and unhappy. He was kind of babbling, and his speech wasn't as coherent as I was used to. It was choppy and kind of rambling," Ted Bitter recalled. "I asked him, 'What's bothering you?' and he would put me off and not be real specific at that time. He was in a despondent state—depressed, disoriented—and I questioned him. 'Is my money okay?' and he said, 'Oh yeah, it's fine. There's nothing to worry about.'

"That satisfied me for a while, but about a month after Marty got back to Toledo he admitted in a telephone conversation that my money had been involved in a 'disaster,' and what was left was inaccessible to me because it had been impounded in a bank in Chicago. It was a very painful disclosure for me. It was devastating. I got very emotional, and it took a while to scrape myself off the floor."

Bitter had in fact broken down in tears—not just because he had learned his life savings were gone, although that was the major reason, but also because he had been betrayed by someone he had trusted and befriended.

"Marty didn't have the guts to tell me this in person. He did it over the telephone," Bitter said. "He was surprisingly cool when he told me what happened, but I, of course, made up for that. I was crushed. I let him have it how I trusted him and he violated my trust. Realizing that your life savings had been ripped away from you, that's difficult enough. But what really stunned me even more than that was the fact that Marty could have done that to me after all the hours I talked with this guy. You know, personal conversations—he would tell me family secrets, that kind of stuff, and I felt the guy could be trusted. It really blew me away that Marty could do that to me of all people."

At the same time, Frankel was trying to convince Bitter that Maxwell was entirely responsible for stealing the money. "Doug stole it, and now I'm the one who's going to be persecuted for it," he cried.

"Some of the things Marty was saying to Ted during the summer of 1988 were very telling," said Bitter's attorney, Jeff Creamer. "He told Ted that he still had some of the Frankel Fund money, and was saying how he should just steal the money and disappear. Ted said that at that point Marty was saying stuff that clearly indicated he had gone over the hill, and had started really to think like a criminal.

"This is when he really started talking about Vesco. He was saying things to Ted like, 'If I'm going to be persecuted, then I might as well just do what I've always wanted to do,' that is, if he stole really big he would be okay. This is the point where the real Marty Frankel came out of the closet. He went through a transformation. There was less of the 'I'm really a good guy, I'm really an honest guy trying to do an honest thing, and I'm just misunderstood,' to 'I'm a genius—a persecuted genius—and I'm not appreciated, which therefore justifies whatever I'm doing.'"

It was around this time that Frankel checked himself into a Toledo hospital. While some say he had suffered a nervous breakdown, Bitter's lawyer believed Frankel had simply been in need of a safe sanctuary as he saw his life spinning out of control.

"After the Frankel Fund collapsed, Marty was hospitalized for several weeks at least, but I think that was because he thought they were going to catch up to him and he was anticipating punishment for what he'd done," Creamer said. "I mean, by that time he was really into it. He had been lying to people, issuing false statements, making up false account statements, using people's money to live on—pissing away people's money down in Palm Beach and living the life of Riley."

In November 1989 Bitter and Herlihy sought to reclaim their money by filing suit against Frankel and Maxwell in U.S. District Court in Toledo. The complaint fueled a fraud investigation by the U.S. Securities and Exchange Commission.

With the feds and clients' lawyers now breathing down his neck, Frankel was beginning to fall apart. An FBI special agent showed up one day at the Stanhope Drive residence looking to interview Frankel, but he was met at the door by Leon Frankel, who ran interference for his son. The agent was not allowed in the house, and as he peered inside he was unable to see who else was home because the interior of the house was shrouded in complete darkness. But then the agent heard the high-pitched voice of what sounded like a little boy.

"Daddy, tell the man he can't come in," the voice said. "Daddy, tell him he'll have to leave."

A private detective working for the lawyers who were trying to reclaim the money that had been stolen from Bitter and Herlihy had a similar experience when attempting to serve Frankel with a subpoena ordering him to appear for a deposition. This time Amy Frankel answered the door.

"What's this about?" Amy asked.

"I have some papers for Marty Frankel."

"I don't know if he's here or not."

"Well, I have a check for him," the process server honestly stated, since he had also brought Frankel's nominal deposition attendance fee.

The mention of money had the desired effect. Frankel rushed to the door. "I'm Marty Frankel," he said, and excitedly tore open the envelope that was handed to him. But while glancing over the documents, Frankel's face suddenly turned bright red. "These are court papers!" he screamed.

"Yeah, you've been served," the investigator replied.

Frankel shouted at his tormentor as the private detective walked toward his car. "I'm not Marty Frankel! I'm not Marty Frankel at all!" he yelled, throwing the papers out into the front yard. He continued to rant as the private detective drove away.

"I'm not Marty Frankel," he screamed while shaking his fist at the moving car. "You can't do this, this isn't legal. I'm going to call the police."

Frankel cloistered himself in his room for days on end, his mind working overtime with thoughts of how to escape his predicament. One possible solution he came up with was to go on the attack. He called Shirley Herlihy one night and threatened that if her husband did not immediately withdraw his lawsuit, he would countersue and take the elderly couple's house and whatever little money they still had.

"This gives you some insight into what this guy's personality was," observed Bitter's attorney, Creamer, who also represented Herlihy. "Frankel's threats made Shirley a nervous wreck. She had never been involved in anything like this, and here comes this vicious bastard calling up the people he's already ruined, and tries to terrorize them into dropping the case."

Creamer said Frankel's call to Shirley Herlihy marked the only time in his legal career that he felt genuine hostility toward another party in a legal action.

"I'm not a fighter by nature, but I'll tell you, if I'd gotten my hands on Frankel that night, I would have beaten the shit out of that punk," Creamer recalled. "In my twenty years of litigating I'd never felt that way about anybody. But for him to threaten the Herlihys, who were these real down-to-earth, very nonconfrontational people, I just could not stand for that."

The day he was deposed for the civil lawsuit, Frankel was driven by his mother to the downtown Toledo office of his former clients' lawyers at Shumaker, Loop and Kendrick. He fidgeted and squirmed as he sat at a conference room table across from attorneys Davis and Creamer.

"As we went through the questions he got more and more agitated, because it was dawning on him that, 'Christ, they've figured out what I'd done,' and it got to the point where he really began losing it," Creamer recalled. "I would ask him something like, 'Isn't it true that you applied the Herlihys' and Bitters' money for your own private uses?' and he'd come back with something like, 'Isn't it true that you're stealing from your clients? Isn't it true that you wouldn't have an office building like this if you weren't stealing from your clients?'

"It was real childish stuff. You know, I've been chasing crooks for years on this job, and some of them are actually quite funny—you know, they have a wry sense of humor about the whole thing and can actually get a couple of digs in. But it wasn't like that with Frankel. His reaction was like that of a child who was being punished by the teacher and was smarting off back."

Maxwell had a much cooler approach when it was his turn to be deposed. "Throughout the deposition, Maxwell refused to answer questions, and he would read from this card when taking the Fifth Amendment," recalled Davis. "Finally he just got up to leave the deposition and he gave us the card and said, 'Here, read this for every answer to every question.'"

When it came time to give testimony to the SEC, the arrogance and cockiness Frankel had displayed during his Toledo deposition evaporated. Finding himself face-to-face with the power of the United States government, Frankel turned suddenly meek. He was also extremely flustered.

When SEC compliance examiner Michael Schnitzer on May 24, 1988, asked Frankel to describe the genesis of the Frankel Fund, Frankel had an impossible time keeping his story straight. "It was Doug's idea, but you'd have to say it was both of our ideas," Frankel said. "It was his idea first to have me do a limited partnership. But he wanted me to—it's almost as if he planted a seed. He didn't plant a seed in my mind, we both together decided."

And when confronted with copies of Frankel Fund checks bearing his signature—indisputable evidence that he had spent investors' money on himself—Frankel clumsily tried downplaying his larcenies. "I didn't go on any spending sprees with clients' funds," he told Schnitzer. "I spent bare necessities, didn't do any of the things I had to do. Never went out to dinner, almost. Ate at home and just ate canned stuff. I lived on canned fish and stuff. I mean, I was not extravagant."

At first it appeared that Frankel was cooperating entirely with the SEC's investigation, turning over records and voluntarily submitting to questioning. But when the SEC demanded his bank records and other financial data, he balked. The SEC investigators then threatened to take him to court to force him to produce the records, at which time Frankel settled the case on what at first might seem harsh terms. In 1992 he agreed to pay the government more than $200,000 and accepted a lifetime ban from the securities industry. Also that year Frankel settled the civil lawsuit by paying Herlihy and Bitter an undisclosed sum.

At the time, the SEC may have been willing to settle with Frankel so quickly because it thought it had been dealing with what amounted to an insignificant money manager. Had it dug deeper, however, the SEC might have learned that Frankel had been lying to them all along. Far from being destitute, as he had claimed, Frankel had embarked on a new enterprise that was secretly controlling millions of dollars and moving large sums into a Swiss bank account. And he was using a variety of aliases to set up dummy corporations, which he used to buy a house, luxury car, and other expensive items.

In fact, Frankel was gearing up for a final and spectacular run at greatness, but one that would come to a fiery conclusion, leaving the public not in admiration of his genius but gawking at him as if he were a sideshow freak.

Chapter Four

While Frankel was busy fending off former clients and the United States government, he did not notice the men who were slinking about in the darkness outside his Stanhope Drive home. They were private detectives, and they were finding all kinds of interesting things as they picked through the garbage pails by the curb.

John Schulte had hired the investigators in his relentless pursuit of his daughters, who were being kept away from him by Sonia in spite of court-ordered visitation rights. Frankel had taken Sonia under his wing, and he was trying to keep her hidden from Schulte by frequently moving her to different apartments, which he paid for. It was a role to which Frankel had grown accustomed. Frankel once confided to a friend that he had even coached Sonia on how she could leave finger marks by squeezing her own neck before making a spousal abuse complaint in order to make it look as if Schulte had assaulted her.

Some of the documents that were fished out of Frankel's trash indicated that he was now involved with a new investment vehicle called the Creative Partners Fund. Other documents seemed to show that far from being destitute, as he had claimed to the SEC, Frankel was secretly controlling millions of dollars that he moved between offshore accounts and a bank in Switzerland. The information was forwarded to the SEC, but it appears the SEC never pursued matters with regard to the Toledo money manager any further than their Frankel Fund investigation.

The Creative Partners Fund was an unregistered limited partnership that Frankel set up in October 1989, with the initial contribution coming from Frankel himself—the $24,000 that remained from the Frankel Fund.

The Creative Partners Fund might have seemed like a scaled-down version of the Frankel Fund, as it required minimum investments of only $10,000 rather than $50,000. But over the two years of its existence, and with the several sales representatives it had employed, the Creative Partners Fund would attract dozens of investors and is said to have grown to include as much as $14 million.

Another major difference was that instead of keeping him hundreds of miles from home, in a foreign land and surrounded by sinister strangers, Frankel could run the Creative Partners Fund with the comforting knowledge that Mom and Dad were nearby should anything go wrong. And this time Sonia was intimately involved with the endeavor, supervising a staff of between eight and twelve sales representatives. One of the fund's Chicago-based sales reps, Mark Shuki, said he dealt with Frankel only through Sonia.

"She used to call us and tell us what were the returns in the partnership," Shuki recalled in a June 1999 interview. "She would call us with what was going on with paperwork, new accounts, accounting forms."

More important, what the new and old funds had in common was that they were both used by Frankel as his personal bank accounts.

On June 20, 1990, Frankel incorporated a shell company that he called the Donar Corporation. Donar—another name for Thor, the Norse god of thunder—is believed to have been capitalized with money belonging to Creative Partners Fund investors. The day after its incorporation, on June 21, Donar paid $70,000 cash for a house at 3415 Stanhope Drive. It was directly across the street from Leon and Tillie Frankel's house. Three months later, Donar paid $73,000 cash for a new Mercedes-Benz. After setting up a pickup date for his new car, Frankel rescheduled it when his horoscope wheel told him of a more fortuitous day.

Whatever sense of security Frankel had from continuing to reside so close to Mom and Dad was short-lived. Soon after settling into his new residence, he caught on to the fact that he was under frequent, if not constant, surveillance. If he had not learned of this by catching glimpses of the men who were lurking outside in the dark, then he did find out as a result of a chance occurrence. John Schulte had begun dating the woman who managed his failed state senate campaign, Judy Stout, who one day let it slip that she knew some of the Creative Partners Fund's confidential financial information.

One of the mutual fund's investors, a disabled railroad worker named Edward Anderson, financed a new van for $28,000 and arranged for it to be paid out of his Creative Partners Fund account. "I had Sonia set up monthly payments of $600, because I figured I might as well start drawing some money out of that fund," Anderson said. "I never told my kids, and the information never left the house. It was between the wife and I. Well, the wife and I were out eating one morning and we ran into Judy Stout in a restaurant, and she came over and sat down and started talking, and she said to me, 'You have a new van, haven't you?' I don't know how she knew that.

"And then she said, 'I understand you're making $600-a-month payments on it,' and I asked her, 'How do you know that?' She said, 'Oh, you know, it's street talk.' Well, I came to find out that when they were sending me $600 a month they had copies of the checks, but the checks went into the garbage. And John Schulte was going through the garbage. I tell you, we found ourselves right in the middle of a real soap opera."

Schulte's activities made Frankel so nervous that he hired private investigators to make a security assessment of his new property. He accepted their recommendation to install an electronic alarm system, but after the PIs suggested that he replace the drywall inside the house with steel plates to protect against bullets, Frankel realized he was just being jerked around for extra money, so he fired them.

Feeling vulnerably exposed in his lightly constructed ranch house located only yards from the street, Frankel decided he would look for a more secure property, preferably one in a private neighborhood and tucked away behind high walls and gates.

Browsing through local real estate listings, he thought he had found the perfect place. On July 27, 1991, Frankel created a new horoscope wheel and placed in its hub the question, "Should I buy farm?" The alignment of the planets that day told him the answer was yes.

The "farm" in question was a 1926 Normandy-style mansion set on three secluded acres in Toledo's most exclusive section, Ottawa Hills. The estate had once been owned by Toledo industrialist Ward Canady, and it included horse stables and servants' quarters. The asking price was $1.2 million.

Still possessing a valid real estate license, Frankel telephoned Shriner Realty in Toledo and told owner Don Skaff he wished to place his license with Shriner so he could broker the sale of the house and earn the entire commission. Skaff not only informed Frankel he would have to settle for the standard broker's commission, he told him that because of his inexperience in the field he would have to attend a broker's orientation.

Frankel was driven to the orientation a couple of nights later by his father, who sat beside him in the conference room at the rear of Skaff's offices. "He showed up with this old guy who slept through the whole thing and snored like a banshee," Skaff said. "Afterward, he explained, 'That's my dad, and I didn't have anything for him to do so I brought him along.'"

After the orientation, Skaff told Frankel that there would be an open house at the Ottawa Hills estate the next day, and that he would accompany him on an inspection of the property. When Skaff arrived the next morning he found Frankel and Sonia already there, waiting just outside the main door. The trio was then joined by the listing agent, Michael Miller, who said something startling.

"Well, Don, you can come in, but that guy's not coming in," Miller said, angrily pointing at Frankel.

Skaff recalled, "Before I could ask why, Frankel said something to Michael, and that really set Michael off. And before I knew it the two of them were really going at it. I was stunned, because Michael Miller is this short, quiet, and reserved guy, and I've never, ever seen him get mad at anybody."

Skaff later learned that Frankel had previously met with Miller in an attempt to make the same arrangement with the listing agency to get the entire sales commission. When Miller told Frankel such a deal was out of the question, Frankel unleashed a torrent of epithets.

Despite having met Frankel so inauspiciously, Miller told Skaff to call him the next day to make arrangements for Frankel to inspect the property some other time.

Nevertheless, Frankel informed Skaff, "I'm going to walk around the grounds anyway. If I'm going to buy this house, I have a right to inspect it." He then stomped away toward the rear of the estate.

"I remember he had these big brown rubber wading boots on that went up past his knees," Skaff said. "I found that very odd, and I thought to myself, 'This guy sure is a weirdo.'"

A few days later Miller gave permission for Skaff to accompany Frankel on a tour of the mansion. As soon as Frankel entered the foyer of the main house, he looked up and was delighted to see that the zodiac had been intricately painted on the ceiling. He knew right then he had to buy the place.

A couple of days passed before Frankel called Skaff to say he wanted to make an offer. Skaff said that was fine but told Frankel he would first need to furnish proof he could secure a loan. Fully intending to pay cash for the house, Frankel needed to think quick.

"But I'm a stockholder of a bank out east, and they are actually going to put the property in their name," he said. "You can expect a letter from them explaining who they are and what the financing arrangements will be."

Skaff responded, "That's not good enough. I don't care who puts what property in whose name, but until you have the financing secured and I've got a commitment letter, I'm not writing an offer."

"Okay," Frankel said, and hung up the phone. He called again the next day and told Skaff, "I've been thinking things over, Don, and now I really don't think this house is for me."

Discouraged by the financial scrutiny such a major purchase would bring, Frankel resigned himself to having to live and operate in Lincoln-shire. Maybe the planets had been wrong.

Then, seemingly from out of the blue, Frankel received a phone call.

"Mr. Fwankel, I am calling you because I am looking to put together a gwoup of investors to buy a bank down here in Tennessee," said the speech-impeded southern drawl coming out of the receiver.

Thus began a long-term relationship between two incredibly dissimilar men who would come to do millions of dollars in business together, yet who would not meet face-to-face until several years later. They spoke by tele-phone for hours on nearly a daily basis, and in this way Frankel came to learn about John Alvis Hackney, a forty-two-year-old businessman from Franklin, Tennessee.

Franklin is similar to Greenwich in the sense that it is the wealthiest community in its state. Instead of Fortune 500 CEOs and Wall Street hon-chos, Franklin's moneyed class is made up of horse-breeding barons and Nashville music moguls.

But Hackney had originally come from more humble origins. Born in 1949 to a dentist and his wife in Lawrenceburg, Tennessee, Hackney even-tually graduated from Middle Tennessee State University with a degree in marketing, and tried his hand at selling respiratory equipment to hospitals. Hackney moved to Franklin and in the early 1980s was hired as purchasing manager for the local First American Bank. Hackney lived with his wife,

Ann, in a comfortable but modest house they bought for $175,000 in a new subdivision, but apparently Hackney, who fancied himself a deal maker, saw that residence as a mere way station en route to bigger and better things.

In the mid-1980s the portly glad-hander attempted what would be his first stab at becoming a player in the mergers and acquisitions game. He and another local businessman, Richard Herrington, were among a group of local investors interested in buying Franklin National Bank. According to people involved in the transaction, the sale went forward without Hackney because he did not come up with the minimum share of $50,000.

"When the time came to belly up to the bar, John chose not to participate," Herrington recalled.

Hackney persisted in his efforts to buy a bank, however, and about a year after he failed to get in on the Franklin National Bank deal he went shopping for a different bank that could be bought solely with Frankel's backing. He reportedly entered into negotiations to buy a bank in western Tennessee but pulled out when it became clear that Frankel's wish to keep his involvement quiet wouldn't survive the intense scrutiny that banking regulations required.

Despite the setbacks, the backslapping, ever-smiling Hackney remained a popular man in Franklin, where he served on the board of the Williamson County–Franklin Chamber of Commerce, and was president of the Downtown Franklin Association.

One of Hackney's good friends was U.S. congressman Burt Gordon, who recalled with fondness their days together at Middle Tennessee State University. "If you needed help moving into a dorm, John would always be someone that you could count on to help," Gordon said.

In 1991 Hackney again saw an opportunity to become a big-time deal maker. After hearing about the struggling Franklin American Life Insurance Company, he set out to organize another group of investors. Franklin American Life was founded in the mid-1980s by former Tennessee insurance commissioner Richard F. Keathley, but at the end of the decade it became so mired in financial problems brought about by mismanagement that it was placed under administrative supervision by the Tennessee Department of Commerce and Insurance. In 1991 the state was virtually begging for buyers to come along and take Franklin American Life off of its hands.

Hackney has not publicly said a single word about his involvement with Frankel, but through one of his attorneys, James Sanders, Hackney stated that in his search for investors to acquire Franklin American Life, he came across a Toledo money manager by the name of Eric Stevens—a new alias that was being used by Frankel.

"John Hackney was a fellow who had been raising money—his jobs and past experience had been raising money to put into investments, and that's when he ran into this fellow Eric Stevens," Sanders said. "Hackney can't recall just how he got put together with Stevens, but when you're a money finder you make lists—like a politician makes lists—and he came across this Stevens guy."

Contrary to his lawyer's take on the relationship, Hackney apparently knew full well with whom he was dealing, after having already tried to buy Frankel a bank. He knew the Toledo resident well enough to have spelled out in a handwritten document that the number one thing to do in the case of "my death or inability to work" was to "call Marty Frankel" and "tell him what happened. He will of course take care of the investments."

Another of Hackney's attorneys, Aubrey Harwell, explained the document was written after Hackney's father asked him to be executor of his estate, prompting Hackney to evaluate the eventuality of his own death. The senior partner of the law firm that Sanders and Harwell belonged to was James Neil, a prominent lawyer who had been the senior Watergate special prosecutor who tried H. R. Haldeman, John Mitchell, Maurice Stans, and other high-ranking Nixon administration officials.

As the long-distance communications between Frankel and Hackney continued, it became apparent that with the amount of money under Frankel's control, the new partnership did not have to content itself with buying just one insurance company. There were many other companies in the same dire fiscal straits as Franklin American Life, and they could be bought for a song. And the companies, like Franklin American Life, would be worth much, much more than their purchase price because of the millions of dollars in reserves they maintained in order to pay off on policy claims.

The new partners dreamed of creating an insurance dynasty. They would use the reserves of each new company they bought to buy still more companies. And Frankel made it clear to Hackney what their respective roles would be: "I'll handle all of the finances," Frankel said. "You'll be the charming front man."

The first step Frankel and Hackney needed to take in building their empire was to fulfill the Tennessee requirement that an irrevocable trust be formed, one that cannot go out of business, for the protection of policyholders. So in September 1991 they incorporated Thunor Trust. Like Frankel's Donar Corporation, the trust was named after a Norse thunder god.

During negotiations for the purchase of Franklin American Life, Hackney told the insurance company's representatives that the principals of Thunor Trust were securities brokers in Chicago who "wanted to gain the insurance company as a new client." An attorney for Franklin American Life at the time, Charles Welch, said he had never heard of such a thing—buying a company whom you want as a client. "That part of it seemed a little unusual," Welch said.

Another unusual aspect of the transaction was that none of Thunor Trust's principals was disclosed until Tennessee insurance regulators insisted. In its incorporation papers, Thunor Trust listed three "silent investors"— Frankel confidant Sonia Howe (formerly Schulte), childhood acquaintance Edward Krauss, and Creative Partners Fund sales rep Mark Shuki. All three would later deny having supplied any of the $3.75 million that Thunor Trust used to purchase Franklin American Life, although Shuki later admitted that he consented to his name being used after being told that "we were going to set up an insurance company and prospect for bigger accounts, and in order to do this we had to set up the paperwork." He said he never bothered learning the details.

Krauss, a childhood friend of Frankel's brother, Robert, who years later would work for Frankel as a personnel consultant, denied ever giving Frankel permission to use his name. In 1999, when shown his signature on a Thunor Trust affidavit that had been filed with the Tennessee Department of Commerce and Insurance, Krauss said it was an obvious forgery.

Thunor Trust bought its first insurance company in October 1991, when for $3.75 million it acquired a controlling interest—52 percent—in Franklin American Corporation in Tennessee. The corporation owned 100 percent of Franklin American Life Insurance Company. Franklin American Corporation would become one of two holding companies for additional acquisitions under the umbrella of Thunor Trust, the other being International Financial Corporation, which was incorporated in Oklahoma in 1993 as a wholly-owned subsidiary of Thunor Trust. Its principal place of business was in Tennessee.

The Creative Partners Fund was shut down soon afterward, and its investors were handsomely repaid. All of the investors thought they had earned large profits, with some realizing returns of as much as 300 percent, and that Frankel with his remarkable talents was responsible. Little did they know that the money did not come from any actual investments.

One such investor was Wallace Powell, a fifty-nine-year-old worker at the Jeep assembly plant in Toledo who had put an initial amount of $10,000 into the Creative Partners Fund; after being shown a statement stating he had doubled his money in four months, he forked over another $20,000. By the time the fund was shut down, Wallace's money had been in it for a little more than a year. He was presented with a final check for $110,000. "The guy is a genius," Wallace said of Frankel in 1999. "I'd follow him around like a puppy if he were here now."

The real story, however, seems to be that Frankel had just masterminded a pyramid scheme that essentially robbed Peter to pay Paul. All of the Creative Partners Fund investors apparently were paid off with money that was looted from the $18 million in Franklin American Life's reserves.

In its simplest terms, a pyramid scheme works like this: Paul gives you money in return for a promise to make him a profit. Instead of investing the money, you keep it or spend it for yourself. Then along comes Peter, with whom you make the same deal. So, if Paul ever asks to see his money, you show him Peter's and reassure Paul that it's his. The pyramid exponentially grows as you suck Tom, Dick, Harry, and a host of others into the scheme. Then you just reflow the capital accordingly in order to keep everyone happy.

The ruse is also commonly known as a Ponzi scheme, named after Charles Ponzi, an Italian immigrant who used such a fraud to become extremely wealthy during the 1920s in Boston. He had claimed to be buying International Postal Union coupons at a tremendous discount in war-torn Europe. Contending he needed more money in order to buy more coupons, he advertised for investors, promising them huge returns on their initial investments.

In actuality, Ponzi had used one investor's money to pay another. When the scheme came crashing down, the truth was revealed. There were no International Postal Union coupons, and Ponzi was just taking money in one door and shoveling it out another, holding on to enough of it for himself in order to line his pockets. He served a five-year prison sentence and was deported to Italy.

In Frankel's case, he and Hackney used what remained of Franklin American Life's reserve assets—after Frankel paid off the Creative Partners investors—to go hunting for more companies to buy. With each purchase, the amount of money at their disposal from all of the companies' aggregate reserves grew exponentially.

In this way, Thunor Trust went on a buying spree over the next several years that saw the acquisition of Protective Services Life Insurance Company, also in Franklin, Tennessee; the Family Guarantee Life Insurance Companies in Mississippi; First National Life Insurance Company in Alabama; Farmers and Ranchers Life Insurance Company in Oklahoma; and International Financial Services Life Insurance Company in Missouri.

Hackney was installed as the president and chief executive officer of each company, and another Tennessean, certified public accountant Gary L. Atnip, was made chief financial officer. The principal officers for all of the companies were either friends or allies of Hackney: Dennis Lee Roos, Frances Burnette, Wade Willis, Gene McKinney, Terry Porter, and Judith Lowry, who was the niece of Keathley, the former Tennessee insurance commissioner.

The assets of all the insurance companies were invested with a Toledo brokerage called Liberty National Securities, whose money manager was none other than Eric Stevens, one of Frankel's many aliases. Liberty National Securities had originally been incorporated in Toledo by a former Frankel associate, Robert Guyer, who then later reregistered the firm in Dundee, Michigan. The brokerage firm's name, however, was apparently illegally appropriated by Frankel for use in his fraudulent schemes over nearly the next decade.

The manner in which each insurance company was managed after being acquired by Thunor Trust should have raised immediate questions among state insurance industry regulators. It didn't. The way things went for Protective Services Life Insurance Company in Tennessee under Thunor's control is a case in point.

Protective Services had been founded in Franklin by James F. "Jack" Robinson, who also ran it as president for thirty-eight years. Tired of having to keep up with ever-changing state regulations that each year seemed to require more money to be spent on administrative and accounting costs, Robinson decided to sell his company in March 1995 and devote all his efforts into turning his funeral home business into the finest in the South.

That was when he was approached by Hackney, who told him about the trust he headed for a bunch of rich northerners and the genius of the trust's remarkable money manager. "He said Thunor Trust was made up of a lot of Jewish investors from the northeastern part of the United States, and that they had selected him to manage all of this money," recalled Robinson. "I told Hackney that I had never heard of black-eyed boys turning their money over to a blue-eyed boy to manage. That was the first thing that didn't add up.

"Then he talked about this guy who managed all the money—some super brain named Eric Stevens who also lived up north. He said this guy was a real money guru and he traded U.S. government bonds all over the world, trading as many as three times every twenty-four hours, and he told me how this person stayed in his bathrobe thirty-six and forty-eight hours without letup studying stock and bond trades, earning 18 percent returns.

"Well, anyway, he convinced me that his investors wanted to buy Protective Services Life and were willing to pay a reasonable amount for the company. Now, you have to remember, we are dealing with big egos and a 'very important' person who's out buying insurance companies and wheeling and dealing with millions of dollars available to him—the Donald Trump type. People were anxious to meet him, and we all believed him."

Robinson and Hackney agreed on a sales price of $6 million, and almost immediately after it was sold the company underwent a name change, to Franklin Protective Life Insurance Company.

But that was not the only change. All of the company's employees were fired, even those Hackney had guaranteed jobs to in the purchase agreement. The pink slips were handed out beginning the day after Hackney threw a large party to celebrate the acquisition.

One of those who was shown the door was Robinson's daughter and company secretary, Margaret Lauro, who knew the business inside and out. She was replaced by Kim Presley, a friend of Hackney's who reportedly had no previous insurance experience. One of the company's most loyal employees, Charles Wilbur, who had been in charge of policy records and underwriting, was fired after over thirty years of service. Within two weeks he was dead from a heart attack.

A stipulation of the sale had required that Robinson remain with Franklin Protective Life's board of directors. That placed him in a position to see the many changes that would occur under the new administration. The most drastic and troubling change the former owner witnessed came

when Hackney eliminated the insurance company's claims review committee and in its place instituted a policy of paying off all claims within twenty-
four hours and without question.

"I was totally at a loss to know what this man was doing," Robinson
said.

At the company's very next board meeting, Robinson questioned the new
policy and made a motion to re-form the claims committee so that the company would have the necessary records should it ever be audited. The motion
was overwhelmingly defeated. The next day Hackney sent Robinson a letter
asking for his resignation.

After months of reflection, Robinson said he came to believe that
Frankel had ordered Hackney to honor all claims just so that Franklin Protective Life—and, ultimately, Thunor Trust and Martin Frankel—would
not come under scrutiny as the result of lawsuits for failure to pay policyholders.

Hackney was now playing his role as a big shot to the hilt. Taking a page
from Frankel's playbook, he greatly embellished his background, telling
people that his "extensive" experience in the banking industry was what led
a group of wealthy investors to select him to head up Thunor Trust.
Franklin-area businessmen were flocking to him, asking about his powerful
connections and wanting to make deals.

In 1994 Hackney and his wife, Ann, sold their house and bought a new
one for $515,000 in a much nicer section of Franklin. Built in 1874 and
known as the Blackburn House, the Hackneys' stately new yellow home,
with a pool in the backyard and a Mercedes-Benz in the driveway, was listed on a walking tour of historic Franklin buildings.

Franklin civic leaders might want to consider one day revising walking
tour brochures to show that when the Hackneys moved into the house at
211 Third Avenue South, they did so as a result of the generosity of one of
the most infamous con artists in American history. Frankel had paid for the
house as a bonus to his Tennessee business partner. On October 12, 1994,
Frankel wired $515,000 from his Swiss bank account to Hackney so that the
house could be discreetly bought under the name of Middleburg Investments, yet another shell company that had been set up in the British Virgin
Islands.

• • •

At the same time Hackney was busy down south, slapping backs and making deals, Frankel was also hard at work, laying the groundwork for a global network of shell corporations that would allow him to quietly shuffle around large sums of insurance company money at will. And in Toledo he was assembling a small group of helpers—the nucleus of what would become a large and unwieldy personal staff.

With Sonia Howe already performing her customary role as bookkeeper, the first helper to be hired was a young Malaysian woman, Sow Chin Tee. "Tee," as Frankel called her, was also working as a sales representative of the Creative Partners Fund, and at the time was dating another of the sales reps, William Kok. Frankel gave her a promotion, making her his personal assistant.

Because he was afraid to leave his house for fear of a confrontation with John Schulte, Frankel told Tee Sow he needed someone who could work part time buying newspapers and food and running other errands. She enlisted a friend of hers from Singapore, Beng Wan Tan, who was attending the University of Toledo on a student visa and who needed extra cash to support his wife and young daughter.

Frankel explained to Beng his situation with Schulte and instructed Beng to always refer to him as Mike King, another alias Frankel had adopted for security reasons. He told Beng he would be working for a company he owned called Gates Investments.

One day Frankel asked Beng, who was majoring in electronics at UT, if he knew anything about televisions, because one of Frankel's sets was emitting a constant low-level modulation that was driving him crazy. Beng found a new television set that agreed with his new boss, and by the end of the summer of 1992 he was working for Mike King and Gates Investments on a full-time basis. Putting his knowledge of computers and electronics to use, Beng would become an indispensable member of the Frankel organization—its top information technology (IT) guy.

From January through March 1992, Frankel formed three offshore dummy corporations that would play integral roles in future schemes: Fletcher International, Sundew International, and Bloomfield Investments, all of which were incorporated in the British Virgin Islands.

Sundew's managing director and sole shareholder was a young German woman named Kaethe Schuchter, who would become the lieutenant of Frankel's vast criminal enterprise. Kaethe also acted as Frankel's European intermediary with Banque SCS Alliance S.A., the multibillion-dollar Swiss bank Frankel used over the next seven years.

Because of the lifetime trading ban that resulted from his settlement with the Securities and Exchange Commission over the Frankel Fund, Frankel set up his relationships to make it appear as though he only offered investment advice to his shell companies.

"This bank [Banque SCS Alliance S.A.] had legally domiciled with it several investment and finance companies—Sundew is such a company," Frankel wrote in a later communication to one of his attorneys in preparation for a tax audit. "The bank often introduces various money managers, such as George Soros, etc., to its clients and/or the investment companies that bring the bank clients; the bank introduced Mr. Frankel to Sundew. Sundew trades, for its own account, through Banque SCS, and Mr. Frankel gives investment advice. But Sundew makes its own trades, without any control from Mr. Frankel. Mr. Frankel simply gives advice, for example, on the direction of the prices of currencies, bonds, and stocks, and Sundew is free to follow that advice or not.

"Sundew's trades are not directed by Mr. Frankel, and its accounts are not controlled by Mr. Frankel. Frankel's brain is 'picked' by Sundew, so that Sundew can make its own decisions on, for example, the direction of the relative prices of foreign currencies."

In the same communication, Frankel goes on to explain that even if he wanted to trade he couldn't because of his nagging psychological affliction: "Mr. Frankel has suffered from a severe case of 'trader's block,' a condition in which it is very easy for him to correctly pick investments, but one where it is very difficult for him to 'pull the trigger' on investments. He even consulted therapists in order to help him overcome this problem.

"After the stress he experienced during the shut-down of the Creative Partners Fund, he decided to pursue only an investment advisory position with a foreign firm, because the position he was offered is very congenial with his psyche and talents. He is much more a talented stock picker than he is a trader; it is very easy for him to give correct investment advice, and much harder for him to actually take advantage of his 'picks.' He is much better at giving investment advice than at 'pulling the trigger.' Therefore, this way of working—where he is paid not on the basis of specific trades, but rather with a long-term contract as an investment advisor for an overseas entity, relieves him of the pressure and makes it easier for him to work."

To create the illusion he was drawing an income rather than pilfering an insurance company, Frankel claimed that his "long-term contract" with Sundew International provided generous compensation.

But in the communication with his attorney Frankel downplayed the amount he was supposedly receiving for his services. He wrote: "A consulting agreement that provides for a $700,000 consulting fee, with a total compensation package of 1.4 million dollars, is very small compared to the sums received by other investment professionals with the same level of expertise as Mr. Frankel."

In setting up his new companies, and in his dealings with the Swiss bank, Frankel had assumed yet another alias—David S. Rosse. There was an actual David Steven Rosse, however, a person who came into Frankel's life in 1991 and who would continue to be associated with Frankel up until 1999. After deciding to remain on Stanhope Drive, Frankel realized that John Schulte was still a threat. He was still in love with Sonia and wanted to be able to protect her and the two Schulte girls. No matter where he moved Sonia to, Schulte had managed to find her. Each day Schulte mailed Sonia one of the postcards with the formerly happy family's smiling portrait, and she presented authorities with a batch of 360 of them to prove she was being stalked. After his previous bad experience with the local private investigators, Frankel decided to look out of town for help.

Through a friend of a friend, Frankel was referred to a security expert in San Jose, California, named David Rosse. Rosse, who owned the American Security Agency and volunteered as an auxiliary officer with the local sheriff's department, seemed to fit the bill. In extended telephone conversations, Frankel told Rosse about how he and Sonia were being "stalked" by Sonia's ex-husband, who had sexually abused his two daughters. Rosse empathized.

"Marty Frankel was a little nerdy, and he couldn't protect himself," Rosse recalled. "And I hate bullies. Schulte is a bully toward anyone who shows any fear. He smells fear and attacks."

Rosse agreed to a meeting, and so he flew to Toledo in order to discuss the situation further with Frankel. After Rosse arrived, Tee Sow and Beng knew something significant was going on because Frankel had ordered them to stay away from his house while he and Rosse went behind closed doors for three solid days.

"When I met him I felt so bad," Rosse recalled. "Reading all those documents about him, Sonia, and the kids, I said, 'This is a fucking travesty of justice.' I like kids. I hate child molesters." So Rosse accepted the job. "I was doing it just for justice," he said. "Schulte was the kind of guy who would walk into a house, shoot everybody, and then kill himself."

Also by the end of the three-day conference, Frankel had reluctantly agreed on the security plan Rosse had mapped out.

"I told Marty, 'If you stay in this neighborhood, you'll never get rid of Schulte, because even if he goes to jail, he'll get out. The best thing you can do is move, quietly in the night. Pack up your shit and get the fuck out of Dodge and start up somewhere else, because you've got nothing here anyway.'"

Frankel heeded Rosse's advice and began to look for a new place to live. Frankel decided he would like to move to the New York City metropolitan area, to be close to the world's financial nerve center. He began looking in Westchester County—the region contiguous to the Bronx, New York City's northernmost borough—that is dotted with many of the city's affluent bedroom communities.

The first Westchester town he tried was Armonk, where in February 1992 he seemed to settle on a nine-thousand-square-foot house on three secluded acres overlooking a lake. The newly built dwelling had six bedrooms, a guest apartment, a maid's wing, an indoor pool and gym, and a Jacuzzi in the master bedroom.

On Frankel's instructions, Rosse flew to Westchester County Airport, only a few minutes from the estate, in order to make an inspection. Frankel, who was deathly afraid of commercial airliners, later joined Rosse after taking an Amtrak train from Ohio. Frankel proposed leasing the house under the name of one of his limited partnerships, Sundew International, but homeowner Louis J. Margan Jr. insisted that the lease had to be in Frankel's name. Frankel then offered to buy the property for an even $2 million and said that the money would be wired from a Swiss bank account. But Margan would not go below $2.25 million, and negotiations collapsed.

A comparable house—but one without a lake view—was soon found just over the nearby Connecticut border. Frankel entered into a long-term lease for a secluded three-acre estate in Greenwich. The property, 889 Lake Avenue, was on a cul-de-sac in one of the town's most prestigious areas. It seemed to be the perfect spot for a big-time money manager to settle. All five of the Connecticut residents found on *Forbes* magazine's list of the four hundred wealthiest Americans made their homes in Greenwich, including billionaire Leona Helmsley.

The town's main commercial thoroughfare is sometimes referred to as "Rodeo Drive East." As with Hollywood's more fabled boutique row, double-parked limousines outside Saks Fifth Avenue and Baccarat are common sights on Greenwich Avenue. It is where the common and sublime regularly converge. A bricklayer living in one of the town's public housing complexes on his way to pick up a prescription at CVS drugstore could very well walk past pop diva Diana Ross, up from her estate along Long Island Sound, sauntering toward brunch at a favorite bistro.

The neighbor across the street from Frankel's new digs, Charles Davidson, did for real what Frankel only dreamed of doing—trading successfully on Wall Street. So did another neighbor, Joseph Jacobs, president of the Greenwich-based Wexford Management money management firm, which managed a portfolio of assets worth over $1.5 billion.

Only four years earlier, in 1988, one of the nation's most notorious confidence artists had lived down the street at 776 Lake Avenue. John Peter Galanis, who promoted himself as a financial genius, had cheated taxpayers, investors, financial institutions, and shareholders out of an estimated $150 million. Instead of investing the money entrusted to him, he used it to finance a lavish lifestyle that included fancy cars, extravagant parties, and expensive homes. At the age of forty-four, Galanis received one of the stiffest prison terms ever meted out to a white-collar criminal—twenty-seven years for convictions on charges that included fraud, bribery, and racketeering.

Since Frankel was familiar with the life and times of Robert Vesco, it's not unlikely that Frankel also knew who Galanis was. If he did know, Frankel might have believed lightning could not strike the same place twice.

Frankel moved to Greenwich in March 1993 with Sonia, the two Schulte girls, Rosse, Tee Sow, and Beng Tan all in tow. He also brought along one of Sonia's cousins, Turner Simpson, who had become the handyman around the Stanhope Drive property and would continue to work in that capacity in Greenwich. He was also the baby-sitter for Leslie and Elizabeth Schulte, earning him the nickname "Peter Pan."

The other residents of the private cul-de-sac made an attempt to be neighborly, with Charles Davidson inviting Frankel and Sonia across the street to an outdoor party at his home. Davidson was a corporate buyout specialist who for ten years had worked beside hedge fund superstar Michael Steinhardt. Although slightly odd in appearance and behavior, Frankel did not arouse any suspicions among Davidson and his other guests, who accepted Frankel's story that he was a successful money manager, too.

Afterward, Sonia's two daughters were often invited to go swimming in Davidson's pool. Frankel and Sonia reciprocated by having the neighbor's children over to swim in theirs.

Outside occasional sightings as they rode their bicycles around the cul-de-sac, Frankel and Sonia were rarely seen following the party at Davidson's. Their reclusive lifestyle was respected in a town that vehemently cherishes its privacy.

That acceptance began to change three years later, after Frankel began renting a second estate, at 881 Lake Avenue. He wanted to use the dwelling and its six acres of land as both a guest house and living quarters for his assistants.

Soon after signing the lease agreement, Frankel had a six-foot-high fence erected around the entire perimeter. The fence blocked a bridle path that had been used for years by the Greenwich Riding and Trails Association. In an attempt to rectify the problem, one of the association's members went to the front door of 881 Lake Avenue and rang the doorbell. She was startled by her gruff reception. "Who are you and what do you want?" demanded an electronic voice coming from an intercom. The frightened woman ran away.

A second go at diplomacy was made by an immediate neighbor of 881 Lake Avenue, Fred Nives. "When I went there a Mr. King answered the door, and as we spoke in the doorway a camera on a tripod followed me around," Nives recalled a few years later. "It was very eerie." According to Nives, a Mr. King promised to install a gate in the fence so that horseback riders could pass through his property, but the commitment was never kept.

After that the gossip about the reclusive newcomer to Greenwich began in earnest. Who was this man? Was he really a money manager, or was he with organized crime or part of a drug ring?

At the same time, almost as if not to disappoint his neighbors, a darker, more sinister side of Martin Frankel began to emerge.

Chapter Five

Martin Frankel might have been just an ordinary thief, but the ways in which he spent the stolen money was extraordinary. He had become lord of a manor on a hilltop overlooking Long Island Sound below, with the spires of Manhattan's financial towers faintly visible in the hazy distance. His fingers were tightly wrapped around the purse strings of tens of millions of ill-gotten dollars that he'd squirreled away in Swiss bank accounts.

Now, with his persecution at the hands of greedy lawyers and the U.S. government just an unpleasant memory, he could enjoy himself a little. Conditions for the debauchery were ripe, and Frankel allowed himself to be seduced by the trappings of power and wealth.

With money as plentiful as water from the tap, Frankel threw his stolen cash around to create his own Xanadu. He filled his estates with women half his age to satisfy his desires, which included a growing appetite for sado-masochistic sex. He also created a caste system of sorts, peopling his private kingdom with assistants at the top, who enjoyed certain privileges, to servants on the bottom, who were not worthy to say his name or be in the same room as "the boss."

In a rare encounter with a neighbor, Frankel had bragged how when he wanted to relax with a glass of ginger ale, one of the women would fetch it from the refrigerator, another would pour it, and a third would pull up his chair so he could sit back and enjoy his cold beverage.

Some speculate that Frankel's penchant for abusive power and sadomasochistic sex stemmed from his increasing inability to forge a lasting romantic relationship with Sonia—just as James Gatz, in the fabulously wealthy guise of the Great Gatsby, had failed to win the love of his precious Daisy Buchanan.

While preparing for his breakout from Toledo, Frankel had continued playing the role of Sonia's great protector. He had her and the two Schulte children spirited away to a safe house in California, a state where the laws favored mothers in child custody matters. It nearly worked, but Schulte managed to find out the location of the safe house after Sonia returned home for a high school reunion and gave some friends her phone number.

But now Sonia, Elizabeth, and Leslie Schulte had been reunited with Frankel in Greenwich, where they could all safely await the outcome of John Schulte's prosecution in federal court. And it was in Greenwich that Frankel would try to create a semblance of a family environment.

Except for the fact that Mom and Dad were no longer across the street, it was almost as if Frankel had never left home. David was there to protect him. Tee was seeing to it that all of the administrative chores got done, and Beng made sure the computers and financial monitors ran smoothly. Turner was the handyman and all-around gofer who cheerfully watched over the two Schulte girls, never minding that he was being paid a mere $2 an hour.

Frankel must have thought that he would finally win the recognition as a financial genius that, in his mind, he so richly deserved, and perhaps Sonia would be the one to share in all the glory.

The idyll didn't last too long. Frankel and Sonia found themselves constantly at odds, bickering over even the most inconsequential of matters.

Frankel had appropriated the living room, the nicest and most spacious of the dwelling's twelve rooms, and there he reconstructed the "trading room" in which he had toiled back in Toledo. With his La-Z-Boy recliner at the center of this sanctuary, he arranged in horseshoe fashion the "lucky" folding tables he had brought from Ohio. Atop the rickety stands he precariously stacked his computers, market monitors, and television sets.

As for the rest of the house, there was no clear plan. For more than a month, much of their belongings remained in boxes that were scattered haphazardly about. Frankel mostly just wanted to be left alone with his machines, but he was unable to concentrate as his irritation grew with each new argument over what needed to be done next. Rosse found himself wondering about what kind of crazy situation he had gotten himself into, as he juggled the roles of peacemaker, mediator, and security chief.

One of the major underlying tensions was the realization on Frankel's part that a marriage between him and Sonia was not in the stars. Sonia was more interested in going out for a good time, while Frankel was the stay-at-home type. They tried enhancing their relationship with kinky sex, which they both found to be highly arousing and entertaining. But even then, whereas Sonia might want to spice things up even further, such as by suggesting to Frankel that they try having sex in a Times Square peep show booth, Frankel was content with practicing S&M within the safe confines of his home. His affinity for perverse sex was growing, and the amount of pain he wanted to inflict was going beyond his partner's tolerance. This led to more arguments, with Frankel complaining about how his needs weren't being satisfied.

Frankel's paranoia reached new levels when he became concerned that Sonia and Rosse, acting either individually or in concert, might be plotting to take his money, and that they might even kill him to do it. And Sonia's insistence on venturing outside of the twelve-room fortress terrified him. He often thought that she would make another slip like the one she had made at the high school reunion and blow his cover in Greenwich.

The atmosphere within the mansion had become oppressive. Beng Tan, the computer technician, was so unsettled by the constant fighting that he and his wife, who was expecting their second child, moved to Florida. Frankel felt lost without his trusted technician by his side to safeguard his precious machines, and for weeks he would call Beng, pleading for him to return.

Then Tee moved back to Toledo, at which time she was accused by some of Frankel's minions of stealing a large sum of cash. Rosse followed Tee to Ohio, where he is said to have threatened her about what would happen if the money wasn't returned. Tee went back to Malaysia soon after that.

Then Sonia bailed out, and the self-appointed financial guru's personal life came crashing down around him. She demanded a lump sum separation payment of $2 million, which Frankel refused to give her. She returned to California but soon moved again after John Schulte's private detective managed to track her down, causing her to pack up her belongings and her children in the middle of the night and leave for Jupiter, Florida. Any lingering hopes for wedded bliss Frankel may have harbored were dashed when Sonia fell in love with Stefan Radencovici, the thirty-nine-year-old owner of Jupiter Catering. Sonia and Stefan married and settled down in Charlotte, North Carolina, where she began operating yet another brokerage firm, PDS Partners.

Sonia was by no means out of Frankel's life, however. In fact, she continued to play a significant role in his business affairs, regularly returning to Greenwich to handle the bookkeeping for Frankel's bogus corporations. It became apparent that once someone was firmly entrenched in the great luxury and wealth of Frankel's universe, it was extremely hard to just walk away. So Sonia stuck around on the business side of things, and her most important responsibility became managing Liberty National Securities' trade confirmations—the sleight-of-hand transactions that kept the Thunor Trust insurance companies believing for years that their reserves were safely ensconced in government bonds and earning millions of dollars at Frankel's capable direction.

Elaborate arrangements were made for Sonia's monthly trips to Greenwich. In the beginning, she took commercial flights from North Carolina to Westchester County Airport; later, after Frankel bought his bodyguard a 1995 Turbo Commander airplane, Rosse would personally pick her up and pilot her back. And each time she came back, the chauffeurs who met her at the airport took a different circuitous route to the Greenwich mansion in case Schulte had placed a tail on his former wife.

It is unknown exactly how well Sonia was being compensated, although Frankel had once complained about how he was sending $50,000 each month to her in North Carolina. Whatever the amount was, it apparently enabled Sonia and Stefan to make a comfortable life for themselves in Charlotte, where they bought a house for $185,000 and enrolled Leslie and Elizabeth at a private school with a yearly tuition of $25,000.

Frankel's small surrogate family was disintegrating before his eyes. Luckily for him, Beng was having a rough time in Florida. His wife had found a good job there, but the thirty-three-year-old University of Toledo electronics graduate was unable to land decent employment with a company that would sponsor him for a work visa. When, during one of his frequent telephone calls, Frankel promised that he would get him a visa, Beng finally relented and agreed to return to Greenwich.

Reunited with his "IT guy," Frankel could sleep a little easier knowing his precious machines were again being closely cared for. Beng would be instrumental in expanding Frankel's computer system to include a network of 150 PCs connected to four servers that provided an uninterrupted flow of the latest financial information from dozens of sources. Later, after the phone system had grown to include more than two dozen lines, the head IT guy would help to successfully negotiate with NYNEX for the installation of a T-1 fiber-optic cable. Getting the cable required digging up the entire five-mile length of Lake Avenue from U.S. Route 1 in downtown Greenwich to Frankel's compound. Frankel would later tell people he had been considering moving because he was experiencing difficulty in getting the T-1 cable, but that the problem was resolved when he asked for help from his "friend," the telephone company's chairman.

Even though Beng was now back in the fold, the only people Frankel had around him were men. He had always felt more comfortable with women, as well as less threatened, and so he set out looking for the best female companionship his money could buy. And he began his search knowing that if he found someone who was unaware of his humble beginnings in Toledo, he could make his Gatsby-like transformation complete.

He turned to the personal pages of newspapers and magazines, promoting himself in small classified advertisements as a wealthy investor looking for a partner with whom he could explore the delights of sado-masochistic sex.

The first one to bite was Miriam Fischer, a forty-year-old, green-eyed Manhattanite who happened to remind Frankel very much of Sonia. Miriam was a graduate of the Parsons School of Design, but her main ambition was to make lots of money playing the markets, so she had taken business courses at New York University. She then worked as a securities broker with a series of firms, including Smith Barney Harris Upham, Oppenheimer and Co., Shearson Loeb Rhoades, and Daiwa Securities.

At the time she met Frankel, Miriam had just left the Stamm Personnel Agency, a Wall Street headhunting firm, and was running her own company, Miriam Fischer and Associates, out of her West Twenty-third Street apartment. She described herself in a resume as an "executive recruiter specializing in institutional equity sales, trading, and research for the brokerage community," with experience as a "position trader in Japanese, Scandinavian, Dutch, and UK securities."

Frankel and Fischer began their relationship through extended telephone conversations in which they discussed sex, but they also talked for hours about what they shared most in common—the markets and trading strategies. After a while Miriam began visiting Frankel in Greenwich, where they consummated their physical and intellectual relationships. The more they discussed business, the more Miriam's confidence in such matters shone through and the more she reminded Frankel of Sonia. In turn, Miriam was impressed with Frankel's financial knowledge and very much enamored with his fat bank account.

Frankel took on Miriam as an associate, and she quickly made herself indispensable in helping with his affairs in and out of the bedroom. Frankel marveled at how, for example, when Miriam went to Boston to meet with representatives of Reuters, she was able to successfully negotiate lower rental rates for news wire terminals that saved him thousands of dollars a month.

Former associates said that Miriam was Frankel's first post-Sonia S&M partner, and after a while became known as the "queen bee" when she began recruiting additional playmates for her kinky new friend, who was now beginning to experiment with group sex.

But Frankel was still hurting from the void created by the departure of his oldest and dearest friend, Sonia. Dating agencies were providing him with hundreds of photographs so that he could go through them searching for women who looked like the farm girl from Elmore.

Frequently he poured out his heart in long-distance calls and e-mails to Kaethe Schuchter, as he had grown entirely comfortable confiding in the young German woman, who by this time had been the Swiss banking liaison and titular head of Sundew International for two years. Kaethe felt sorry for the lost and insecure-sounding voice coming over the phone, and in 1994 she agreed to join Frankel in Greenwich.

For the next year the petite young woman with light brown hair lived the life she might have only dreamed about while watching *Dallas* reruns on German television. She was given her own chauffeured Mercedes-Benz that took her on extravagant shopping sprees at the trendiest shops and boutiques, where she freely used an American Express platinum card to buy the latest in designer clothes.

In return for his generous patronage, the middle-aged bunko artist was given the best sex of his life, with the most attractive and eager-to-please woman he'd ever been with. Kaethe was seemingly without inhibitions, as she would sometimes walk about the Greenwich mansion in the nude, completely visible to Frankel's lower-level employees.

Already a proven business partner, Kaethe would make herself even more valuable to Frankel, rising to what could be considered the rank of lieutenant in his criminal enterprise. He had recognized the young woman's business acumen and became her mentor in the ways of the markets. Frankel imparted to her the secrets of his informational analysis system, and she was the only one of his girlfriends to be given her own stock quote machines and news wire terminals. And Kaethe, by some accounts, managed to put those tools to good work by actually building up a sizable nest egg as she traded for herself in her second-floor office at the Greenwich compound.

But Frankel had also seen the potential usefulness of Kaethe's social charm, good looks, and other talents. He set up a base of operations for Kaethe at the swank Metropolitan Tower apartments on West Fifty-seventh Street, under the alias Kaethe Moreau. To satisfy his need for cash, Frankel regularly had packages of $50,000 in American Express traveler's checks shipped from his Swiss bank to Kaethe's apartment. Kaethe also used the apartment to host frequent parties in which she thrilled guests with ice sculptures and a selection of fine wines.

By 1996 Kaethe was becoming well known on the New York City party circuit, where she befriended Dewi Sukarno, the wealthy jet-setting widow of the founding president of Indonesia, Achmed Sukarno. When Kaethe told Frankel about her new rich buddy, Frankel tried enticing Sukarno into investing with his Columbus Investment Fund, yet another shell company he'd incorporated in the British Virgin Islands.

At some point—perhaps because Sukarno failed to invest with Frankel—Sukarno and Kaethe had a nasty falling-out. The hard feelings were still evident when they bumped into each other at a 1997 Halloween party. A New York *Daily News* gossip columnist described the encounter as a catfight, in which Sukarno slapped Kaethe and pulled her hair. Sukarno would later talk about Kaethe as though she were no more than bait that had been cast out by Frankel as he fished for suckers.

"Kaethe Schuchter always picked up the bill in the restaurant, bought the tickets, provided the black stretch limo," Sukarno said. "In New York, if you have a black stretch, with a driver, twenty-four hours a day, you are intriguing. People loved to go to restaurants, they loved to go to parties, using her car. And Kaethe knew people were tricked by her car, and this is how she became popular. Unfortunately, where money smells, people are like bees all over a sweet cake. Kaethe was the sweet cake."

The third wife of the deceased Indonesian president may have been onto something. After all, it was Kaethe who would apparently later seduce Thomas Corbally—an elderly, flamboyant international businessman with a penchant for gold, caviar, and intrigue—into using his connections with people in high places while he played a major supporting role in Frankel's charade.

Perhaps because Frankel favored and trusted her above his other former girlfriends and female assistants, Kaethe had an attitude befitting her position. She was the most arrogant of the Frankel elite and was secretly despised by the servants.

"She was extremely difficult—she went through drivers every other week," said one of Frankel's former chauffeurs, Patrick Vecchio. "Kaethe thought she was royalty. She'd tell you to pick her up at six A.M., and she'd keep you waiting until seven. When you'd take her shopping she'd go back and forth between the stores, passing by the car each time to make the driver get out and open the door even though she wasn't getting in. And every time she got out of the car she wouldn't close the door, so the driver would have to go and do it."

After Kaethe's sexual fling with Frankel had ended, Adriana Rodrigues, a Brazilian who came to this country as a nineteen-year-old film student to attend Hunter College in New York City, stepped into the picture. While staying at a youth hostel in Manhattan in the early 1990s, she met Carlos Gustavo, an aspiring photographer from a wealthy family in Brooklyn. They soon married, but Adriana divorced him after gaining her U.S. citizenship.

Not too long before the divorce, in 1995, Carlos demanded to know from Adriana where she had been disappearing to for hours on end, and sometimes even overnight. She admitted that she had met a rich financier in Connecticut, that she had begun working for him at his mansion in Greenwich, and that she sometimes stayed over.

"All of a sudden, when she met this guy, Adriana became like this socialite, wearing Rolex watches, riding in limousines, and doing lots of cocaine," Gustavo said. "She would never want to talk about this guy and what went on up there in Greenwich. I would find torn-up pieces of paper with names on them, and these business notes that talked about hundreds of thousands of dollars. She was becoming very secretive and sneaky."

What she didn't reveal was that she had begun perusing the *Village Voice* personal ads, where she found Frankel's listing in the alternative lifestyles section. "It was for a dominant-submissive relationship," Adriana said of the ad in a later interview with the *New York Post*. "He said, 'I'm looking for someone that I can love and cherish and spoil.' It was very sweet. I thought, 'This would be a sexual adventure with someone who sounds like he could give me a good time.'"

After talking a few times on the phone, Frankel asked Adriana out on a date. In one of the rare occasions he wore a suit, he picked her up in New York and they went to a French restaurant. They talked during the entire meal, and Adriana found Frankel to be attractive in a nebbishy way.

"He had a nice face," she said. "He doesn't exercise a lot, so his body wasn't taken care of in that sense, but yeah, he was cute, really cute.

"We talked about the ad and what we were looking for. I had never done anything like this before, so to me it was all new and exciting. We also talked about astrology. He loved astrology. He told me that before we'd met he'd done my chart to see if we would be compatible. . . . From the very beginning I could tell he was very eccentric, and I liked that."

After dinner, Frankel brought Adriana straight home. When she returned to her apartment from work the following day, waiting for her outside the door was a vase of red roses Frankel had sent.

Soon afterward Adriana accepted an invitation to visit Frankel in Connecticut, and she stayed overnight. Then she began going there every weekend, and true to the promise in his personal ad, Frankel began spoiling his new girlfriend by lavishing her with gifts.

"The first gift he gave me was clothes," Adriana recalled. "He took me to the mall in Stamford and we bought a bunch of clothes. He bought me casual skirts, little dresses, and one nice dress that cost $300. I was a little wary because it was such a fairy tale. I thought, 'There's something wrong with this.' I didn't want to feel indebted to him."

But Adriana apparently ignored any warning bells she heard, because after a few months of regularly dating Frankel, she complied when he asked her to quit her job and move in with him. Adriana found life in the Greenwich mansion to be much to her liking.

"It wasn't a pompous, millionaire kind of home. It was relaxed and simple," she said. "He loves wood—cherry wood—and simple Shaker designs. He had couches that were good to sit in—not just to look at—and lots of plants, which I loved. There were very few things on the walls. It was a clean space, but it wasn't minimalist or pretentious. His bedroom was simple. He had two dressers with a TV on each one so he could watch different programs. He also had a long built-in dresser, a king-sized bed, and two bedside tables. He liked cotton white sheets from Bed Bath and Beyond. He was allergic to down, so he had a synthetic comforter."

In the November 1999 interview Adriana described what went on inside the simply appointed master bedroom.

"He bought all these little toys, like whips and handcuffs," she said. "But he is a very delicate person and the last thing he wants to do is hurt someone physically, so it was interesting for him to play the dominant role because even with something like handcuffs, he bought the softest, most comfortable handcuffs you could buy. He would put them on me and say, 'This is not hurting you, is it? Are they too tight? Are you okay?'

"I felt safe with him. I felt that if he tied me up I had nothing to worry about because he was not going to turn into a madman. And we always had time limits for what we did and what we played. He was the dominator all the time."

When talking to others about the great sex he was having, according to former associates, Frankel referred to the Brazilian woman as "my super bitch."

About six months into the relationship, Frankel began talking about wanting to meet other women. Adriana did not object when he resumed placing personal ads, but the few dates that resulted never amounted to anything. In one instance, two women arrived from Germany, only to take off after embarking on a shopping spree that had been financed by their wealthy American host.

Frankel and Adriana ended their physical relationship in the fall of 1996. "We stopped getting along," Adriana said. "Things didn't feel right anymore. We were bickering about the silliest things, and our sex life had faded away."

After she moved back to New York, Adriana received a call from Frankel. "He said, 'My office manager is really screwing up and I would like you to come in and work for me,'" Adriana recalled. She agreed, taking advantage of the $3,000-a-month salary and the use of a company car. Frankel also put her up in a posh apartment at 477 Central Park West in Manhattan.

Frankel recruited dozens more women through alternative-lifestyle personal ads—in newspapers, on the Internet, and through telepersonals— in which he always made sure to mention his wealth, which he now knew to be surefire bait.

Often when he met a woman but found her to be unattractive, he would ask her to remain with him as an "employee." A master of manipulation, he put into practice his own theory that submissive women—and especially the homely, overweight ones–would make the most loyal of employees. He was right. The women fitting this profile whom Frankel hired adored their new boss, and they would do anything he asked with the hope that they would one day become one of his girlfriends.

Frankel was smart enough to realize the prettier women would find nothing attractive about him except for his bank accounts. "Without money, there is no freedom," he once confided to an associate. "If I was living in my mother's house and I was a garbageman, do you think I would be attractive to most women? You can't be in love with a woman unless you are free. Money buys love."

Frankel devised a system with one of his chauffeurs, Sheldon, that weeded out the most unattractive women without his ever having to meet them. Dozens of young women were flown in from all across the country, and when Sheldon met them at the airport he would call Greenwich to give Frankel physical descriptions of the women.

"If she was real fat, she would go right back on the plane," another associate said.

The search for women became such a time-consuming task that Frankel eventually delegated the purchasing and placement of personal ads to some of the women on his staff.

When initially speaking with a woman over the telephone, Frankel would tell her up front that he was a millionaire, and that if he liked her she could live with him in Greenwich, where he would take care of her every need. He would come across as being highly intelligent and sensitive, and in the initial conversations, which sometimes lasted for hours, he impressed the women with his vast knowledge of many different subjects. When a woman agreed to come to Greenwich to meet Frankel, one of Frankel's assistants would call her before making the trip to find out what kind of food she liked.

Frankel assistant Mona Kim recalled how after Sheldon had picked her up at the airport and brought her to the Greenwich mansion, she was greeted at the front door by Miriam, who escorted her into the living room. She was instructed to wait there and told that Marty would be with her shortly, but it took Frankel over half an hour to work up the nerve to leave his room.

"When he finally came out he was really friendly, but he was not at all as I had imagined," Mona recalled. "He was tall and really skinny, wearing these flowing clothes—huge jeans and a huge white shirt—and he had this tiny, tiny little head. He said to me, 'Well, I put on this white shirt and shaved, and this is as good as it gets, so you should be honored.'"

Frankel and Mona sat and talked for a very long time. Well, it was mostly he who did the talking, rambling for a couple of hours on a host of subjects. Mona was bowled over by Frankel's breadth of knowledge. She found out that she shared an interest in astrology with her host and that Frankel had prepared charts for both of them that indicated they were kindred spirits, or so Mona was told.

The evening appeared to be progressing extremely well. Claude Dechappe, the French chef, served Mona an assortment of sushi. She had thought it "sweet" that prior to meeting Frankel, his office manager, Karen Timmins, had phoned to ask what she would like to eat when she came to Greenwich.

When they finished their meal, Frankel asked his guest if she would accompany him to his bedroom and undress. According to Mona's version of the encounter, her host's request was what caused the evening to come to an abrupt end.

"That made me very uncomfortable," Mona said. "I told him I wanted to be taken to the airport." Nevertheless, it was apparent that Frankel liked what he saw in the intelligent young woman. Although Mona already was doing well for herself on the West Coast as an import-export broker, Frankel remained in touch with her and eventually offered her a position.

"He called and offered me a job doing anything I wanted to do, basically," Mona said. "Even though I had a good job, a house on the beach, and a nice car, I was in a rut, and he was saying, 'I'll get you out of your rut. Screw your car—I'll get you a better car. I'll get you whatever you want. Screw everything. Everything is workable.'

"What it basically came down to was him saying he could take care of me because he had the means to do it. He was very adamant that I come the very next day. He acted like a little kid who wants something right away."

As was the procedure for each woman who became either a girlfriend or an office assistant, Mona first had to undergo a background check that Rosse, using the information off her driver's license, performed for Frankel before a firm offer could be made. Sometimes Rosse would give unfavorable reports when he discovered that women had criminal histories, usually involving arrests for such misdemeanor offenses as drug possession and prostitution. But Frankel would often ignore Rosse's warnings and invite the women to join him in Greenwich anyway.

Because of the harsh economic hardships being endured within the republics of the recently dissolved Soviet Union, Frankel knew that there were scores of materialistic young women there, particularly in Russia, who would do almost anything to get to the promised land of America. He began placing personal ads in English-language Russian publications, trolling for the women he would refer to as "shish ka-babes."

The first Russian Frankel met this way was a woman named Inna, but her stint as a girlfriend was short-lived, as Frankel soon concluded that she was a seasoned prostitute. If that were the case, having sex with a prostitute would be intolerable for Frankel. Even though he had his girlfriends tested for HIV, he always wore a condom, even for oral sex.

Although Inna had fallen out of favor as a "girlfriend," she continued an association with Frankel in a new capacity. She and her brother Dimitri came to be known as the boss's "girl brokers."

Frankel instructed Inna and Dimitri to recruit other young Russian women for him, insisting that they must be pretty but simple. A "country girl" is how he described his ideal girlfriend. He apparently wanted to stage his own production of *Pygmalion* by molding an innocent from the farm into a charming metropolitan beauty.

Inna evidently did not follow the instructions Frankel had given her.

"What he had wanted was some sweet, innocent, and unsophisticated girl," recalled a woman who was turned down for the job of girlfriend but was hired as an assistant instead. "But Inna basically just recruited her hooker friends."

The girl brokers had found a seventeen-year-old named Oksana Boudanoval from Riazan, a town outside of Moscow, as well as another young woman named Katia, a musically talented Russian who dreamed of becoming an American rock star. The two new girlfriend recruits had been warned that the American man they would be living with had an S&M fetish, but that they would only have to endure a maximum of five minutes of pain each day.

As with all of Frankel's prospective girlfriends, Oksana and Katia had to undergo complete physical examinations. An extreme hypochondriac, Frankel feared all types of diseases, but especially sexually transmitted ones. "His ultimate fear was that one day his penis would fall right off," a female assistant said.

Oksana and Katia had been in Greenwich for nearly two months before Frankel said he wanted to see what they looked like and what they could do. He gave one of his assistants a video camera and told her to tape the Russians as they performed Frankel's favorite game, "clipping and whipping." After several futile attempts were made to explain to the newcomers what the game consisted of, it was decided that they had to be shown. One of Frankel's assistants removed all of her clothes and allowed another female assistant to apply alligator clips to her outer labia. The second woman then picked up a four-foot-long riding crop and whacked off the clips one by one from the body of her gleefully grimacing partner.

The Russians studied the performance and dutifully complied when told it was their turn to "clip and whip" for the video. After watching the tape, Frankel decided that Katia would be his "girlfriend."

Frankel treated the tall, slender blonde very well, buying Katia a white Steinway piano for $70,000 so that she could practice her music in the mansion and booking time for her at a recording studio so that she could make a CD of her singing. But the relationship did not last too long, and soon Oksana was given the honored position of girlfriend. This created tension and jealousy between the two Russian women, and during the rest of their time at the Greenwich compound they constantly fought as they vied for their rich American benefactor's attention.

"Watching Katia and Oksana fight was entertainment for Marty," one of Frankel's female assistants said. "But that's just the way he was. He would manipulate people to turn one against another so that they would fight. Miriam once described the people around Marty as his chess pieces because he was such a genius at manipulating people. He told one really large girl he was going to make a project out of having her lose weight. Marty said to us, 'We're going to document this and turn this girl into the next Susan Powter.'"

One of Frankel's chefs recalled how his employer used to have fun at the same woman's expense by saying, "'I'd love to see you in a French maid's outfit.' It was really mean, because this woman must've weighed close to four hundred pounds."

At the same time, some of those around Frankel thought they saw a paternal streak in their employer when he intervened in a child welfare matter. As it turned out, however, he had only acted in his own interests, not the child's. Upon learning that one of his assistants, a single mother from Texas, was leaving her eleven-year-old daughter alone at her home in Westchester while visiting her boyfriend on Long Island, Frankel "bought" the girl for $65,000.

"The boss would get so afraid that someday people would begin asking questions, so finally he said [to the girl's mother], 'All right, if you cannot take care of your daughter, I'm going to buy her and I'm going to get a baby-sitter so that there's no problem when it comes to the police asking where you work,'" a Frankel employee recalled.

Frankel moved the girl into the house he was leasing across the street from 889 Lake Avenue, where his most recent prospective girlfriend, a woman from Canada named Debbie, lived with her three young children.

It was hardly a wholesome environment for young children. Debbie, who was fond of wearing leather, appeared to have been kept strictly for entertainment value. Even though she had been recruited as a possible girl-friend for Frankel, she was the only one who was not made to undergo testing for HIV because after meeting her, Frankel decided he would not have sex with her. He would only watch her perform with others.

Once Frankel woke up an assistant with a telephone call late at night for advice concerning the woman he kept across the street. "Debbie had been basically brought over to be a sex toy for other people," the assistant said. "One night he called me up just to ask me, 'Should I have Debbie come over and give Tom a blowjob?'" It would seem, then, that having sex with the women around Frankel was one of the perks that the money manager's business associates readily enjoyed.

Another of Frankel's former girlfriends, who used the margins of her appointment calendar as a sort of diary, noted that one Tuesday evening in March 1999, Tom had taken her to dinner at Manhattan's 21 Club, and that afterward he took her home, where "I give BJ." The next night she wrote on the calendar, "Tom takes me to a S/M dungeon. I am tied up and beaten very hard. . . . I go shopping afterwards, and I go to Jean-Georges for a drink. I am extremely unhappy." The day after that, the former girlfriend wrote, "I am really upset. I go to the duck pond and to church. I can't deal with M any-more. Tom comes to my house. I fall asleep at eight P.M." A day after that,

"Tom spends the night with me and piss in my mouth and BJ." The next day the woman noted that she had lunch at the Drake Hotel, and later, "Tom takes me to Patsy's. We have sex—BJ."

Because they had been intimate with Frankel and had thus gained personal knowledge of the fraudulent schemes through pillow-talk confessionals, Adriana and Kaethe, along with another former girlfriend, Jackie Ju, were among the elite at the Greenwich compound, where a caste system of sorts had evolved. In addition to having their own offices on the second floor of the main house, former girlfriends were also given the privilege of washing Frankel as he showered.

At the bottom of this hierarchy were the servants—the maids, chauffeurs, chefs, handymen, and general gofers. They were under strict orders to refer to Frankel only as "the boss," for fear they might someday slip and reveal their employer's true identity while talking to the wrong people. Paid either with traveler's checks or checks from the personnel accounts set up under Frankel's dummy Good Luck Corporation and Lucky Stars Investments, the servants were not allowed to venture farther than the kitchen in the main house, in order to prevent them from seeing or hearing anything concerning the true nature of Frankel's business.

The servants complied by calling Frankel "the boss," feeding his constant desire to be revered. "He wanted you to look up to him as a god," a female associate said.

The maids were never allowed to go into the trading room, so the chore of cleaning up in there each morning—carting away empty Evian bottles and tidying up stacks of newspapers and file folders—fell to one of the office assistants. When it came time to make the bed in the master bedroom, the maids wouldn't be allowed inside until Frankel removed himself to the bathroom, where he could not be seen by unworthy eyes. The mess the maids often were confronted with, however, could hardly have been less befitting a deity—used condoms amid the twisted bedsheets, and an oversized dildo on the nightstand.

Then there were the servants known as "nannies," the misleading job title given to a group of women whose job was not to take care of children but to constantly shadow Oksana. Frankel employed a total of three nannies at a time, each of whom would work an eight-hour shift, to ensure Oksana was being watched twenty-four hours a day. He wanted Oksana to have such close supervision because he believed she was a nymphomaniac who would jump into the sack with virtually anyone. He especially didn't trust her around one of his own IT guys, Gregory Wiktor.

Perhaps Frankel was jealous because he saw a little of himself in the twenty-two-year-old computer technician. In a biography/resume he prepared for his boss—one that was strangely reminiscent of a resume that was composed in Toledo nearly two decades earlier—Wiktor described himself as having "an unusually high IQ" and someone who as a child related better to adults than other kids. He went a step further in the truth department than Frankel ever did, however, boasting of how at a young age he had learned how to beat the system.

"During ninth grade the school principal loved me since I was the only student he ever knew who made a master key for all the school lockers from scratch," Wiktor wrote. "That's why I got special treatment in the ninth grade. In tenth I was teacher's pet in the computer lab. The teacher figured she could not protect herself against me, so she might as well use me, and she did. We became good friends as well."

Wiktor took his knack at beating the system a step further the next year while attending Briarcliff High School in Briarcliff Manor, New York. "As a junior I was selling 'Red Boxes,' which are devices that allow anyone to make free calls on pay phones. I was making AT&T Alliance teleconference calls across the world at the age of fourteen or so. . . . I didn't pay for the calls, no, but they costed [sic] upwards of $3,000 since there were usually thirty to forty people on via an 800 number across the country."

Explaining how he had been placed in special-education classes due to low test scores in classes that failed to hold his interest, Wiktor bragged to the boss about how his state-subsidized status enabled him to coast through school.

"This began the free ride," he wrote. "From that point up everything was easy, and I definitely took advantage of it. For examples [sic], Briarcliff High School, working during schol [sic], and receiving paychecks from the state for it, private mentors, leaving school when no one else could, etc."

Interestingly enough, Wiktor's father was a criminology professor at an area college. The young man's devious nature fit in perfectly with the environment at the Greenwich compound, which is why Frankel probably let him stay on despite his fears of a tryst with his Russian girlfriend. Another reason was that Wiktor was indeed a young wizard who could diagnose and troubleshoot a technical problem in less than an hour, where it might take others days.

Ignoring the advice of others to simply fire Wiktor, Frankel juggled all of the IT guys' work schedules so that Wiktor would begin his job in the morning rather than the afternoon, when he would be least likely to encounter Oksana, who would normally be out of the house shopping, at school, or visiting her family.

When Oksana was sleeping in her bedroom, located down the hall from Frankel's, a nanny would be seated just outside the doorway just in case she tried sneaking out to see Wiktor. If she were to wake up in the middle of the night and want a bottle of Evian, the nanny would accompany her to the kitchen and make sure she returned to her bedroom. If Frankel were to summon Oksana at any time of the day or night, the nanny would deliver her to the master's bedroom and take a seat in the hallway until they were through.

Sometimes the nannies would see a second woman join Oksana in Frankel's bedroom, and other times they would hear screams coming from the other side of the closed door.

"Oksana would have this empty look in her eyes when she came out of his room," recalled one of the nannies, Tess Berbano, a U.S. Army veteran from Yonkers, New York, who took the job to supplement her income as she studied to become a nurse. "I saw that same look many times. She would be smiling, but her eyes weren't."

Interestingly, Berbano noticed that same look in Frankel. "In spite of all of the wealth the boss had around him, you could see it in his eyes—they were empty too."

Frankel had enrolled Oksana at Pace University's nearby Pleasantville, New York, campus, where she majored in psychology. He also paid for one of her nannies to register as a student, fearing that Oksana would flirt with other students.

Oksana resented the constant chaperoning, but even more seemed to loathe herself for what she thought she had become. "Once she said to me, 'How can I have respect for you when you're nothing more than a slave keeper,'" Berbano recalled.

Another of the nannies, who requested anonymity, said she had become sort of a confidant to whom Oksana would talk about her hopes of one day living the American dream. "She was confused, because she had come from

Russia at a time when there were really big problems there, and the only way she saw that she could escape it was with the help of the boss. But she didn't realize she would end up in this type of situation," the former nanny said. "She said she wanted to finish her psychology studies and someday open up a clinic of her own, and maybe even write a book about people like herself, about Russian girls who are in the same situation that she was. Oksana is very intelligent and very qualified—very smart and interesting. So she had to make the best of the situation. She knew that if Marty got fed up with her, he would just dump her and maybe send her back to Russia. She knew if she put up with it she would eventually become like Kaethe, Adriana, and everyone else." Oksana began undergoing psychotherapy as she tried to cope with the situation she found herself in.

Another of Frankel's fears was that Oksana would leave him to return to Russia. Even though he lavished her with such gifts as a $70,000 Mercedes-Benz 600 and a $50,000 sable coat—which she had to return to the Greenwich Avenue Saks Fifth Avenue after Frankel developed an allergy to it—Oksana had grown homesick for her family in Riazan. After she wrote a letter to Frankel informing him of her intentions of leaving, a security guard wielding an electric cattle prod told her she had better stay. Then Frankel said to her, "You're being unpredictable, and I don't know what to expect of you. How do I know you won't hook up with some Russian Mafia and tell them about me?" Jackie Ju thought she had scored some real points with Frankel by suggesting that Oksana be fitted with an electronic monitoring bracelet, like the ones criminals on probation are made to wear to track their movements, but the idea was vetoed by some of the other female assistants.

Frankel tried desperately to placate Oksana by paying for her mother and grandmother to join her in Greenwich. First he put them up at the pricey Hyatt Regency Greenwich, but later moved them to the local Howard Johnson Motor Lodge. Oksana would be driven for regular visits at the hotels by a nanny, who would wait outside the room like a dutiful sentinel.

Oksana wasn't always allowed to see her mother and grandmother when she wanted, however. Whenever Frankel prevented a visit, the Greenwich mansion would rattle with the Russian woman's screams about being held prisoner. Frankel would remain steadfast in the face of these verbal torrents but would sometimes compromise by having a chauffeur pick up Oksana's family members for visits at the compound. To help keep the older members of the Boudanoval family occupied, Frankel spent tens of thousands of dollars for them to learn English at the Stamford Berlitz.

Frankel discouraged familiarity between servants and those above them in the hierarchy, such as that which had formed between Oksana and her nannies, and so he found ways to create frequent turnover before the lowest-level employees could learn too much about what went on in the compound. One of the nannies was suddenly dismissed on a fabricated charge of passing a love letter from Oksana to Wiktor. Another was let go after being accused of sleeping on the job.

Frankel's mistrust of Wiktor apparently dissipated somewhat over time, because in the summer of 1998, as the expiration date of Oksana's visa approached, Frankel asked him to marry Oksana so that she could remain in the country. Wiktor said that was okay by him but demanded payment of $100,000 in return. The twenty-two-year-old Somers, New York, resident and the Russian "sex slave" were wed in June 1998. Even so, Oksana continued on in her capacity as Frankel's girlfriend and remained under orders to keep away from her legal American husband.

Slightly above the servants and nannies in Frankel's pecking order were the security guards—the twenty-one off-duty police officers who were handsomely compensated for providing Frankel with around-the-clock protection from Schulte and other potentially dangerous outsiders. The officers came from various police departments in Westchester County, as well as from New York City. They worked as subcontractors for Rosse, who had renamed his private investigations company Judicial Investigation Agency and relocated it to Peekskill, New York. It was in Peekskill that Rosse cultivated relationships with local police officers and tapped into their network of friends and colleagues when recruiting for security guard positions.

The security guards packed guns in shoulder holsters as they roamed the grounds at 889 Lake Avenue and kept a vigilant eye on the surveillance monitors. They were paid "at least $200 more per shift" than the other employees, according to one of Frankel's former chefs, Bryan Rodriguez. "The cops would say if you worked for [Frankel] long enough, he'd buy you a new car," Rodriguez said. The off-duty police officers also "told me never to ask any questions about what was going on there. And when I did ask questions, it got me fired."

Robert Randolph, another of Frankel's former chefs and brother of Bryan Rodriguez, said when he was driven by his girlfriend for his first day of work at the Greenwich compound, he was greeted by three security guards who immediately made it known that they were armed. When they opened their jackets to reveal holstered semiautomatic handguns, the new chef's girlfriend began to cry, wondering what Randolph had gotten himself involved in.

Although none of the officers was accused of criminal wrongdoing, some ran afoul of their departments' side job policies, which forbade them from working as security guards. And one of the officers, a patrolman who later married one of Frankel's office assistants, was said to have been present when evidence of Frankel's fraudulent schemes was shredded and burned at the Greenwich compound. That same officer is also said by some to have been among those who looted the compound of stereos, television sets, and other electronic goods the day after Frankel vacated the premises.

The lower-level Frankel employees got to be chummy with the chefs as they passed the time in the modern and spacious kitchen of the main house. With granite countertops, an attached chef's office, its own fireplace, and a huge aquarium stocked with tropical fish, the kitchen was a comfortable place to hang out. The chauffeurs waited there to be called on for rides, and nannies watched the closed-circuit television monitor in case Oksana tried wandering about unattended. The monitor would also be a source of entertainment. Once an IT guy rigged a VCR to the security video system and popped a hard-core sex tape into it, delighting some of the other guys and embarrassing the nanny who was dutifully monitoring Oksana. The tape had come from the household's extensive collection of X-rated videos, which were stored in a box that was appropriately labeled Porno Tapes.

There was a couch in one corner of the kitchen where the help could put their legs up and watch television, and also a computer station where employees spent many hours surfing the Internet. They all enjoyed sampling the fine cuisine served up by the chefs, who were skilled culinary artists who had graduated from the Culinary Institute of America. Rodriguez gave up a teaching position at the New England Culinary Institute to go work for Frankel; Randolph, who had once served as a private chef for many of Greenwich's wealthiest residents—including hotel queen Leona Helmsley, who lived at stately Dunnellen Hall on nearby Round Hill Road—left some good gigs behind to join Frankel.

When Frankel's security guards weren't patrolling the grounds, they were normally confined to the security office, one of several offices that were created when Frankel had the garage of the main house partitioned with plywood and plasterboard. But they were also frequent visitors in the kitchen, and Rodriguez referred to them as "the best-fed cops in the world."

Frankel loved most types of seafood, but he abhorred flounder, crustaceans, and any other "bottom feeders," which he thought were contaminated. If seafood wasn't prepared the day it was bought, the chefs were under orders to throw it out. Among Frankel's favorite meals were Chilean sea bass and sea trout. He also favored truffles and different rice dishes, but never wanted anything cooked in oils, or anything caramelized or charred for fear those cooking processes produced carcinogens.

The chefs also became familiar with the food preferences of Frankel's business partners who were regular guests at the mansion. Thomas Corbally, an elderly international businessman, for example, had an unquenchable hankering for sushi. Another frequent guest was a flamboyant Catholic priest named Father Peter Jacobs, who lived in Rome yet visited the Frankel mansion a few times a month.

"There always had to be caviar for Father Jacobs," Rodriguez recalled. "This stuff cost $170 per quarter ounce, and he would eat tons."

Then there was Tom Quinn, another one of Corbally's contacts and a convicted stock swindler who rented a house near the Frankel estates, who enjoyed eating almost as much as he liked talking with the chefs about the dishes they prepared. "Tom would say, 'I don't understand it. I'm here all day and all I want to do is eat,'" Randolph said. "He really loved to eat, and he loved to talk to me about cooking."

With so many hungry mouths to feed, the chefs made daily trips to local food markets, each time spending between $400 and $500. Randolph, who was used to operating under Leona Helmsley's tightfisted budget, was amazed at how little money seemed to mean at the Greenwich compound. When he would tell Frankel's assistants he needed cash for food, they would sometimes give him hundreds more than what he required, telling him to keep the change.

The office assistants comprised the next highest group in the Frankel hierarchy, and they included Mona Kim, Donna Silver, Cindy Allison, Alicia Walters, Karen Timmins, and Karen's sister Christina, among others. They were all women who had responded to Frankel's personal ads but who had not been sexually appealing to him.

These women were each given their own office at 889 Lake Avenue, and each had specific duties. Christina, for example, was in charge of the chauffeurs, Karen was responsible for rounding up all credit card receipts, and Mona handed out expense money to the chefs and chauffeurs and approved each day's dinner menu.

All of the assistants were at their boss's beck and call for every slightest whim. Once they found themselves rummaging about every Radio Shack they could find for handsets with round earpieces in order to replace the square ones Frankel couldn't stand that came with the new telephones he had just gotten. Another assistant went on a weeklong search for a specific brand of dried peas that Frankel preferred.

It was important to Frankel's self-esteem that he be seen as a dynamic businessman for whom time was money. The second Frankel set foot into his trading room each day at around nine A.M., he would begin paging his assistants and assigning them their tasks. First he would need one of the women to bring him a glass of ginger ale and ice. Then he would hand another a stack of file folders, some of which might contain only a single memo he had jotted down for something that occurred to him in the middle of the night. "Get so-and-so a new car" or "Make sure to get the insurance for so-and-so's vehicle," the memos would read.

"Every single idea he ever had, he had to make a file folder for it," Mona Kim said.

All of the assistants took turns answering the telephones that rang incessantly throughout the day. They were instructed to answer certain phone lines by saying, "Liberty National Securities, may I help you?" If one of the Thunor Trust insurance companies was calling to inquire about its investments, the woman would have a financial statement, which Frankel had prepared in advance, to read from. John Hackney would call at least three times a day from his office in Tennessee.

Some of the assistants were also trained to run a sophisticated program that had been written especially for Frankel's bogus operation by a New York City computer whiz named Mark Burgess. According to a source with intimate knowledge of Frankel's schemes, Burgess' program generated false earnings statements to the Thunor Trust insurance companies that led them to believe their investments were earning hundreds of millions of dollars and not sitting in Frankel's Swiss bank account.

"The way the computer program worked was it monitored actual market trades, so when the client got the statement and checked on a particular security—by looking in *The Wall Street Journal*, for example—the computer-generated earning would match exactly with what it would have actually earned," the source said. "Say Marty wanted to show an insurance company their investments earned $20 million. The program would come up with the trades to match that amount."

Another important daily task for Frankel's assistants was to make printouts from his stock quote machines, which he stressed were crucial for his informational analysis system. One of the assistants brought the wrath of the boss on herself for being late in printing out the information one day. "You stupid bitch," he screamed at the exasperated woman. "Do you know what you've done? You've cost me millions of dollars because you couldn't do your fucking job!"

The assistants learned to grin and bear the verbal lashings, however, because the financial benefits of working for this dictatorial man with such unpredictable behavior and violent mood swings were so great.

Karen Timmins was slightly more useful to Frankel than some of the other assistants, as she allowed herself to be listed as an officer for some of Frankel's fraudulent enterprises, including treasurer of Liberty National Securities and vice president of the Jupiter Investment Fund. She also lived in an apartment Frankel rented for her on West Fifty-fifth Street in Manhattan, another of the addresses Frankel had his $50,000 packages of traveler's checks sent to. That is probably why Frankel further compensated Karen by allowing another of her siblings, her brother, Jimmy, to be one of his gofers. Frankel also had taken the unusual step of buying a car for Karen's mother.

Among the lower-level employees who were constantly guessing as to what kind of business was really run out of 889 Lake Avenue, these higher-level women were known to be "in the loop."

Their duties were often changed, as Frankel played upon the women's desire to feel that they were more important than the others. Fights would break out as they argued over who would have the privilege of serving Frankel his morning glass of orange juice.

Many of the disputes were over money. If the women learned one of the others had gone on a $10,000 shopping spree, for example, then they would all start screaming to Frankel about what they wanted to buy—which, of course, would cost more than $10,000—and Frankel would always cave in.

Bickering among the female assistants was constant as they vied for

Frankel's attention. They emptied glasses of water in each other's faces and hurled insults and threats as they argued over everything from who got the latest-model office safe to who drove the nicest car. Some assistants would sabotage paperwork their cohorts were preparing for Frankel, hoping that he would fire them for incompetence, and some of the women would pocket cash and then blame others for stealing it. Men working at the estate had dubbed one brouhaha "the limo wars," and all of the bemused male employees made a game of trying to guess who the latest "queen bee" would be.

Some of the assistants would try to make Frankel jealous by coming on to the men at the compound. Once, when electrical contractors were working on the first floor of the main house, an assistant watched them from the balcony above, wearing a short skirt and no underwear. That same assistant also had one of the heartier appetites at the house, but she wanted to retain a figure that she hoped would be appealing to the boss. Often after meals, the woman would excuse herself to the bathroom and force herself to vomit what she had just consumed.

Most entertaining of all for the male help, and most frustrating for Frankel, were the frequent "catfights" among the former girlfriends at the Greenwich compound. One such altercation that former Frankel associates continue to talk about began when Kaethe was walking toward her office in the main house and accidentally bumped into Adriana, causing the Brazilian woman to strike her head against a ladder that was in the hall. Without offering a word of apology, Kaethe entered her office and sat down at her desk. Adriana, now deeply incensed, stormed into the office and screamed, "You pushed me into the ladder and I hit my head. You don't even say excuse me?"

"You're excused," Kaethe drolly retorted.

According to the people who witnessed it, the incident escalated into what became known as the "tampon war," with one of the women removing a bloody tampon from her body and throwing it in the other woman's face. The war's sole casualty marched into the trading room demanding of Frankel that he have the other woman retested for HIV. He agreed, and the test came back negative. After the incident, Frankel forbade Kaethe and Adriana to ever be in the house at the same time.

Frankel may have been bothered by the constant turmoil among his brood, but he also used the distractions as a convenient excuse—in addition to that old standby, trader's block—for why he was unable to do any trading. "I can't get anything done around here because they got me all screwed up," he would lament, and then proceed to ignore a close associate's advice that he simply give each of the women a wad of cash and their walking papers.

The catfights and jealous rivalries would prove to be only minor annoyances when compared to the tragic manner in which one of the women ended up leaving Frankel's brood. Frances Burge, a confused girl from Shirley, New York, was found hanging on the afternoon of August 8, 1997, at the Frankel house at 881 Lake Avenue.

Chapter Six

Life in Greenwich had been good for Martin Frankel by the time the summer of 1997 rolled around. By then, his fraudulent insurance empire had been steadily growing, and his Swiss bank account was getting proportionately fatter.

One of Frankel's biggest buying binges with the use of embezzled funds had taken place in 1994, when Thunor Trust acquired Farmers and Rancher's Life Insurance Company in Oklahoma and International Financial Services Life Insurance Company in Missouri. The following year, the acquisition juggernaut swallowed up Protective Services Life Insurance Company in Mississippi, and in 1997 negotiations had begun for the purchase of First National Life Insurance Company in Alabama. The First National deal would successfully conclude before the year's end.

As hundreds of employees and agents went about their daily business of selling the policies the Thunor companies specialized in—policies that allowed people of modest means to plan and prepay their own funerals—they remained unaware of the pipeline that was methodically draining their firms' cash reserves and emptying them into Frankel's pocket. One documented transaction showed that in November 1994, $4.3 million from Franklin American Life's account with First American National Bank in Tennessee was wired to Frankel's brokerage account with Dreyfus Corporation in New York City. The following year, Franklin Protective Life's bank account was depleted by over $8 million. And so it went into 1996 and 1997, when a total of over $50 million made its way from the Tennessee bank into Frankel's hands up north.

"Business" had gotten so good, in fact, that Frankel began considering buying the mansion that he had been renting the past four years. He liked the privacy that backcountry Greenwich afforded, and had decided it was there that he would remain.

It must have come as an immense shock, then, when a crisis that erupted in his Xanadu brought the dreaded authorities intruding on his private world. The name of that crisis was Frances Burge, and of all of the stories of victims left in the wake of Frankel's rise to power, hers was the most tragic.

Born September 21, 1974, in Shirley, New York, a blue-collar village on Long Island, Frances Burge was the daughter of Clarence, a truck-driving Mormon, and Gabriella, a Jewish clerical worker. Raised in her father's faith, Frances was overweight and very plain in appearance. She fought and lost constant internal battles waged over her self-esteem and was hospitalized twice for severe depression after suicide attempts.

While Clarence and Gabriella Burge were going through a divorce, mother and daughter lived together for a time in a homeless shelter. At seventeen Frances gave birth out of wedlock to a daughter, and three days later the infant was given up for adoption.

Soon after, Frances set out for San Francisco with the hope of leaving her problems far behind. But any promise of a new start in California was quickly and rudely dashed. Arriving in the city by the bay penniless and unable to find a decent job, Frances began working for an escort service.

It didn't take long for the girl from Long Island to realize that traveling over two thousand miles had not put her one step ahead of whatever it was from which she had been trying to escape. Less than three months after saying good-bye to Shirley, a despondent Frances called her father and said she wanted to come home. Clarence sent his daughter an airline ticket back to New York.

For a while it seemed as though Frances might be getting it together and developing a sense of direction. By 1996 she had earned a high school equivalency diploma. She got a job as an assistant manager at the local Blockbuster Video store in Shirley.

But Frances was still searching for a better life, or at least a different one. One place she looked was in the personal ads of the *Village Voice,* the New York City weekly alternative newspaper. How many ads she responded to is not known. But one thing is for certain: In the summer of 1996 Frances left a message in voice mailbox number 2440. It was in response to a listing under the "Anything Goes" section that read: "A SUBMISSIVE WOMAN WANTED. Do you want to be financially secure, treasured & cherished? SWM, 40, very rich investor wants to share your dreams & fantasies. You must want to give complete submission."

When the wealthy man returned Frances' call, he said his name was Marty. Marty immediately put Frances at ease, as he came across as an extraordinarily good listener and a compassionate human being. Without thinking of the potential pitfalls of disclosing personal information to a total stranger, Frances found herself telling the sympathetic-sounding voice her entire tragic story, and of her longing to have a strong-willed man take over and impose order on her life.

Frankel often spoke about his own sad childhood marked by physical and emotional abuse, so it would have been very easy for him to connect with Frances. Based on recollections from other Frankel assistants, his boyish charm could be very disarming: "You've had a very difficult time, and so have I," Frankel might have said to Frances. "But that's all behind me now. Now I'm a very wealthy man, and the people who used to look down on me are all green with envy. I can do anything I want. If you come and stay with me, you can start a new and rewarding life."

It was an offer she couldn't refuse.

A couple of days later Frankel dispatched one of his drivers to Shirley to pick up his latest girlfriend prospect. Before stepping into the shiny limousine that pulled up in front of her house, Frances told her parents only that she was going to interview for a job with a rich investor in Connecticut.

Comfortably seated in the back of the black Mercedes-Benz, the normally tedious ride on the Long Island Expressway seemed unusually quick. Soon the car had left Long Island and was gliding across the Whitestone Bridge. As the car traveled toward the Bronx shoreline, out the left window the skyscrapers in the Manhattan skyline glimmered with the promise of an exciting new beginning.

Once past the redbrick maze of Co-op City and slipping from the Bronx into Westchester, the car whizzed by signs on the shoulder of the Hutchinson River Parkway: Pelham Manor, Mount Vernon, New Rochelle, White Plains, Mamaroneck, Rye, Armonk, and finally, Welcome to Connecticut.

Exiting onto Lake Avenue, the Mercedes turned into a hidden cul-de-sac on the left side of the road and up a winding driveway that opened onto an impressive contemporary stone mansion that was barely visible from the road. Passing through tall, solid oak entrance doors, Frances was greeted by another young woman who introduced herself as Marty's assistant. She was then escorted down a long atrium and into a paneled room that was both a study and a dining room. A table with two place settings sat in front of a fireplace amid tall bookcases that were filled with hundreds of volumes.

After being shown to her seat, Frances was told that her host would be joining her shortly, but she waited for over half an hour for him to appear. Then an apparition in faded and baggy blue jeans came through the door.

"Hello, I'm Marty," said the gaunt, pasty-complexioned man to his guest, who rose to accept the bony and extremely white hand he extended. "It's so nice of you to come."

Taking their seats, Frances and her host were served dinner by Marty's personal French chef, Claude Dechappe, who filled Frances' fluted wineglass with a vintage Chardonnay shipped by the case directly from its California vineyard. Into Frankel's wineglass he poured Evian spring water.

In between bites of the exquisitely prepared meal, Marty told Frances about all the great things he was accomplishing from his Greenwich abode. He confided to her about how he had perfected a scientific method for predicting the behavior of markets, which had enabled him to create fortunes for investors as well as one for himself.

"Managing money for others," he solemnly intoned, "is a sacred trust."

In order to be able to fulfill this calling, Marty explained that he relied on assistants to relieve him of having to trouble himself with the mundane. In addition to having a staff of domestic servants, Marty said, he employed young women as trusted aides who performed a number of important tasks. An assistant might be called upon one day to deliver important documents on which a multimillion-dollar deal depended. On other days, one might be invited to the master bedroom.

After Claude left the room with the dishes he had cleared off the table, the host made a most unusual request of his guest. "Would you please stand up and remove your clothes?"

Peering through thick, round lenses, Frankel appraised the naked woman as though she were a side of beef, a commodity to be bought and later sold as a profit. Resting his chin on the backs of interlocked fingers, he narrowed his already squinting eyes. Hoping that Frances' clothes had just been an unflattering concealment for what was underneath, Frankel was disappointed at what he saw and inwardly grimaced.

"Thank you. You may put your clothes back on," he said softly, almost apologetically. Putting on his most earnest expression, Frankel then broke the bad news to his guest. "You know, Frances, I had charted both of our horoscopes before this evening, and unfortunately I discovered that we would not be very compatible romantically. But I like you a lot. You're a very nice girl and I'd love to be able to help you out. I'll tell you what: There's a whole lot that needs to be done around here, and from time to time I need to bring on more staff. If an opening should occur, I'll give you a call, and I hope you would accept any offer that I make."

A year later, when recounting that evening with Greenwich detectives, and relishing playing the role of rich playboy, Frankel would make it sound as though Frances had been the aggressor and that she had disrobed of her own volition.

Knowing that he would not be inviting Frances into his bedroom, Frankel summoned the chauffeur and directed him to take the disappointed young woman back to Long Island. As he had with others who came before her, Frankel remained in touch with Frances. In frequent phone conversations he continued to dazzle Frances with his wide range of knowledge and soothed her with his kind and gentle understanding, but at the same time he probed Frances' mind in order to gauge how loyal she would be if he took her on his staff. By September 1996 Frankel was satisfied that Frances would eagerly do his bidding without posing a security risk to his illegal operation.

And so Frances was welcomed into the growing extended Frankel household, now filled with a curious collection of women from greatly varied backgrounds. The Long Islander appraised her new housemates; none of them was beautiful, but some were highly appealing in a strictly sexual way. They came from exotic, far-off places such as Russia, Germany, and Brazil. She particularly liked Karen Timmins, and the two would in time come to be intimately—some say romantically—involved.

Frances, like some of the other women, began life with Marty as a gofer, although a handsomely compensated one. She was given a bedroom on the ground floor of the six-acre estate at 881 Lake Avenue, where sliding glass doors opened to a swimming pool in the backyard. She was also assigned a "company car"—a new Champagne-colored sedan—and was issued a credit card that she used when she made the three-mile trip into town to run errands for her benefactor. Often she was allowed to charge things for herself.

On her twice monthly visits back to Shirley, friends and acquaintances began to see noticeable changes in Frances, changes that seemed to be for the better. Frances had begun paying closer attention to her appearance, dressing neatly and wearing makeup. Her straight, usually greasy hair was washed and in a French braid. A portion of her discretionary funds went toward the purchase of diet pills, and she had lost a significant amount of weight.

In her new car and equipped with a pager and cellular telephone, Frances stopped by Blockbuster to boast to former coworkers about how she regularly shuttled to a posh Manhattan apartment to make business deliveries for her rich Connecticut investor. While the people she left behind in Shirley had to buck the bumper-to-bumper traffic on the Long Island Expressway in order to cool off at an overcrowded Jones Beach, all Frances had to do was jump into the pool that waited outside the sliding glass doors of her ground-floor bedroom. She bragged about shopping without spending limits, and how she even sometimes helped Marty to make investment choices. Her description of how Frankel often wandered about the house in his pajamas left former coworker Denise Paladino with the impression of Frances' boss as an eccentric "Hugh Hefner type."

Despite the outward changes, Frances Burge was still the same deeply disturbed young woman on the inside. It was about this time that Gabriella Burge was growing increasingly concerned about her emotionally fragile and vulnerable child. In March she took a trip to Greenwich to see just what it was Frances did for Marty and under what circumstances she lived. But while making arrangements for the visit over the phone, Gabriella was told by her daughter that coming to the house in which Frances lived was out of the question.

"It is forbidden," Frances explained cryptically.

So mother and daughter arranged to meet at the Greenwich Colonial Diner for lunch, during which Gabriella insisted on at least being able to see the house from the outside. Frances relented, and they hopped into the sedan Frankel had bought for Frances. But as the car turned into the cul-de-sac, Frances ordered her mother to duck as they slowly passed by the mansion. "I can't let them see you with me," she said.

Clarence Burge was becoming equally concerned about his daughter's well-being. When he asked Frances what she did for "this Marty fellow,"

Frances replied that it was always something different. Sometimes she would drive into Manhattan to make a delivery to the West Fifty-seventh Street apartment Marty rented for one of his ex-girlfriends, Kaethe. Other times, Frances told her father, Marty would direct her to accept package deliveries for him. "She said she once asked Marty what was in those packages, and he said, 'Don't worry about it. It's only money,' " Clarence later recalled.

Clarence Burge actually once spoke with the mystery man in Greenwich, after dialing a phone number he had gotten from his daughter. "Marty picked up the phone, and he demanded to know how I got the number," Clarence said. "I didn't like all this secrecy one bit. Frances used to come home every other weekend, and the funny thing was she would have to be [back] home [in Greenwich] by a certain time. This guy was too weird. He was a total control freak. I told Frances to look around and get as much information she could on this guy in case things backfired on her."

Despite the perks that came with life in Greenwich, Frances began to feel as though she did not belong. She hated the fact that Frankel did not have the least bit of interest in her sexually.

The women who were invited into Marty's bedroom clearly constituted an elite. They were members of an inner circle on whom Frankel heavily relied. They were the only ones who were given access codes to the keypads unlocking forbidden rooms. Only they had their own offices. And only they were constantly around the boss, breezing in and out of the ground-floor trading room where Frankel was said to have executed megatrades that reaped windfalls for investors and bankrolled his lavish lifestyle.

While all this was occurring at 889 Lake Avenue, Frances felt her isolation at the house down the road growing. She was kept on the periphery of the exciting world of high finance. Marty often refused to take her calls, and when she would show up at 889 Lake Avenue she was told that the boss was too busy to see her.

Her funk steadily deepened, and Frances retreated into a world of her own creation, one in which a single, powerful man possessed her so completely that he dominated her entire existence. She remained inside her bedroom for days on end, dreaming of her perfect lover and planning to make yet another break for the new life where she would find him.

And all the while the Frances Burge from Shirley was slowly reasserting dominance over the Frances of Greenwich. She began keeping more to herself, not leaving her room for days at a time. The hard-fought weight loss disappeared. Each pound she had shed returned as she sought solace in a diet of junk food and television. Her hair went unwashed and the shirttails again went untucked.

Frances returned to perusing the same personal columns that had brought her to Greenwich, where the man of her dreams surely awaited. She began collecting magazines devoted to sadomasochistic sex, and when she wasn't reading about bondage, submission, and domination, she watched it on videocassettes.

The last time Gabriella Burge would see Frances was in May 1997, when Frances returned to Long Island for Mother's Day. In a rare frank discussion between mother and daughter, Frances poured out her heart to Gabriella, sobbing about how lonely and more depressed than ever she felt. She confided that she had come to believe that the situation in Greenwich into which she had inserted herself was a charade for something sinister, that Marty was doing "something wrong."

In this last encounter, Gabriella noticed that her daughter had become preoccupied with sex, especially in how Frances spoke of wanting to learn more about sadomasochism. "Marty promised to teach me, and I kept saying, 'What is there to learn?' " Frances recounted for her mother. She then told Gabriella about how she had gone with some of the other Greenwich women to the Vault, a notorious club in Manhattan's S&M scene.

After returning from Long Island to Greenwich for the final time, Frances became as reclusive as her boss. Unable to find salvation through personal ads taken out by others, she decided to take out some of her own. Trying hard to sound alluring, but her words betraying either an interrupted primary education or a very distraught state of mind, Frances composed the following ad: "Young woman looking for a special relationship with that special kinky fun erotic person. You must be attractive, attentive and hold [sic] to acquire my attentions if you feel that your qualifications meet my standards. Left [sic] a message and I might respond to you."

Since Frances had virtually isolated herself at 881 Lake Avenue, she hardly saw any of the other girls anymore. But in a rare effort to be more social, Frances made tentative plans with Mona Kim to go to the Great Adventure amusement park in New Jersey on August 8. The day before the trip, Marty's secretary, Mary Anne Rizzaro, phoned Frances to ask about a letter Frances was supposed to mail, because Mary Anne had been notified that it was never received. Frances assured Mary Anne the letter had been sent.

"The conversation was usual," Mary Anne later told police. "She sounded normal."

That brief conversation would be the last time Frances spoke with anyone.

On August 8, the day of the planned amusement park excursion, Mona drove to the neighboring city of Stamford to buy a book. Upon returning to Greenwich, she dropped off her things at 889 Lake Avenue and took the short walk through the woods to the other house to see if the amusement park trip was still on.

Earlier, as another sweltering midsummer day began to take shape, Frances had parted the sliding glass doors and left her bedroom's air-conditioned coolness. As she walked onto the concrete patio below the wooden deck that looked over the swimming pool at the rear of the house, she was wearing the same blue football jersey, bearing number 87, and same white shorts she had worn for several days straight.

In one hand she held a length of clothesline that she had cut with scissors. With the other hand she grabbed a chair and positioned it directly beneath one of the deck's support beams. She fashioned a slipknot on one end of the rope, passed the other end through the knot's eye, and then climbed onto the chair and fed the rope over the beam, tying it firmly in place. Frances spread the loop at the rope's untied end, placed it over her head, and pulled on the rope until it was nice and tight around her neck. She then stepped off the chair.

An account of what happened next was provided by Mona Kim, in a signed statement she gave to police:

> I arrived at 881 Lake Avenue at about 3:45 P.M. to see if Frances still wanted to go to the amusement park and found the front door open as usual because the front door doesn't lock. I went into the kitchen and dialed extension 33, which is the telephone in Frances' bedroom, and then called to her.
>
> When I got no response from her I went downstairs and knocked loudly on her bedroom door and still got no response. I then opened the bedroom door and saw that her bed was empty.

I then called over to 889 Lake Avenue, the office, where Frances sometimes worked. Mary Anne answered the telephone and I asked if Frances was there. Mary Anne said she was not. I told Mary Anne that I checked her bedroom and that she wasn't there, but that I didn't check the bathroom because I was afraid to. Mary Anne said that I would have to check the bathroom, and that she would stay on the line.

I checked the bathroom and did not see Frances. I then saw the sliding glass door and screen door open, so I walked outside thinking Frances was by the pool. As soon as I got outside I saw Frances from the corner of my eye, hanging from the deck.

Mona let out a piercing scream that was heard by distant neighbors.

Since Mona was still holding the phone, Mary Anne heard the scream too. She called out for Karen and Claude, telling them to go immediately to 881 Lake Avenue and see what was wrong with Mona.

Mona was still on the phone with Mary Anne when the pair arrived. She yelled for them to go downstairs but then tried stopping Karen. Karen pushed Mona out of the way and demanded to know, "Where is she?"

Mona directed her to go through the sliding glass doors in Frances' bedroom and look to the left.

Upon seeing the limp body dangling beneath the wood deck, Karen ran away screaming. Claude took out his pocketknife and cut Frances down, placing her gingerly on the ground. Although the woman had been dead for some time and rigor mortis had begun to set in, the fifty-nine-year-old chef checked for a pulse. Finding none, he began administering CPR. He didn't stop until the paramedics arrived.

After Karen quieted down and the police had arrived, she told the officers the sad story of Frances Burge. "She had a date with Marty and he was not interested," Karen said. "But he thought she was very sweet, and because she had such a sad life, and I could use some help, she could help me. When I first met Frances Burge she was just lovely. Sweet, kind and giving. A wonderful girl."

At the time, Karen was living at another place in Greenwich that was being rented by Marty, and Frances would often make the short drive to the house on Stanwich Road in order to visit. "Then she stopped coming over,"

Karen told the police officers. "She would stay in her room, and not respond to anybody unless I physically went over there."

Karen also told the detectives about the fantasy world into which Frances had withdrawn. "I would go along with her stories because I didn't know what her reaction would be if she knew that I knew she was lying," the thirty-two-year-old woman said.

Among other tales, Frances would tell Karen about how she came from a "warm and loving family." She maintained this charade until one day she opened up to Karen over a cup of coffee at the Greenwich Colonial Diner.

"At this time she told me that she had a horrible family, and how her mother wouldn't even take her to the doctor when she was pregnant; how her father wouldn't let herself and her mother live at home while divorcing, thus the homeless shelter," Karen recounted for the police. "I urged her to get help and she did. She went to a doctor she liked on Long Island and went back on her medication, Zoloft, I think. I haven't seen her since last week, but I took great care to make sure that somebody checked on her every day."

The investigation of Frances' death was assigned to detectives Scott McConnell and Edward Zack. Although the incident scene had been at 881 Lake Avenue, the detectives knew that the center of whatever was going on was just up the road, at 889 Lake Avenue. Using Frances' suicide as a pretext for getting inside for a look around—explaining they needed to dot the i's in their report—the detectives went to the main house and were invited in by Frankel himself.

"We didn't know exactly what was going on," McConnell said. "When me and Zack first got there we saw all these broads. Then we found those S&M tapes, so we had a suspicion this guy was into something sick. So we just wanted a chance to be able to look around."

Frankel had ushered the detectives into his office at 889 Lake Avenue, a converted living room that struck the officers as resembling the bridge on the *Starship Enterprise*. Like a wryly grinning Captain Kirk, Frankel sat in a reclining lounge chair that was surrounded on three sides by as many as thirty computers that were stacked one on top of another on rickety folding tables. The detectives also took note of the several telephones that were within Frankel's reach, and they inquired about the monitors that were mixed in with the stacked computers that flashed constantly changing financial figures and stock symbols.

"I'm a consultant with an investment firm called Sundew International, which leases this house and the other one at 881 Lake Avenue," Frankel explained to McConnell and Zack. "I do all the investing for a major Swiss bank."

He bragged about his many girlfriends, and how in return for "taking care of my needs I treat them real nice."

Then the detectives began asking Frankel about Frances Burge and the circumstances surrounding her death. He gave the following signed statement:

I want to tell you about the situation with Frances Burge and the other females that live at number 881 Lake Avenue. The females are mostly my ex-girlfriends that I met through personal advertisements. I date a lot of women and these girls are special to me. I care about these girls. Some of the females I have had sexual contact with but at no time did I have sex with Frances.

Frances answered an advertisement I placed in either the telepersonals or the *Village Voice*. I sent a limousine to pick up Frances for our first date. She did not look as I expected. She was overweight but a nice person. During that evening Frances had taken her clothes off and wanted to have sex. I did not want to.

Frances and I kept in contact. Approximately during the month of September 1996 I hired Frances as a general helper around my house at 889 Lake Avenue. Frances would actually live at Number 881 Lake Avenue. This house at 881 and my residence at 889 are rented by the company of Sundew International Ltd. I work for this company as a consultant.

In the house at 881 Lake Avenue there are several other females that also live there. Their names are Yvette Bradford, Mona Kim, Adriana Gustavo. All these girls answered my personal advertisements at one time. Mona, Frances, and Yvette, I had no sexual contact with. Adriana is my ex-girlfriend. Some of these girls think that they might be my girlfriend some day. I trust all these girls. The girls do not get paid a salary, but I give them money as they need it.

Besides the other girls I mentioned I also have Karen Timmins, who is actually my office manager. She also manages the houses at 881 and 889. Karen lives at 527 Stanwich Road.

Frances wanted to have a sexual relationship with me. Karen told Frances several times that I did not want to have sex with her. Frances did not handle this well. This has been occurring ever since Frances moved into 881 Lake Avenue.

In January 1997 I had a long talk with Frances about the situation. During this conversation I learned that Frances attempted suicide several times when she was fourteen to sixteen years old. She was placed in a mental hospital because of the attempts. After the conversation I told Karen about it. Karen said we have to get Frances help.

Karen had Frances see a psychiatrist, and the doctor prescribed some types of drugs for Frances. I don't know if Frances was taking her pills. The last time that I have seen Frances was approximately two or three weeks ago. I complimented Frances on her nice looking hair ribbon. She appeared fine. Frances never told me that she had any thoughts about committing suicide.

The way that I found out about Frances was that Karen called me on the phone today and was very upset. She told me Frances had tried to hang herself. I told her to call an ambulance and the police.

The detectives had Frankel sign the statement, and then they reengaged him in small talk. Frankel offered to provide both of them with free investment advice. "I gave him a couple of back slaps and said, 'Marty, you're the best,'" McConnell recalled.

But any further chance to get chummy with Frankel was abruptly quashed when Sonia, who happened to be in Greenwich making her monthly visit, burst into the office. "She came rushing in and shut us down," McConnell said. "She screamed at Marty, 'What the fuck are you doing?' and yelled for us to get out."

Soon after McConnell and Zack returned to the detective bureau they received a call from Michael "Mickey" Sherman, a high-profile local criminal defense lawyer, who warned them to have no further contact with his client, Martin Frankel, unless he was present.

The evening of Frances' death, Clarence and Gabriella Burge arrived at Greenwich Hospital, where their daughter's body was being held before being sent to the office of the chief state medical examiner in Farmington for autopsy. After identifying Frances' body, the Burges met with Detective Zack in the emergency waiting room.

"Mr. Burge advised that he had serious concerns about his daughter living at 881 Lake Avenue," the detective wrote in his report of the meeting. "His daughter advised him that although she worked for Mr. Frankel, she was not paid on a regular basis and that she would occasionally be given traveler's checks as pay, for which she would have to produce receipts for everything that she bought with the traveler's checks and in turn, give the receipts to Mr. Frankel.

"Mr. Burge further advised that his daughter would never tell him exactly what she did for Mr. Frankel. She only told him that Mr. Frankel was a stock analyst. Mr. Burge advised that he will attempt to collect his thoughts over the next few days and that we will speak again regarding this that his daughter had told him about living at 881 Lake Avenue and working for Mr. Frankel."

The Burges returned to Greenwich two days later to meet some of the women Frances had lived with, and to go through their daughter's room looking for any keepsakes they might want. "I hoped I'd be able to keep in touch with Karen and the other girls because they were like Frances' extended family," Gabriella later said.

On September 10 state associate medical examiner Arkady Katnelson officially ruled that Frances Burge had died as a result of asphyxia due to hanging and that the manner of death was suicide. The police concurred and closed their case the following month, informing the medical examiner's office that the rope Frances had used to end her life could be thrown away.

Though grief-stricken, the Burges accepted the official determination of their daughter's death. Still, Gabriella desperately searched for a way to give Frances' death some meaning. "It would make me feel good if this accident helped to expose what Marty Frankel was all about," she said.

As a direct result of the suicide, agents from the Drug Enforcement Agency made some inquiries about Frankel. The agency was tipped off by a lawyer of the neighbor who had heard Mona Kim's screams. The neighbor thought that the death could have been linked to illegal narcotics activity.

Detectives McConnell and Zack did everything they could to make Gabriella's wishes come true. Although they were satisfied with the medical examiner's findings, which were supported by their own investigation, the pair sensed something was terribly amiss at the Lake Avenue compound.

They convinced their superiors that Frankel was probably operating some type of criminal enterprise, persuading them to place the Lake Avenue compound under surveillance. But their efforts were ineffective because undercover officers were legally barred from entering the private cul-de-sac without a warrant. They had to content themselves with parking on the shoulder of Lake Avenue to monitor the comings and goings from the cul-de-sac. In the end, all the police were able to do was confirm that there was an unusually high volume of traffic of vehicles with New York license plates at the Frankel estate. But still they persevered on the off chance of spotting a violation by one of the cars leaving the cul-de-sac, leading to possible questioning of the driver and even a search of the car.

In the meantime, Zack and McConnell tried passing the ball to the Connecticut offices of the Internal Revenue Service. "I spoke with this agent, and I told him, 'Look, I want to make you aware that something doesn't seem right down here,' " McConnell recalled. McConnell told the agent that it was plainly evident that someone named Martin R. Frankel, who despite having been banned from the securities industry for allegedly bilking clients, still seemed to be doing business with a brokerage firm he was running from his home. Making the situation even more suspicious was the fact that Frankel appeared to be using a series of aliases in an attempt to conceal his true identity. The history of police responses to 889 Lake Avenue shows that Greenwich officers had often gone there to check on burglar alarm activations, usually because one of the women there had forgotten the security code. One time the alarm system's owner was listed as Mike King, another time it was Sundew International, and still another it was a Mr. Frankle, when all along authorities knew the owner's name to be Martin R. Frankel.

The IRS sent an agent to Greenwich to meet with McConnell, and on New Year's Day 1998 the detective accompanied the agent to view the two Lake Avenue properties and then filled her in on what he and his partner had seen.

"After that, nothing!" McConnell said. "I never heard another freaking thing about it."

Frankel was shaken by his sudden exposure, and although he was assured by his lawyer that the detectives would not be bothering him anymore, he decided that it would be smart for him to ingratiate himself with the Greenwich police department. Through David Rosse's private investigation firm, Frankel made a large cash contribution to the local police union, the Silver Shield Association, and he paid the way of the union's president and another officer to play golf in Myrtle Beach, South Carolina, with Rosse. When Frankel learned that the union's annual golf tournament was approaching, he said he would pick up the entire tab for the event, earning him a plaque of appreciation from the Silver Shield Association.

Inside the compound, Frankel tried masking his fears by laughing off the suicide, telling associates morbid jokes involving death by hanging. Then he returned his undivided attention to further expansion of his fraudulent empire.

Martin R. Frankel's 1995 driver's license photo. It's one of the few recent photographic images of the fugitive financier.

Frankel in his Jefferson Junior High School yearbook.

A recent photograph of Frankel's parents' house on Stanhope Drive in Toledo, Ohio.

John and Sonia Schulte, with their two children, in a 1988 postcard that was sent to supporters after John's failed state senate campaign.

Ted Bitter, one of Frankel's earliest fraud victims, looks over printouts of the legal expenses he incurred trying to win back his life savings, which were misappropriated by Frankel.

6

The house at 889 Lake Avenue that Frankel allegedly bought with $3 million in embezzled insurance assets. It was Frankel's primary residence and the place from which he ruled his corrupt empire.

7

Greenwich Police Chief Peter Robbins—the man who oversaw the initial investigation into the suspicious fire at 889 Lake Avenue.

8

Frankel's other residence, this one at 895 Lake Avenue, where he housed some of his female employees.

A Greenwich police photograph of Frances Burge's room the day she committed suicide in 1997.

9

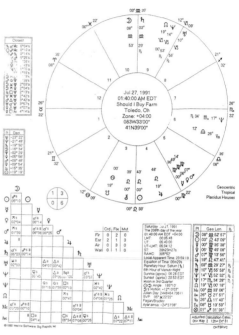

One example of the type of horoscope wheel Frankel used to make most of his major life decisions. This one was for buying or not buying a mansion in Ottawa Hills.

10

The Ottawa Hills mansion that Frankel opted not to buy. He set up his empire in Greenwich, Connecticut instead.

11

Father Peter Jacobs, one of Frankel's associates and his direct link to the Vatican, outside his trendy New York City restaurant in 1983.

12

John Hackney, the Frankel associate who allegedly brokered many of Thunor Trust's insurance company acquisitions, as shown in a 1996 photo.

13

14

Thomas A. Bolan, circa 1985—a former assistant U.S. attorney who allegedly tried to link Frankel's bogus St. Francis of Assisi charity with a legitimate Italian Catholic organization.

15

One of the men who put an end to Frankel's illegal insurance scheme—Mississippi Insurance Commissioner George Dale.

16

Hotel Prem in Hamburg, Germany, where Frankel's four-month international manhunt finally came to an end.

17

*FBI Special Agent Michael Wolf announces at a New Haven press conference
that Martin Frankel was found in Hamburg, Germany, taken into custody,
and charged with money laundering and wire fraud. FBI Special Agent
Robert Marston stands to Wolf's right.*

18

*Assistant U.S. Attorneys Kari
Dooley and Mark Califano—
two instrumental members of
the team that helped bring
Frankel to justice.*

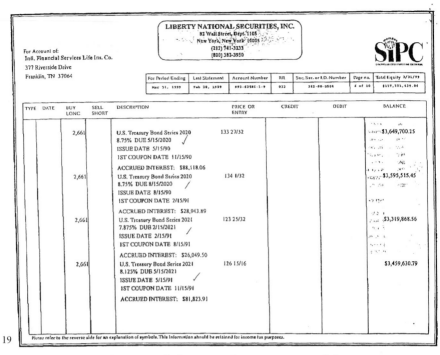

19

A photocopy of a bogus earning statement Frankel sent to the Thunor Trust insurance companies.

20

The prison in Hamburg, Germany, where Frankel was taken after he was arrested at the exclusive Hotel Prem.

Chapter Seven

With Burge's suicide and its subsequent investigation behind him, Martin Frankel concerned himself with thinking up ways to make even more money. One idea that came to him would have actually been a legitimate business venture had it not involved financing with stolen money.

The idea struck Frankel as he was surfing the Internet, which he did for countless hours while others believed he was hard at work behind the locked doors of his "trading room." Because he often found himself cursing the amount of time he spent conducting Web searches only to come up with irrelevant information, he finally thought, "Why not create my own Internet company?"

While pondering this notion, Frankel came to believe that if he assembled the right talent and resources, he could develop an Internet search engine to surpass those that had already been well established by AltaVista, Yahoo, and similar companies. When his search engine would be asked to find out about Robert E. Lee, for example, it would retrieve information *only* on the Confederate Civil War general and not anything for, say, Paul Lee Barristers and Solicitors in Ontario.

The investment of time and money would be great, but Frankel believed he could make a killing when making an initial public offering of stock in the company. "He thought he could make $400 to $500 million because as an IPO, Yahoo or one of the other Internet companies would want to buy him out," an associate said.

Frankel spent much of the year conducting research for his idea, and by early 1999 had gone so far as to begin negotiations to lease ten thousand square feet of office space on Maiden Lane, at the foot of the World Trade Center in lower Manhattan, that would be used as headquarters for the Internet firm.

But 1998 was a very busy year for Martin Frankel for many other reasons. In July Frankel bought the house he had been renting at 889 Lake Avenue for $3 million cash, nearly all of which was wired from his account at Banque SCS Alliance in Geneva. Six months later he bought Chuck Davidson's house across the street, at 895 Lake Avenue, for $2.6 million, also with cash that was wired from the Swiss bank. As owner of the properties that anchored the entrance to the cul-de-sac, Frankel approached the owners of the remaining houses in between and made offers on that land as well.

"He said that if he was able to buy all of the properties, he would connect them all with a covered walkway," a Greenwich real estate agent recalled Frankel telling him. "Marty didn't like to go outside that much. He had all these phobias about ticks that would give him Lyme disease, and he had all those allergies."

The same agent said that on another occasion, when he bumped into Frankel and Adriana as they were riding bicycles in the cul-de-sac, Frankel mentioned he was thinking of buying a "huge" piece of property on which he could build a fifty-thousand-square-foot mansion.

"He basically talked about wanting to build something like the Hyatt hotel," the real estate agent said. "Soon after that, when he had already bought the other Lake Avenue house, I called him up and told him about a great piece of property—thirty-five acres on Round Hill Road that was subdivided into seven lots. I said, 'Hey, this property is perfect for you, you can build your own cul-de-sac, create your own little community. It's perfect.'

"So he sent Sonia out to look at the property, and when she showed up she was driving this new Mercedes 600, wearing a mink coat, and her hair was all done. I mean, she looked pretty good, whereas before, when she was living at the house with Marty, she was plain. She wore cheap clothes, didn't do much with her hair. But when I saw her this time she looked substantial. So anyway, Sonia got back to me later and said Marty wasn't interested, that he was focusing on buying out the other homes in the cul-de-sac where he lived, that he didn't want to get uprooted."

Although his trader's block had persisted into 1998, Frankel was trying desperately to break free of it. After having tried an assortment of counselors, psychologists, and psychiatrists, and for a time regularly attended therapy sessions on Saturdays, he sought the services of Ari Kiev, a New York psychiatrist who had worked with Olympic athletes on performance issues. One of Kiev's specialties was working with securities traders such as Frankel. Kiev had even authored a book on their affliction, called *Trading to Win*.

The counseling may have begun to help. Frankel had maintained accounts with some of Wall Street's largest brokerage firms, including Bear Stearns, Merrill Lynch, and Prudential Securities. He also had an account with Instinet, a unit of Reuters that allowed customers to trade after hours and without using traditional exchanges. His usual method of operation, however, would be to put millions of dollars into an account, only to take it right back out, causing much consternation at the New York brokerages. Bear Stearns once even threatened to close out his account, but Frankel met with representatives of the firm and talked them out of it.

But in 1998, and coinciding with his therapy under Kiev, Frankel did manage to pull the trigger on some trades, making between twenty and thirty transactions worth about $25,000 each and involving Treasury securities and corporate bonds. Toward the end of the year he made one large transaction through Prudential, involving some $80 million in Treasury securities purchased by Thunor Trust–owned insurance companies.

Nineteen ninety-eight also marked the beginning of the most unusual twist in the Frankel saga. For reasons that remain unclear, Thomas Corbally, the international businessman, helped Frankel develop a plan to create a charitable foundation, preferably one that could claim it was directly connected with the Vatican. One possible explanation was that such an organization would lend the con man greater credibility when shopping around for more insurance companies to buy. The other was that Frankel may have seen an advantage to adding yet another layer between himself and the companies he controlled, a precautionary measure for when and if government authorities began snooping into his activities.

One thing was for certain: Each gentleman used the other for entirely greedy purposes.

"Tom Corbally was this quasi-legend, and Marty saw Tom as the person who could make everything happen—and it worked. I mean, Tom did bring Marty the Vatican," said Mona Kim. "And Marty had Tom believing he was a billionaire and was going to make Tom and everybody else rich too."

Corbally was splitting his time between the luxury hotel suites he maintained at the Delmonico on Park Avenue in New York City and Claridge's, the fabled hotel in London's Mayfair district that for generations played host to some of the world's wealthiest and most powerful people.

In his business dealings, Corbally had developed extensive and important contacts throughout the world, on both sides of the straight and narrow. He was thought to have friends within both the intelligence community and organized crime, and Corbally had counted among his acquaintances Howard Hughes, who made billions from defense contracts and is believed to have allowed his businesses to be used as CIA fronts.

For many years Corbally was associated with Kroll Associates, the world's largest private investigation firm, headed by former prosecutor Jules Kroll. For twenty years Corbally dealt directly with Jules Kroll, and he was paid commissions for business and intelligence he steered to the firm. Corbally was also compensated with his own office at Kroll Associates' Manhattan headquarters, where he could be seen arriving in the morning carrying a box of cigars and two six-packs of diet Coke to get him through the day.

Born in 1921 in Newark, New Jersey, Corbally was someone who would have been called a playboy during the 1960s, when he was a divorced businessman who was living and swinging in London. He reportedly threw wild parties in his London flat that culminated in orgies, and he was a regular on the party circuit that included British lords, politicians, government officials, and plenty of "party girls," a polite term for prostitutes. At one party of about twenty guests attired in formalwear, the waiter serving dinner wore nothing except a black hood over his head, with slits for eyes. After dessert everyone participated in group sex, including the waiter, who was said by some to have been a high-ranking British cabinet official.

It was amid this environment that Corbally learned that two of the party girls, Christine Keeler and Margaret Davis, were planning to sell to a London newspaper lists of prominent men they had slept with, including government officials. On January 29, 1963, Corbally went to the American embassy in London and passed along this information to his friend Alfred Wells, secretary to U.S. ambassador David Bruce. He told Wells that among those the prostitutes would name was British secretary of war John Profumo, who would later resign amid the growing scandal.

Three decades later—in his mid-seventies, but still partying heavily—

Corbally came across another young woman who would soon find herself at the center of an international scandal, Kaethe Schuchter.

Corbally met Kaethe on the Manhattan party circuit in the spring of 1998, at which time he learned of the eccentric but brilliant man in Greenwich named Marty who generously subsidized the attractive German woman's posh apartment and chauffeured limousine, as well as other extravagant perquisites. Kaethe described her benefactor to her elderly new friend as not only the owner of a small insurance empire but "the biggest trader on Wall Street."

Corbally, of course, was intrigued. He wanted to meet this Marty guy. When he went to Greenwich in May 1998, Frankel found himself in the unusual position of being the one doing most of the listening as his guest recounted spellbinding exploits around the globe. Then Frankel told Corbally of his latest and most ambitious insurance company acquisition plan, in which he intended to accumulate $100 billion in assets. When he told Corbally he would give him 1 percent of that amount if he would use his business connections to help put his plan into action, Frankel found himself with an exciting new business partner.

"One percent of $100 billion is $1 billion," Corbally later said, explaining why he so readily joined forces with the man whom he said seemed nearly as eccentric as Howard Hughes. "I've never been exposed to that kind of money in my life."

Frankel was equally impressed with the aging, gravel-voiced swinger, who because of a lifelong cigarette addiction needed to suck oxygen from a tank whenever his emphysema robbed him of breath. He believed it when Corbally boasted of being a CIA operative.

In turn, Corbally may have believed that Frankel was a hugely successful investor, but he was flabbergasted by the hodgepodge operation he found at the Greenwich mansion, likening the haphazardly constructed offices filled with young women who had little or no business experience to a rabbit warren. "If we're going to do business together, we're going to do it the right way," Corbally told Frankel, and in the months to come, he put his magic Rolodex to work for the new partnership. Calling on some of his many associates and contacts, he assembled an impressive team of talent that would seem to be able to make the ambitious business plan happen. At the same time he became a frequent guest at the Lake Avenue compound, and he and Frankel talked on the phone daily, often several times a day.

Although he was not drawing a salary during this time, Corbally was given what amounted to an open-ended allowance that he used liberally to support the lavish lifestyle he had been used to. As the relationship wore on, Frankel began to grouse about his partner's spending habits, and at one point considered limiting Corbally to $50,000 per month. Corbally's denials to the contrary notwithstanding, one person with intimate knowledge of the relationship said Frankel had no choice but to give the elderly businessman what he wanted because "Tom had Marty by the balls because he knew full well what was going on in Greenwich. So Marty had to appease Tom at any cost."

The first order of business of the Frankel-Corbally partnership was to line up the lawyers and accountants who would be needed to draw up business prospectuses and contracts. Corbally shot a call to Texas billionaire Robert Strauss, the former U.S. ambassador to the Soviet Union and former chairman of the National Democratic Committee, who was senior partner of a high-powered law firm in Washington, D.C.—Aiken, Gump, Strauss, Hauer and Feld. Another of the firm's senior partners was President Bill Clinton's close friend and adviser Vernon Jordan.

Strauss said he would consider helping the Greenwich money manager with his plan for a charitable organization but first wanted to meet with him. On Memorial Day 1998 Frankel and Corbally met with Strauss at the lawyer's suite at the Watergate, the infamous hotel in the nation's capital that nearly three decades earlier was the scene of a third-rate burglary that led to the resignation of President Richard Nixon.

Although Strauss never personally handled any of Frankel's business, he referred the Greenwich money manager to a partner at his firm, Kay Tatum, who would become such a frequent caller to the Greenwich mansion that Frankel's assistants immediately recognized her voice. None of the law firm's principals would publicly comment on their dealings with Frankel, which a spokesman said consisted only of "certain transactional matters." Those matters brought the firm hundreds of thousands of dollars in billings.

Another topflight attorney for the cause was found closer to home. As lawyers go, they don't come much better connected than Thomas Bolan. From 1953 to 1957 Bolan served as assistant U.S. attorney in the Southern District of New York. His specialty was prosecuting fraud cases.

Upon entering private practice, Bolan became law partner of the late Roy Cohn. Cohn had earned fame as the pit bull chief counsel to Sen. Joseph McCarthy and the House Committee on Un-American Activities during the Red-baiting days of the 1950s. His later years were marred by charges of tax evasion, perjury, and disbarment. Through the good and the bad, Bolan remained Cohn's loyal friend throughout their thirty-year association. He was one of only two other people who knew and kept Cohn's secret that he was dying of AIDS, to which he finally succumbed in 1986.

Bolan also was a close friend of President Ronald Reagan, who served on the board of Reagan's alma mater, Eureka College. Cohn used to like to boast how his law partner could pick up the phone and get through to Reagan at any time he chose. Although he never held elective office, Bolan was politically active. For the Reagan administration he was a key advisor on many different matters, especially concerning the federal judiciary, and had served as a director of the Overseas Private Investment Corporation at Reagan's request. Bolan helped to found the New York Conservative Party, and he chaired Senator Alfonse D'Amato's federal judge selection committee.

Bolan was a member of the elite and staunchly conservative secret society known as the Sovereign Military Order of Malta. Others included New York's Cardinal John O'Connor, automobile executive Lee Iacocca, and three former CIA directors. Another member of the order was William F. Buckley Jr., publisher of *National Review* and former CIA operative who had been a staunch supporter of Senator McCarthy.

Bolan had extensive business experience and contacts, having served as executive officer and director of numerous corporations and financial institutions, including the Mercantile National and Gateway National Banks. But more important, as far as Frankel was concerned, Bolan was a devout and prominent Catholic. In addition to being Cardinal O'Connor's brother Knight of Malta, Bolan's law firm, Saxe, Bacon and Bolan, had the Archdiocese of New York as a client. Bolan served on the board of St. John's University and as a St. Francis College regent. When Pope John Paul visited Alaska in 1981, Bolan was flown there on Air Force One to greet the Pope as Reagan's personally designated representative. Also in the 1980s, Bolan was again loosely connected with the Holy See when his law firm represented Michele Sindona, the Sicilian banker who swindled millions of dollars from investors by abusing his ties with the Vatican Bank.

Among the many prominent Catholics in New York Bolan came to know was Father Peter Jacobs, a controversial priest who had become somewhat of a celebrity.

Jacobs was born in Berlin, New Hampshire, the son of a Jewish father who labored at a local mill and a Catholic French-Irish mother from County Cork, Ireland. As a young seaman aboard a U.S. Navy ship during World War II, he had a life-altering experience. He read a biography of St. Francis of Assisi, the young Italian aristocrat who gave away all his worldly possessions to dedicate his life to helping the sick and the poor. The story inspired Jacobs to begin attending mass, and after the war he entered a seminary. Jacobs was ordained in 1955 by the Archdiocese of Washington, D.C., and later transferred to New York City, where he became chaplain of two inner-city schools, Power Memorial Academy and Rice High School.

After his arrival in New York, Jacobs became well known, both within and outside the Catholic Church, for good works that were keeping in the spirit of St. Francis. He tirelessly ministered to modern society's castoffs—runaways, drug addicts, and prostitutes—and maintained five phone lines and always wore a beeper should he be summoned to aid one of his unfortunate sheep.

In 1964 Pope Paul VI made the first papal trip ever to the United States, and while in New York City his motorcade stopped at the corner of 124th Street and Lenox Avenue for an unscheduled visit to the all-black Rice High School. As stunned teachers and jubilant students poured out of the building to greet the Pope, the journalists who were on hand reported the visit as a gesture of interracial harmony by the pontiff. What they didn't know at the time was that the Pope had wanted to say hello to Father Jacobs.

In 1982 Jacobs inherited a restaurant in the heart of Manhattan's theater district and, contrary to the wishes of his superiors in Washington, he turned it into a trendy French bistro called Palatine 313. A portion of the restaurant's proceeds helped fund scholarships at Power Memorial and Rice.

Affectionately called "Father Jake" and "Father Pete" by friends and patrons, Jacobs made Palatine 313 into a fashionable place to eat and, more important, to be seen. He hired an authentic French chef from Lyons, and off-duty firemen tended bar for the priest, who served as their chaplain in the New York City Fire Department. Usually attired in a FDNY T-shirt beneath his black sports coat, Jacobs had performed the last rites for half of the twelve firefighters who died while fighting a fire at Broadway and Twenty-third Street in 1965.

Located on West Forty-sixth Street—New York's "Restaurant Row"—Palatine 313 was a regular dining stop for Jacobs' celebrity friends, including Walter Cronkite and Gloria Steinem. It was where Prince Albert of Monaco celebrated his twenty-fifth birthday in March 1983.

Jacobs thrived in the reflected glitter of the rich and famous. He attended charitable balls with the likes of Bianca Jagger, bellied up to the bar with writer Pete Hamill, and enjoyed the friendship of Jacqueline Kennedy Onassis and Grace Kelly. After Princess Grace of Monaco was killed in a 1982 car crash, Jacobs officiated at the private mass that was held in the Monaco palace chapel.

But Jacobs never forgot his downtrodden flock. One night, while attending a fashionable dinner party, his beeper went off, summoning him to intervene in a teenager's threatened suicide. When he returned to the party he opened his hand to show *Ms.* magazine publisher Patricia Carbine and other dinner guests the six bullets he had removed from the teen's gun.

Jacobs had already amassed a thick file of Church infractions, including a few for performing interdenominational marriages, and when the restaurant opened, Washington archbishop James Hickey had had enough. He did not buy Jacobs' comparison of Palatine to restaurants operated by priests in Madrid, Paris, and elsewhere in Europe or his argument that "if the diocese can have a big Inner City Scholarship Fund banquet at the Waldorf Astoria, then I can have a restaurant to help poor kids." In 1983 Hickey suspended Jacobs of his "priestly duties."

Jacobs continued to greet diners at Palatine 313, while at the same time performing those duties from which he had been barred, including celebrating mass and performing weddings, such as the union of orchestra leader Peter Duchin and writer Brooke Hayward in 1985. The Church later invalidated those weddings.

Jacobs finally relented to pressure from the Church in 1987 when, following a meeting with New York's Cardinal John O'Connor, who had also frowned on the idea of a priest running a restaurant and bar, he agreed to get out of the business. He sold Palatine 313 and donated the proceeds and the rest of his earthly assets, which totaled nearly $1 million.

Jacobs continued to live with his mother in a Manhattan brownstone he owned until 1996, at which time he sold the home and moved with Mrs. Jacobs to an apartment in Rome owned by someone he had met at an FDNY memorial service. Mrs. Jacobs died in 1997. "She was 101, and she died drinking a Jack Daniel's and smoking a cigarette," Jacobs said.

When Frankel was put together with Bolan in the summer of 1998, the former federal prosecutor was told that Frankel planned to give at least $50 million to Catholic charities immediately, and that the Greenwich money manager wanted Bolan's help in arranging an audience with senior Catholic clerics to discuss the gifts. That was when Bolan introduced Frankel to Jacobs, who eagerly signed on with Team Frankel and pledged to use his friendship with people inside the Vatican to make the plan happen.

Frankel had done his homework on Jacobs and knew from previously published news articles about how Jacobs, who was seventy-two years old in 1998, had been inspired to become a priest by St. Francis of Assisi. To prepare for his ultimate con, Frankel immediately set out to become an expert on the Catholic Church and on St. Francis of Assisi in particular. He sent his helpers out on a mission to scour bookstores and the Internet for every possible volume they could find on the subjects. Dozens of books on St. Francis and other Catholic saints soon made their way into Frankel's library, including Alban Butler's classic *The Lives of the Saints*. One of the assistants even found a videotape of Franco Zefferelli's film about St. Francis of Assisi, *Brother Sun, Sister Moon*, which Frankel watched over and over again. It was not long before Frankel could give a complete recitation of the thirteenth-century saint's life and also discuss papal encyclicals.

"He had actually read the encyclicals," Jacobs would later say with a touch of amazement still in his voice. "Even I hadn't read them all."

Frankel made simultaneous forays into the charity business in August 1998, sending Bolan to Rome and a Corbally associate—an Italian business consultant named Fausto Fausti—to Florence. A former air force pilot, Fausti worked for many years as press spokesman for the Italian helicopter manufacturer August SpA and was a member of the Union of Italian Aerospace Journalists. After leaving August in 1985, he got a job as a private pilot in the United States. At the time he hooked up with Frankel, he was running two businesses—a publishing concern called Edizioni Barone, and Fausti and Associates, a legal and business consulting Internet site. Fausti had told others of also having arranged financing for a supermarket chain seeking to build stores in the Middle East.

On August 6, 1998, Fausti showed up unannounced at the office of Father Christopher Maria Zielinski, prior of the San Miniato al Monte monastery atop a hill overlooking the city of Florence. Although Zielinski originally hailed from Cleveland, Ohio, he had become an influential person in his corner of Italy, a country in which Church officials are as intimately linked with politics as are their governmental counterparts. In 1994 Zielinski recruited American lawyer Michele Spike to set up Genesis Center, a nonprofit, nondenominational Delaware foundation that sponsored seminars and meetings in fulfillment of its mission of encouraging interreligious and intercultural dialogue. Only a small portion of the center's work was charitable.

Minutes after meeting Fausti, Zielinski was on the phone to Spike: "Michele, there's someone in my office offering us $50 million! Would you come here right away?"

With the attorney now seated beside him, the monastery's prior asked Fausti to repeat what he had just told him.

"There is this extremely wealthy financier in Connecticut who has made a lot of money in the stock market and has decided he would now like to give a certain amount of money to charity," Fausti explained in Italian.

The deal was that the financier, whom Fausti identified as David Rosse, would establish an account in the Genesis Center's name. Rosse would have exclusive control on how the money was managed, and the center would receive 100 percent of the income off the principal and use it for charitable purposes.

Spike was skeptical at first, but any doubts she had were somewhat allayed when Fausti told her that David Rosse's attorney was Robert Strauss, and that Jules Kroll and Lee Iacocca were among those who would be serving on the board of directors for the enterprise. Kroll and Fausti had met about a decade earlier. When Kroll's son was studying in Italy, he had become friends with Fausti's son, Alfredo.

Dropping the names of a former U.S. ambassador and a legend in the American automotive industry was impressive indeed, but it took only the mention of Kroll's name to dispel Spike's initial concerns. While practicing law in New York, Spike had called on Kroll Associates numerous times to do background checks, corporate searches, and other investigative work. At times she had even spoken on the phone with Jules Kroll himself.

When Spike told Fausti they would seriously consider the proposal, the businessman advised her that Mr. Rosse's business partner, Tom Corbally, would first need to see Genesis Center's certificate of incorporation, the letter of tax exemption status from the Internal Revenue Service, and the organization's banking information.

Then a red flag shot up.

When Corbally and Spike got on the phone with each other—while Fausti was still sitting in the monastery office—Corbally asked Spike how much the Genesis Center spent on charity each year. When Spike replied the amount was only about a mere $15,000, Corbally then asked whether a sudden infusion of $50 million into the Genesis Center "would raise the eyebrows of the IRS."

Spike responded by saying she didn't care what the IRS did with its eyebrows, as long as she and the center did not do anything illegal. She then faxed Corbally the documentation he had requested. Corbally had told her she could expect to get a visit the following day from Tom Bolan, who would be bringing the brokerage agreement that she would have to sign to get the transaction rolling.

On the afternoon of August 7 Fausti and Spike lunched together at the monastery as they awaited Bolan's arrival. The businessman used the opportunity to talk to the attorney about concerns he had for his son. Now in his mid-twenties, Alfredo Fausti had studied law at La Sapienza University in Rome and spoke English fluently. As a result of Fausti's new association with Mr. Rosse, Alfredo had been made an offer to live at one of the financier's homes in Greenwich while Mr. Rosse paid for him to attend law school at Yale University. What most anguished Fausti was that Alfredo had fallen in love with Mr. Rosse's "personal assistant," Kaethe Schuchter. Fausti told Spike that not only did he consider Kaethe to be somewhat of "a tramp," but he also believed she was the rich American's girlfriend. Fearing that his son was being drawn further into the Frankel organization, Fausti told Spike that should the arrangement between Rosse and the Genesis Center go forward, he hoped that the center would hire Alfredo to help administer the income from the $50 million fund, a move that would force his son to remain in Italy.

When the stretch Mercedes-Benz limousine that Spike and Fausti thought was carrying attorney Bolan pulled into the monastery's courtyard, Fausti's jaw visibly dropped as soon as the driver opened the door for his passengers. Directly in sight of the Byzantine gold mosaic of Christ bestowing his blessings on the city below, out stepped Alfredo with Kaethe. Kaethe was hardly attired appropriately for a visit to a monastery—she was provocatively dressed in lavender silk hot pants, a chartreuse halter top, and lizard-skin high heels. Both of them were slightly disheveled. It told the exasperated businessman that his son and the skinny young woman he despised had been intimate with each other on the ride to Florence.

The couple spoke excitedly about having flown into Rome from the United States on the supersonic Concorde. Kaethe apologized for Bolan's absence, explaining that the attorney was in a meeting in Rome that he was unable to get away from. She presented Spike with a Federal Express package containing the documents that needed to be signed.

Having introduced herself as David Rosse's personal assistant, Kaethe was asked by Spike to explain what her understanding of her boss's proposal was.

"Mr. Rosse has to buy an insurance company, and he needs a charity to do that," Kaethe told the attorney sitting across from her. "If you do this for him, he will give something to you, but we don't know what."

This was the first time Spike had heard anything about an insurance company.

"Well, can you tell me what the source of the funds is?" Spike asked.

"No, you cannot know that," Kaethe said.

"Can you tell me, then, who is going to be on the board of directors, and would we have a seat on the board of this insurance company—I mean, who's going to manage the insurance company?" the attorney asked.

"David Rosse is," Kaethe replied.

"This is preposterous," Spike thought, and then quickly concluded in her own mind, "That's the end of this transaction."

Wanting to learn more, however, the attorney asked to see the documents Kaethe had brought. She was startled upon seeing that one of them was authorization for David Rosse, through a British Virgin Islands entity, to have blanket power of attorney for all transactions involving the Genesis Center alliance. The other document would have indemnified Rosse from all liability. Neither document made mention of any income for the Genesis Center.

"Thank you very much, but there is no way we could get involved in this," Spike informed Frankel's emissaries.

"You obviously don't understand the documents," Alfredo Fausti interjected. "We should call Mr. Bolan so he can explain everything."

Spike responded, "Alfredo, you can read English. You read these documents. Let's read them together and then tell me what they say. You show me where the Genesis Center's rights are."

In a last-ditch attempt to save the fast-sinking ship, Kaethe called Frankel in Greenwich and then handed the phone to Spike.

"First of all, Ms. Spike, let me tell you just how impressed I am with the Catholic Church," Frankel said, in the guise of David Rosse. "Quite frankly, I am a Jew, although I have not been involved in organized religion for some time. But I can't tell you how much I admire the Catholic Church for all the good works it does in helping the poor and working to alleviate suffering throughout the world. I am also a great admirer of St. Francis of Assisi, and now that I have made so much money, I believe the time has come for me to follow the example set by St. Francis and give back part of what I've earned."

When Spike told Frankel that as an attorney she found the documents that had been given her to be "egregious," the apologetic voice on the other end of the phone line blamed his attorneys.

"Apparently my lawyers have not understood what I am trying to get at," Frankel said.

Spike told him she was sorry but the Genesis Center could not do business with him. Frankel tried one last ploy to salvage his plans.

"Would you consider selling me the charity?" he asked.

"Yes, that is something we can consider," Spike replied.

"If you sold me the charity," Frankel asked, "can I have Father Christopher's name?"

Spike was adamant. "No. Absolutely not."

And that was the end of the conversation.

After Kaethe and the Faustis left, Spike came to the conclusion that what had happened was an attempt had been made by some organization to use the Genesis Center to launder money. Because Spike had taken Kaethe's accent to be Slavic instead of German, the attorney surmised that she might have been involved with the Russian Mafia. So on August 10, Spike wrote to Kroll in New York, telling him that he should be aware that "David Rosse" and his associates "are trading off of your good name." Kroll replied in his own letter that while he knew the Faustis, he was unfamiliar with Rosse or his insurance venture. Spike then advised the Genesis Center not to get involved with the American's scheme.

Soon afterward, Spike fired off a letter to Connecticut: "Dear Mr. Rosse: It was a pleasure to talk to you about your charitable intent, and I wish you the best of luck in all you do. But I did spend a day of my life on this project, and if you were going to give the Genesis Center $50 million, surely you could at least pay for my time." She suggested that he make a $2,000 donation to the center.

Receiving no immediate reply, the attorney then faxed Frankel a copy of Kroll's letter stating that Kroll Associates had no knowledge of David Rosse or his charity-insurance plan. That got Frankel's immediate attention. The very next day, Fausto Fausti arrived at the monastery bearing a check for $2,000 and a donation of a portable computer.

Frankel never profited from his relationship with the Italian businessman and his son. Although Fausto would later help Frankel in his flight from prosecution in 1999, the Faustis only ended up costing Frankel time and money.

During their fling as lovers, Kaethe and Alfredo were frequent fliers on Frankel's tab, whether it was jetting to Rome on the Concorde or getting away for a romantic weekend at the Breakers in Palm Beach. Around Christmas 1998 the real David Rosse received an urgent page from Frankel. When the bodyguard called his boss, Frankel was frantic. "The Faustis are here and they're trying to extort money from me," he said to his bodyguard. "I'm afraid they're going to kill me."

Rosse raced over to the house, but by the time he got there the Faustis had gone. "Marty had given them $2 million, and he told David that everything was okay now," an associate recalled.

What supposedly really happened was that the Faustis had gone to see Frankel to ask him to kick in $20 million for a microchip business they wanted to start. But the appearance of the father and son, along with a couple of other Italian businessmen, caused Frankel's mind to flash to *The Godfather*, and he freaked out, thinking he was being made an offer he couldn't refuse.

"Alfredo approached Marty with this dumb business proposition, which basically said, 'You give us $20 million and we'll give you 10 percent of the business,'" a Frankel associate said.

Although Frankel had been defeated in Florence, he had much better luck with Thomas Bolan in Rome.

Soon after his recruitment by Frankel, Father Jacobs had gotten on the phone with a friend who was a retired Vatican official, Monsignor Emilio Colagiovanni. Colagiovanni was judge emeritus of the Roman Rota church tribunal and was editor of *Monitor Ecclesiasticus,* a Vatican City–based Church canon law review journal established by Pope Pius IX in 1876.

The two priests had met in 1994 at the Istituto per le Opere di Religione (IOR)—the Vatican Bank. *Monitor Ecclesiasticus* maintained an account there, and Jacobs had gone to the bank to visit friends who worked there. One of Jacobs' specialties had always been performing interfaith marriages, and Colagiovanni accepted Jacobs' invitation to assist with the wedding of Edgar Bronfman Jr., a Jew and one of the richest men in the United States, and Clarissa Alcock, the Catholic daughter of an oil executive in Buenos Aires.

Colagiovanni was thrilled that he had been able to participate in a high-society wedding, and so when Father Jake called on him for a favor in 1998, the monsignor was more than willing to help.

"He was inviting me to go to New York because a rich and generous Jewish man wanted to make donations to the Catholic Church, and specifically to the Monitor Ecclesiasticus Foundation, for charitable purposes," Colagiovanni recalled.

Soon afterward the monsignor received another telephone call, this time from Bolan, known for ties with the New York Catholic community, who vouched for David Rosse's good intentions.

Colagiovanni flew to New York for a brief meeting with Jacobs and Bolan, and the three of them then drove to Greenwich to meet with Frankel. The monsignor was highly impressed with the Jewish man's knowledge of Catholicism and the current Holy See hierarchy, and marveled at Frankel's vast library, which was filled with religious books. He politely listened as Frankel earnestly expressed a desire to help use his vast wealth to help the less fortunate, and how he felt the best way to accomplish that would be through Catholic charities that had the blessing of the Vatican and the Pope himself.

The monsignor thanked Frankel for his good intentions but informed him that all such matters needed to be handled by the Secretariat of State of the Vatican. He promised he would do what he could to help. The next day Colagiovanni telephoned the Prefect of Economic Affairs for the Holy See, Archbishop Francesco Salerno, and told him of Frankel's wishes. He mentioned that two of Frankel's representatives—Bolan and Jacobs—would be traveling to Rome to meet with him concerning a proposal to establish a Vatican charitable foundation.

That meeting took place on August 6—the same day Kaethe and the Faustis were meeting with Father Christopher and Michele Spike at the

Genesis Center in Florence—after Frankel flew Bolan to Rome on the Concorde. In addition to Salerno, they also met with Monsignor Gianfranco
Piovano, an official with the Vatican's Secretariat of State.

The proposal Bolan pitched to the high-ranking priests was that David
Rosse would establish a new foundation in Liechtenstein, and it would have
a set of secret bylaws stipulating that Rosse would be the original grantor of
$55 million. That money would be wired from a Swiss bank, they said, and
of that amount, $50 million would be forwarded to a brokerage account
set up in the United States under the foundation's name and would be
controlled exclusively by Frankel. They told the priests that the leftover $5
million would be a donation to the church, to be placed into an account
controlled by the Vatican.

The conditions of the "donation," plus future such contributions to the
Church, were outlined in an August 22 letter from Frankel to Bolan: "Our
agreement will include the Vatican's promise that the Vatican will aid me in
my effort to acquire insurance companies" by allowing a Vatican official "to
certify to the authorities, if necessary, that the source of the funds . . . is the
Vatican."

On September 1, Bolan faxed Jacobs a letter that Colagiovanni had sent
him, in which the monsignor stated: "I have talked this morning with Salerno and Piovano . . . [they] reaffirmed the willingness of the Holy See to erect
a new foundation in the Vatican whose president should be Mr. David."
(Colagiovanni had often referred to Frankel's alias that way.) The monsignor's letter went on to state that "an account in U.S. dollars in the IOR
[Vatican bank] can be opened by Mr. David."

About a month later, officials in the Vatican began to be concerned
about allowing Mr. David to have control over his own foundation within
the Holy See. A new relationship was thus forged, in which Frankel would
form the St. Francis of Assisi Foundation, which could claim links to Colagiovanni's Monitor Ecclesiasticus Foundation.

On October 19 Colagiovanni wrote to Jacobs to inform him that the
Vatican Bank would be issuing a declaration affirming its links to Monitor
Ecclesiasticus "as suggested by Mr. David." But the monsignor said that
before the declaration could be sent out, he wanted to know more about the
Connecticut money manager. That same day Frankel sent Colagiovanni a
twenty-page biography/resume, which contained his Swiss bank reference as
well as the usual fluff about having used "informational analysis" to lead a

fabulously successful career as an investment adviser. But this time it included new falsehoods, such as an embellishment of the real David Rosse's history, talking about how during his two years in the U.S. Army he had been "in charge of all security for the nuclear missile site" in Key Largo, Florida.

On November 3, after Frankel's Swiss bank reference was checked out, the Vatican Bank's director general issued a declaration, which was provided to Frankel, that noted the IOR's "uninterrupted relation" with the Monitor Ecclesiasticus Foundation.

Frankel was then able to use the declaration as a stage prop in the legitimization of the St. Francis of Assisi foundation in his subsequent dealings with American insurance companies. Even though he was unable to forge the direct Vatican ties he had hoped for, this was the next best thing. After all, Pope Benedict XV had once declared that the Monitor Ecclesiasticus Foundation's canon law review was "published with the special authorization of the Holy See." And in 1978 a top aide to Pope Paul VI wrote to Colagiovanni to tell him that the pontiff's "favor to Monitor Ecclesiasticus is no less than that of his Predecessors." The letter continued by stating that "the Holy Father is happy to impart to you . . . president of the foundation, his apostolic blessing and pledge of continued divine assistance."

And in his dealings with Team Frankel, Colagiovanni had repeatedly asserted that as the Monitor Ecclesiasticus Foundation's president, he was approved by the Vatican's Secretariat of State. In addition, the monsignor had said, the Monitor Ecclesiasticus Foundation's directors included Salerno and three other top Vatican officials, and the foundation's bylaws, updated in 1983, were "approved by the Holy Father."

In a letter addressed "Dear Mr. David," Colagiovanni said that "any fund or donation given to the Monitor Ecclesiasticus Foundation" was protected by the "very strict confidentiality and secrecy" laws that apply to any entity linked to the Vatican Bank. Continuing, the monsignor wrote that "only the Pope personally" had the authority to disclose information concerning IOR accounts.

Even before the declarations were issued, but soon after Frankel had begun his overtures to the Vatican, the St. Francis of Assisi Foundation was officially launched as a charitable trust in Tortola, in the British Virgin Islands.

Out of all the bogus documents that were created by the computers in Frankel's Greenwich fortress, the chef d'oeuvre has to be the 115-page opus titled "The Saint Francis of Assisi Foundation, to Serve and Help the Poor and Alleviate Suffering, Deed of Settlement."

The document is marred by poor grammar, bad syntax, and obvious repetition. It contains numerous run-on sentences and historical passages that seem lifted from textbooks. But when allegedly presented by a priest professing a desire to right the wrongs of the world with the blessings of the Pope himself, mistakes and amateurish prose are easily overlooked.

The deed of settlement described the new foundation as follows:

In the spirit of Saint Francis of Assisi, and through his amaranthine example, we must feed, comfort, and medically aid the poor; at the same time we must send social workers and educators to help the poor: This is the key that will allow poor people to uplift themselves, with God's help, out of poverty.

A primary goal of The Saint Francis of Assisi Foundation, to Serve and Help the Poor and Alleviate Suffering, is to educate social workers, who will become educators, so that these educators establish schools, in order to lift the people of the world from poverty.

The work of The Saint Francis of Assisi Foundation, to Serve and Help the Poor and Alleviate Suffering is a continuation of the work of Saint Francis of Assisi. The Sons of Divine Providence and the Congregation of Christian Brothers are two among many charitable Orders and Congregations of the Church that do much to further the work of Saint Francis of Assisi. Monitor Ecclesiasticus Foundation, through The Saint Francis of Assisi Foundation, to Serve and Help the Poor and Alleviate Suffering, aims to assist all such worthy charitable enterprises, both inside and outside the Holy Church.

In its bylaws, the St. Francis of Assisi Foundation vowed:

1. To alleviate human suffering, by helping the poor and needy throughout the world.
2. To rescue homeless and needy children, in any part of the world, and to feed, clothe, shelter, and educate these children so they may learn to support themselves through professions and trades.
3. To prevent cruelty to children.

4. To help needy migrants and refugees.
5. To provide to the needy medical treatment, including hospital-ization, where necessary, throughout the world.
6. To make grants to any person or persons or class of persons or company or unincorporated body, whether technically classi-fied as a charity or not, that the Foundation determines is advancing the above-stated goals of the Foundation.

After a nine-page history lesson on the Sons of Divine Providence, con-cluding with founder Father Louis Orione's proclamation to "Always do good, good to everyone; never do harm, to anyone," the deed explained how the Monitor Ecclesiasticus Foundation was "desirous" of creating a $51 mil-lion trust to make acquisitions and investments. The "beneficiaries" of the trust would include: Mother Teresa Hospital in Tirana, Albania; Boys Town of Italy and Girls Town of Italy; Medicins Sans Frontieres (Doctors Without Borders); Infant Jesus Pediatric Hospital; Sacred Heart University Medical School's Gemelli Hospital; Oxfam; and the Royal Society for the Prevention of Cruelty to Children. Many of the causes close to Jacobs' heart were listed as potential beneficiaries as well, including Rice High School in Harlem.

The St. Francis deed of settlement gave control to the trust fund to the board of trustees' "investment adviser," which was Frankel using his favorite alias, David Rosse. "The adviser may act in relation to the investments as if he were the sole and total owner of the funds under management as he in his absolute discretion shall determine," the document declared. The invest-ment adviser could not be removed without approval of "the Protector (if any)," but the deed does not define what a protector is or does.

The deed also permitted Frankel to deposit trust money in any bank or financial institution in the world, and to "keep the whole or any part of the trust property within or without the jurisdiction of the Proper Law." The new foundation's bylaws state that its main office would be located within the Vatican and may have additional offices wherever else it sees fit. The office in the United States would later be listed as being in Bedford Hills, an exclusive community in Westchester County, New York. The address was actually for a Mail Boxes Etc. location in Bedford Hills.

Although the foundation's bylaws named Jacobs as the only trustee, it authorized him to appoint all other St. Francis officers.

By the time Frankel had drafted the foundation's "Hospital and Life

Insurance Company Acquisition Business Outline and Mission Statement," Bolan had been named as another St. Francis trustee, along with Edward D. Collins, former director of one of the world's largest conglomerates, Hanson Trust Plc. John Hackney and Gary Atnip, Thunor Trust executives, were named as well.

The St. Francis of Assisi Foundation also boasted an advisory board with such luminaries as Walter Cronkite, the retired *CBS Evening News* anchorman once known as having the most respected voice in America, and automobile executive Lee Iacocca, who had saved the Chrysler Corporation from bankruptcy. Although it was an impressive lineup on paper, Cronkite and Iacocca would each later claim his name was used without permission.

Cronkite learned of his name's involvement with the bogus foundation in a phone call from *Greenwich Time*. "Father Jacobs is an old acquaintance, and he asked if I would be on the board. He said they just wanted my advice on where to put this billion dollars they had," the newscaster told the newspaper. Cronkite said he politely declined but told Jacobs he could call on him whenever he wanted some informal advice.

"I didn't want to be formally connected with something I knew nothing about," Cronkite explained. "I told them I would not be on the board and, apparently, they went ahead and listed me as such."

Iacocca refused media requests for interviews but said through spokespeople that he also had declined an invitation to serve on the St. Francis advisory board. Iacocca declined despite accepting Frankel's loan of a private jet, which he flew to Milan, where he attended to some personal business.

In the St. Francis business plan, Frankel droned on for more than a dozen pages about the good deeds of Father Louis Orione, and then he went on to explain the insurance acquisition concept with such sophomoric redundancy, it's a small wonder that anyone bought the sanctified snake oil:

The Saint Francis of Assisi Foundation believes its ownership of insurance companies will help the Foundation better fulfill its mission to help alleviate human suffering. The Foundation's mission can be helped because we believe the Foundation's investment in insurance companies will be equivalent to the Foundation investing in a stock that can return many times the initial investment to the investor. We anticipate the growth in value of the insurance companies owned by The Saint Francis of Assisi Foundation will help provide more assets to fulfill the mission of The Saint Francis of Assisi Foundation.

There are many ways our insurance companies will serve both our specific clients and all humanity. Serving our clients will enable us to serve humanity; our insurance companies will fund, in perpetuity, hospitals which shall aid forever all who are in need.

Our life insurance companies plan to produce scientific breakthroughs which can lead to the cure of human disease. We shall accomplish this goal by providing funding for researchers' efforts to cure diseases which afflict us all. Our efforts may take many years, but the payoff will be significant. How has mankind progressed, except by taking both a short-term view, in order to insure immediate survival, and also a long-term view, in order to insure a better future for our children? All caring human scientific progress has come from inventors, researchers, and thinkers who took many years to develop their innovations and discoveries.

Our life insurance companies can help play a small role in curing disease. Our companies can use the forces of the marketplace to aid in the search to cure disease. By providing capital for fledgling medical research companies, we can enlist the forces of the marketplace to achieve a multiplier effect. Through this multiplier effect, we can leverage our assets to achieve significant medical progress. As Archimedes proclaimed, "Give me a lever and I will move the world."

Thus, we have established the mission of the life insurance companies owned by The Saint Francis of Assisi Foundation: Our mission is to acquire life insurance company assets, and to manage these assets wisely, so individuals can have a safe, secure environment, so their medical needs can be met, and nurtured, and given a better world than the one we have found. Through this process, our life insurance companies' success will enable us to fund the acquisition and operation of many hospitals, which will serve as beacons of love and care for all who are in need.

There are so many needy, hungry and afflicted children in the world. It is the mission of The Saint Francis of Assisi Foundation to establish hospitals and assistance programs for these needy children, and for all who are afflicted and suffering, for all who are in need of caring, loving medical assistance.

Nowhere does the business plan state that the insurance companies would be subsidizing its investment adviser's decadent lifestyle in Greenwich, Connecticut.

Then Frankel made a bold move in what may have been a gamble to forge actual and direct ties with the Vatican Bank by currying favor with the Pope himself.

Pope John Paul II had expressed a desire to be the first pontiff ever to visit Russia, but the trip had been blocked by Patriarch Alexy II, leader of the Russian Orthodox Church, which had long viewed the Roman Catholic Church with suspicion. The Russian patriarch had torpedoed just such a visit at the last minute two years earlier.

Frankel decided he would do what he could to make the historic papal visit happen. If he could pull that off, he thought, the least the Vatican could do was provide him with what he referred to as a "Pope letter," a document signed by John Paul II himself that surely no one could question.

Setting his plan in motion, Frankel sent Jacobs to Rome in September 1998 to meet with a former Italian army general, Gianalfonso D'Avossa, who resigned from the military in 1996 amid allegations of official corruption and of consorting with members of the Russian Mafia. Jacobs told D'Avossa, who was widely known in Italy for his recent work with Russian Catholics, that an American benefactor he knew, David Rosse, was prepared to donate millions of dollars to the Russian Orthodox Church. Rosse would give the church as much as $50 million if it would only cease its opposition to a visit by Pope John Paul II to the former communist country.

D'Avossa was a career military officer with forty-two years of service. Before his resignation he had been president of the Commission of the Chamber of Defense and had been head of the Center of High Studies for the Defense. D'Avossa was relieved of commanding the Italian army's 132nd Brigade in January 1996 for allegedly misusing military vehicles while on a peacekeeping mission in Yugoslavia. A military tribunal found him not guilty on the basis of insufficient evidence. Prior to that, the general had been convicted of fraud and related charges stemming from the construction of military buildings. While his conviction was later overturned on appeal, the appellate court of Verona sentenced him to seven months of "military reclusion" for "injuries to a subordinate."

D'Avossa resigned from the army in September 1996, citing damage to his reputation caused by the military tribunal's investigation. Later that same month, a member of the Italian parliament called for another investigation, this time looking into alleged corruption within the military. Two months after that, in November 1996, the Ministry of Defense launched a probe of D'Avossa's alleged connections with Russian organized crime. In March 1997 two Italians and eleven Russians were arrested by Italian police as part of "Operation Checkmate," but D'Avossa was not among them.

By early 1997 D'Avossa had resurfaced in St. Petersburg, Russia, where he was living and working on behalf of Catholic–Russian Orthodox unity. During this time he had become chummy with the mayor of Moscow, Yuri "Little Czar" Luzhkov, a popular politician and aspirant to the Russian presidency.

With Jacobs using his influence in the Vatican on one end and D'Avossa using his Russian connections on the other, the two arranged for Luzhkov to have a private audience with the Catholic pontiff during Pope John Paul II's upcoming trip to Romania.

The trip went ahead as planned, and when Pope John Paul II arrived in Romania on May 7, 1999, he became the first Catholic pontiff ever to visit a mainly Orthodox country. Luzhkov did indeed meet privately with the Pope in Romania, but whatever plans they discussed for his visiting Russia were for naught because three days earlier, on May 4, Frankel had fled the United States as a fugitive from justice.

It is unclear whether Frankel actually channeled any of the stolen insurance money to Russia. On the advice of legal counsel, Jacobs refused to discuss the matter. Colagiovanni said, however, "Jacobs told me he was managing to pay some money to the patriarch over there [in Russia]. He said Rosse was supposed to pump in some money to the patriarch over there, but I would doubt the patriarch would accept any money just for having the Holy Pope go over there."

While Frankel's religious connections were busy entertaining unprecedented visits by the pope, Frankel's financial connections were busy getting the St. Francis of Assisi Foundation rolling. For the purposes of identifying insurance companies that the new foundation might buy, and then to broker the deals, Frankel hired Merger Acquisition Profiles, a firm specializing in insurance company takeovers headed by Jerry Wolfe in Century City, California. Wolfe tapped into his firm's network of attorneys and accountants, who identified possible takeover targets and then tried to facilitate the deal.

One of the Merger Acquisition Profiles team's first targets was Western Annuity and Life Assurance Company, owned by Metropolitan Mortgage Group in Spokane, Washington. In December 1998, John Hackney, Father Jacobs, and some of the Merger Acquisition Profiles team, including Wolfe, flew to Spokane to meet with Metropolitan Mortgage's CEO, C. Paul Sandifur Jr., in order to make an offer for Western Annuity and Life Assurance. In the meeting, the St. Francis of Assisi Foundation was described as both a successful operator of a string of insurance companies and a charity that counted many wealthy personalities as benefactors.

"They mentioned at the time that Walter Cronkite was a friend of these guys, and that Cronkite and Lee Iacocca supported this thing," Sandifur recalled. "Father Jacobs showed me a picture of himself with Mother Teresa, and basically said he hobnobbed all over the world with these types of people."

Sandifur said it struck him as odd how Jacobs seemed to be making a much greater attempt to dazzle him with his association with celebrity than Hackney was in making a pitch for Western Annuity and Life. Even so, Sandifur said he wanted to believe the claims that the foundation would use profits from investments made with insurance company assets to fund Catholic hospitals and other charities around the world. So he wrote a letter to the Vatican seeking verification.

"The [St. Francis] foundation claims to be an agent of the Holy See and desires to engage in a business transaction of $120 million," the insurance CEO wrote. "The foundation also claims that it was established by the Monitor Ecclesiasticus . . . which they represented as a Vatican foundation."

Twelve days later, the Vatican's third-highest official responded to Sandifur in a terse and carefully written letter. "No such foundation has the approval of the Holy See or exists in the Vatican," wrote Archbishop Giovanni Battista Re.

When Sandifur brought the bishop's letter to the attention of Aiken Gump, the law firm representing the St. Francis foundation, Colagiovanni signed a new declaration, which this time omitted any mention that the money came from the "Holy Father," but did note that the Monitor Ecclesiasticus Foundation was "existing under the laws of the Vatican."

Dated February 13, 1999, the declaration stated:

I hereby certify and confirm to you that Monitor Ecclesiasticus Foundation is the grantor of funds to the Saint Francis of Assisi Foundation, to Serve and Help the Poor and Alleviate Suffering, a British Virgin Islands trust. Monitor Ecclesiasticus Foundation has contributed approximately $1,000,000,000 (One Billion Dollars) to The Saint Francis of Assisi Foundation since the creation of The Saint Francis of Assisi Foundation on August 10, 1998. Such funds were received by Monitor Ecclesiasticus Foundation from various Roman Catholic tribunals and Roman Catholic charitable and cultural institutions for Monitor Ecclesiasticus Foundation's charitable purposes. These funds have been donated by Monitor Ecclesiasticus Foundation for use by The Saint Francis of Assisi Foundation for The Saint Francis of Assisi Foundation's charitable purposes.

Still unsure of what kind of deal he was getting involved in, Sandifur traveled to Vatican City on February 26 to meet with Colagiovanni so that he could find out for himself just what type of clout the Monitor Ecclesiasticus Foundation's president's imprimatur carried. "We met in an office near the Vatican, and we did tour the grounds, so I had every reason to believe the monsignor had access to the Vatican that went beyond public access," Sandifur said.

The trip to Rome had been just a waste of the Spokane insurance executive's time, however. Negotiations for the sale of Western Annuity and Life abruptly ended in April. The original asking price for Western Annuity and Life Assurance had been $110 million, but Sandifur had upped it to $120 million. Team Frankel balked.

"They called us one day and said Mr. Hackney had withdrawn the offer," Sandifur said. "Obviously, I'm very happy we didn't make the deal."

The Hackney-led acquisition team did have some success, however. In March 1999 Frankel made it look on paper as though the St. Francis of Assisi Foundation had assumed control of Thunor Trust. Kay Tatum and Leah Hudson of the Aiken Gump law firm prepared a "Memorandum Summarizing the Saint Francis of Assisi Foundation," which Frankel freely distributed to bolster the credibility of his acquisition machine. The memo not only listed the bona fides of Jacobs, Hackney, Bolan, and Edward D. Collins, but stated as a fact that "The Advisory Board members include, among others, Walter Cronkite and Lee Iacocca, who have graciously agreed to serve in such capacity." Now firmly under the cloak of charity and religiosity, the Frankel-controlled Franklin American Life Insurance Company acquired Old South West Life Insurance Company and its $5.3 million in reserves on March 31, 1999.

The following month, the Frankel-controlled First National Life Insurance Company further aggrandized the Greenwich money manager's Swiss bank accounts in a reinsurance agreement with Settlers Life Insurance Company in Virginia. All Frankel had to do was put up $1.75 million to assume liability for a huge chunk of Settlers Life policies, which came along with the $46 million in assets needed to cover those policies. The day after the deal was struck, on April 2, 1999, Settlers Life transferred $44.8 million to First National Life's bank account, and three hours after that the money was on its way to Frankel's Dreyfus account in New York, and then to United Bank of Switzerland, also in New York, and finally to Banque SCS Alliance in Geneva.

Other reinsurance deals, with the Peoples Benefit and Veterans Life Insurance Companies, netted Team Frankel blocks of business worth $15 million, which were promptly transferred to First National Life Insurance Company's bank account and then wired into one of Frankel's brokerage accounts up north.

But not everybody was so easily taken in by Frankel's priest-and-pony show. When Team Frankel tried to buy the Capitol Life Insurance Company in Golden, Colorado, owned by former U.S. ambassador to Jamaica Glen A. Holden, they were thwarted by basic due diligence the company performed that determined fairly quickly that something about the deal didn't smell right.

First, the prospective buyers had provided Capitol Life with a deposit slip purporting to show that the money to be used in the transaction would come from the approximately $50 million the Vatican had placed in a St. Francis account with the Jupiter Growth Fund, a Frankel shell corporation in the British Virgin Islands. The deposit slip, like most of the documentation provided by Team Frankel, "looked like a desktop special," said retired New York City police detective George Trapp, who did the investigation for the Colorado insurance company.

Second, when the insurance company wanted proof that Jacobs had been duly authorized to represent the Vatican, Aiken Gump provided the 1998 Catholic Yearbook, which listed Jacobs. "I said to them, 'What does this show? Where is the official document from the Holy See showing this Jacobs could act on behalf of the Holy See?'" Trapp recalled. "There were just too many questions about the credibility of St. Francis—they just didn't pass the test in Colorado."

The company's president, Joseph L. Blattner, said even though he had wanted to sell, it was doubtful a deal could have been struck because of his state's prohibition of foreign ownership of U.S. insurance firms. "St. Francis was telling us that they were ultimately controlled by the Vatican, but if that was the case, then they could not buy Capitol Life," Blattner said.

Had Frankel somehow managed to buy the company, Capitol Life could have kissed $461 million in assets good-bye.

A much bigger pot was at stake in Louisiana, where Frankel made a bid for United Life and Annuity Insurance Company of Baton Rouge, which held assets worth $1.4 billion. This time a more seasoned version of Team Frankel would be making the pitch.

Corbally, who had been insistent that Frankel involve professionals in his acquisitions gambit, finally got the green light. He formed a new unit that was headed up by Larry H. Martin, a New York attorney with previous, indirect links to securities transactions that had come under scrutiny. He had been an intermediary when in the mid-1990s Osicom Technologies of California bought a controlling stake in Builders Warehouse, a failed home products retailer in Arkansas. Shareholders of Builders Warehouse brought a class action suit claiming they'd been defrauded, prompting an investigation by the U.S. Securities and Exchange Commission.

Martin's right-hand man would be Thomas F. Quinn, a smooth-talking disbarred lawyer and stock fraud veteran whose rap sheet extended back to Frankel's childhood. Even though Quinn had arrived in Greenwich two years earlier, it does not appear he knew Frankel until being introduced to him through Corbally. Quinn's forte was peddling worthless stock to the unsuspecting public in what is known as "boiler room" operations, and he had served prison time in both the United States and Europe. Boiler rooms, also known as "chop shops," are fly-by-night offices from which fast-talking pitchmen sell bogus stock to unwitting victims through telephone solicitations. In 1970 he served six months in the Danbury Federal Correctional Institution after convictions for securities, mail, and wire fraud. He was later ordered by a federal judge in Illinois to surrender $26 million in illegal profits he obtained in connection with the fraudulent offer for sale of securities in GSS Venture Capital and Max Inc.

According to the U.S. Securities and Exchange Commission, the court had concluded that Tom Quinn's "customary business activities appeared to be devoted exclusively to securities fraud."

In the 1980s Quinn was at the center of an international scam that sold $500 million of worthless stock. At the time it was one of Europe's largest-ever securities frauds. Working out of his villa in Mougins, outside of Cannes, Quinn oversaw a vast boiler room operation in which telephone salesmen peddled worthless stocks in as many as twenty countries. For that he was sentenced by a French court to four years in prison in 1991.

When he met Frankel, Quinn and his companion, Rochelle Rothfleisch, were living in Quinn's villa in the south of France. Coincidentally, approximately two years before meeting Frankel, Quinn and Rothfleisch began renting a house in Greenwich, not far from the Lake Avenue compound. Frankel confided to associates how much he enjoyed Quinn's company because his new partner was able to provide a glimpse into the dark side of the business. "And since Tom got caught, Marty thought he could learn from his mistakes," one of Frankel's female assistants said.

The new Quinn-Martin production was called American Life Acquisitions. Its business plan mapped out an ambitious strategy of assembling limited partnerships to raise $1 billion in working capital by the end of 1999 in order to acquire insurance companies with assets totaling $10 billion. Each partnership would require a minimum investment of $25 million. "The fund intends to raise additional funds in the next several years and acquire additional assets of up to $50 billion over the next five years," the business plan boldly declared.

The new team then brought aboard a cadre of professional insurance consultants, accountants, and actuaries. During get-acquainted meetings at Martin's home in Pound Ridge, New York, they were told about how Martin and Quinn had made frequent trips to Europe, where they had lined up a group of wealthy investors, including a Luxembourg bank that had already entered into four partnerships, giving the group an initial amount of $100 million to work with. The new associates were also told about how Martin was courting a few Swiss and French banks to buy into the new fund as well.

As with other Frankel dealings, some of the players who were drawn into the new enterprise thought they were associating themselves with a legitimate enterprise. Manhattan attorney Peter Vigeland, for example, said his law firm, LeBoeuf, Lamb, Greene and MacRea, worked briefly for American Life Acquisitions after being hired by Martin. "The work consisted of doing limited legal research and conceptual advice for the potential acquisition of insurance companies," Vigeland said. "LeBoeuf never set up any companies for Mr. Martin, and there were no implemented transactions. It was very limited in scope and time and in subject matter."

Cheryl Everts, an investment manager with United States Trust Company of New York, was listed in the American Life Acquisitions business plan as a financial reference. She claimed to have known nothing of her alleged involvement until insurance companies began calling her in February 1999, asking her to vouch for their suitors. "I have no idea how they got my name," Everts said. "I can only guess they got my name from U.S. Trust's annual report."

The other financial references American Life Acquisitions were giving out included David Rosse and Karen Timmins, president and vice president of Frankel's Jupiter Investment Fund.

The remaining ALA team members were as follows:

- Eugene Esposito, a consultant with over thirty years of experience in the insurance industry, who once was senior vice president of operations for Home Security Life Insurance Company in Durham, North Carolina.
- John D. Yednock, another consultant with over a quarter of a century of industry experience, who had been senior vice president with United Insurance Company of America in Chicago. He had also held actuarial positions with Teledyne Inc. and TransAmerica Occidental Life Insurance Company.
- Laurence M. Brotzge, a certified public accountant with more than two decades of experience in the insurance industry, who was a former senior vice president of Providian, a multibillion-dollar financial services company, and a senior executive with the Agency Group in Louisville, Kentucky, and Direct Response Group in Valley Forge, Pennsylvania. Prior to that he had been a senior manager with the Ernst and Young accounting firm's Louisville office.

- Donald Heller, who was introduced to the rest of the ALA team as president of J. S. Karlton Co., a Greenwich-based real estate investment and management company. Karlton officials would later vigorously deny Heller had any connection with their firm beyond a limited partnership with one of Karlton's properties. Heller's resume also listed him as chairman of Novatek Medical, a manufacturer of a device that guards against blood transfusion errors.

- David S. Wolfe, who at the time of ALA's formation was said to be corporate finance director for Carty and Company in Nashville and "experienced in all facets of the insurance industry, including product design, employee benefit plans, pension, securities trading, and portfolio management." He was also a former executive vice president of United Resources, a division of Integrated Resources, and had supervised national sales and recruiting for the Equita Group, which specialized in annuities and tax-sheltered life insurance products.

- John D. Mazzuto, who from 1971 to 1989 held a number of positions with Chemical Bank, including managing director of corporate finance, and had served on the bank's executive credit committee. He had also been head of finance in the New York offices of the Asian Oceanic Group, an international merchant bank.

In addition to LeBoeuf, Lamb, Greene and MacRea, ALA listed its legal counsel as the Manhattan law firm of Maloney, Mehman and Katz. The ALA team's accounting firm was Ernst and Young, and providing actuarial services was Tillinghast-Towers Perrin.

Now Frankel had the topflight lineup that Corbally had insisted on, and American Life Acquisitions was formally launched on January 21, 1999. The date was chosen by Frankel because his astrology charts told him it would be an auspicious day for a new business venture.

A series of ALA planning meetings then was held through early February, at the Trump International and St. Regis Hotels in Manhattan; a hotel in Stamford, Connecticut; and the Homestead Inn in the ultraexclusive private section of Greenwich called Belle Haven, where pop diva Diana Ross and Fortune 500 magnates make their homes.

With the new acquisition team in place, Frankel dispatched them to cities throughout the country and around the globe. On expense statements for an American Express card issued to Kaethe Schuchter, the same ALA players could be seen making regular trips to Chicago, Dallas–Fort Worth, Los Angeles, New Orleans, and St. Louis, as well as Rome, Geneva, London, and Luxembourg. And when he wasn't using commercial flights to send his emissaries on business jaunts, Frankel was chartering private jets. The charge card statements show that for the chartered flights, Frankel incurred fuel bills totaling over half a million dollars between December 1998 and March 1999.

ALA's first bid was made for the purchase of United Life and Annuity Insurance Company in Louisiana. But the latest line-up for Team Frankel struck out in its first time at bat. Martin, who did all of the negotiating during the meeting in Baton Rouge, had "talked about some wild scheme of financing through Luxembourg banks into a British Virgin Islands entity," recalled Craig Gardner, Louisiana's highly skeptical deputy assistant insurance commissioner. "We said, 'You need to tell us where the money's coming from,' and he said that was confidential. That didn't work for us."

After Martin and his entourage were sent packing, they decided in February 1999 to take a stab at yet another Mississippi firm—Gulf National Life Insurance Company. Joey Langston, a lawyer from Booneville, Mississippi, who represented Gulf National during negotiations, said he smelled a rat after the one and only meeting with ALA representatives Larry Martin, Tom Quinn, and Gene Esposito.

"The principals in Gulf were not convinced these were legitimate buyers," Langston said. "These people from ALA came into Mississippi acting very flashy, with a nice big jet and a stewardess, and they tried to leave us with the impression that money wasn't an issue with them. Well, money is *always* an issue. They talked like there wouldn't be any negotiations, that even if we were to name a premium price, they would pay it."

During the meeting in a reserved room at a Gulf Coast restaurant the Team Frankel members seemed to work too hard at trying to impress, according to Langston. "Tom Quinn was talking about his house in the south of France, and Larry Martin was talking about going to sleep in one country and waking up in another, and how he couldn't keep track of time zones," Langston said. "Well, that's the kind of talk that makes country people like us skeptical. We thought it was more show than substance."

The owner of Gulf National Life was Jeremiah "Jerry" O'Keefe, the seventy-six-year-old former U.S. congressman and mayor of Biloxi who made his fortune in the undertaking business that his great-grandfather had started just after the Civil War. In 1958 O'Keefe founded Gulf National Life and turned it into the largest insurance company in the state. O'Keefe retired prior to ALA's attempted purchase of his firm, which at the time had $70 million in assets, and he had given all of the stock to his children. But he remained on retainer as a consultant, and Team Frankel thought the best way to convince the new owners to sell would be through O'Keefe.

"I told them the company now belonged to my children, and, besides, the company wasn't for sale," O'Keefe recalled. "But they insisted on coming down, saying, 'We want specifically to meet with you.'"

Like Langston, O'Keefe was not impressed by Team Frankel. "Larry Martin didn't know what the heck he was talking about, and it was obvious he didn't know anything about the insurance business," O'Keefe said. "Martin then began talking about how he'd already bought these three other insurance companies, and when he named them I said to him, 'If what you say is correct, I know a fellow in Tennessee who said he bought those same companies and represents the same money fund that you claim to represent.'"

That "fellow" was Frankel's original partner in the insurance business, John Hackney. O'Keefe had met Hackney at the same time Hackney was trying to arrange Frankel's takeover of Protective Services Life in 1995. The Atlanta insurance broker who mediated the deal, Jim Caldwell, had invited O'Keefe to meet with Hackney at Protective Services' owner James Robinson's office in Tennessee. Caldwell at the time had cautioned his friend Jerry O'Keefe about doing business with Hackney because he would never give straight answers—even to his own associates—as to who the Thunor Trust investors were.

Martin acknowledged that John Hackney worked for the same people that he and Quinn represented, but told O'Keefe, "Well, you see, John just isn't aggressive enough, so now we've taken over."

O'Keefe was wary of the New York lawyer. "I just didn't get along with this Martin fellow," O'Keefe said, "because he was trying so damn hard to impress me with how much he'd been flying all over the world. He said to me, 'Yesterday I was in Amsterdam, and the day before that I was in Brussels and then had to stop in London.' You know, that sort of thing. Like I was really interested in where he'd been. Larry Martin was a very arrogant kind of guy. He thought he knew it all, but he didn't know anything about the insurance business. That was obvious.

"I gave them a very bad report to my daughter and the executive vice president. They met with them for breakfast the next day, and they came away with the same impression of them that I had."

As the Quinn-Martin failures mounted, Frankel was becoming desperate to get his hands on more insurance assets. By April 1999 the St. Francis of Assisi Foundation had unsuccessfully courted at least ten insurance companies, proposing either buyouts or deals for blocks of business. Those companies, some of which had assets of over $1 billion, included American States Life Insurance, a unit of Safeco Corporation; Intercontinental Life, in Austin, Texas; and Grand Pacific Life Insurance, in Honolulu.

Frankel was learning from his failures, seeing that one of the biggest obstacles had been the skepticism of the targeted insurance companies' executives. In the words of Roger Harbin, a Safeco executive vice president, "It was impossible to verify this was a legitimate offer" when the St. Francis foundation made an offer on American States Life.

To mend the credibility problem, Frankel, with the assistance of Merger Acquisitions Profiles and Jerry Wolfe, tried assembling yet another acquisitions team by recruiting two respected executives from the corporate world. One was Victor C. Moses, a Seattle resident and senior vice president of business development at GE Financial Assurance. The other was Bruce I. Weiser, a lawyer from Westport, Connecticut. Only a month before meeting with Frankel, Weiser was head of investor relations for Swiss Reinsurance Corp.'s Life Re unit when the Swiss reinsurance giant shelled out $360 million for the $2.6 billion in combined assets of Royal Maccabees Life Insurance Company of Michigan and its New York subsidiary, Royal Life Insurance Company.

A third prospective recruit was David Ricci, an actuary with American Annuity Group of Cincinnati, who eventually turned down a huge signing bonus and million-dollar annual commissions because he smelled a rat.

The three prospective Team Frankel recruits, along with Wolfe, assembled for a luncheon meeting at the Greenwich mansion on April 13, 1999. All were dressed in business attire, while Frankel, who introduced himself as David Rosse, wore his customary oversized blue jeans and a T-shirt. Upon arriving, the men were "welcomed by [Frankel's] administrative staff—all women in body-length nunlike outfits," Ricci recalled.

The five men went into the conference room next to Frankel's trading room and sat around a table that appeared to have been set for lunch, although no food was ever served. Instead, Frankel's assistants would constantly refill glasses with Evian and other beverages.

"[Frankel] was animated, fidgety, and quick to interrupt, but this was expected since we were prepared by the broker to expect an eccentric personality," Ricci said, adding that Frankel frequently excused himself in order to go to the bathroom—"or at least that's where he told us he was going."

In between his trips out of the room, Frankel breathlessly explained to his guests the trading strategy that would lead them all to the promised land.

"His investment plan was so simple it was a work of genius, according to Rosse," Ricci said. "He would merely trade thirty-year Treasuries based upon his 'feel' for the market, knowing that in the long run Treasuries were headed for fifty-year lows, and that any security bought before that point would always turn profitable if held long enough. Of course there were always rough spots, but with a large enough portfolio he had virtually unlimited earnings potential."

Frankel claimed that his portfolio already consisted of $1 billion, after having doubled an initial amount of $500 million for the St. Francis foundation. "The St. Francis of Assisi Foundation, we were told, was backed by all these funds from the Vatican, funds that would eventually be used to purchase large blocks of insurance company business," Ricci recalled. "Everything seemed to be on the up-and-up. We asked to see financial documents, which he showed us, and we assumed they were legit."

Frankel then told his guests that, with their help, he was going to use that single billion to amass a multibillion-dollar insurance enterprise that would rival Conseco and SunAmerica. "If I had the right people working for me eight years ago, I'd be [SunAmerica Chairman] Eli Broad right now," Frankel commented.

Referring to the aborted deal with Sandifur in Spokane for the purchase of Western Annuity and Life Assurance, Frankel told Weiser, Moses, and Ricci that he needed fresh talent that would be more aggressive in their pursuit of insurance assets. "He went into excruciating detail about a venture that was going bad because the seller wanted $10 million more than the original asking price, saying that it was the fault of his current legal and actuarial team, who didn't understand what the real issues were," Ricci recalled. Frankel told the guests that he didn't really care about how much money he needed to spend to reach his ultimate goal because, Ricci said, "once the assets were under his control, it would be impossible for the venture to lose in spite of the up-front costs."

Convinced of Frankel's earnestness—and especially swayed by the documents Frankel dangled before them, which purported to show how he had doubled St. Francis of Assisi's assets to $1 billion—Moses accepted a $750,000 signing bonus, and Weiser received $600,000. Contracts for both promised millions of dollars more in commissions over the next several years. Neither would ever perform any work for Frankel, however, as the financial guru would suddenly vanish less than a month after the employment agreements were signed.

Ricci turned down a similarly generous offer, as he sensed something wasn't quite right. "There was an investment anomaly that Frankel was never going to resolve to my satisfaction," the insurance actuary said. "The cash-flow characteristics of the life insurance products were long-term in nature, yet his trading scheme reduced the duration of his assets to virtually zero.

"The biggest problem I had was that this one person, Dave Rosse, was the only one answering any questions about the operation, and there seemed to be no way to get behind him to find out what really was going on. Another thing that bothered me was the commissions that were involved were unheard-of."

Looking back on his close call with infamy, Ricci said, "It was easy to see why so many trustful and honorable folks were duped into [Frankel's] scheme. He had a very pleasant yet quirky demeanor, and could have virtually sold anything. It's unfortunate for him, as well as thousands of investors, policyholders, et cetera, that he could not distinguish proper from improper and became one of the world's biggest con men."

Even though he now had reputable professionals willing to do his bidding, Frankel would not be marching into the bright and profitable future that he had envisioned. Dark and forbidding clouds were gathering on the horizon, and by the time Frankel realized that, it would be too late to save his Xanadu from a disastrous end.

Chapter Eight

If Frances Burge's death had earlier foreshadowed disastrous times ahead, subsequent events toward the end of 1998 and early 1999 portended the same.

In November of 1998 Leon Frankel died at the age of eighty-seven. Although Frankel had always seemed to be embarrassed by his family and looked down on his father as a "loser," he was deeply affected by Leon's death.

When he flew home for the funeral, he was accompanied by Rosse and a coterie of armed security guards in case his Toledo nemesis, John Schulte, should show up. Sure enough, Schulte had read about Leon Frankel's passing in the local paper and thought that if Frankel came for the funeral, Sonia would likely be with him. He saw a chance to see his children for the first time in six years.

As Schulte slowly drove down Stanhope Drive and approached the Frankel residence, he spotted two cars with Michigan license plates following him. Realizing he was being followed, Schulte sped up and a chase ensued. When Schulte braked for traffic at a busy intersection, one of the men in the sedan immediately behind him got out and jumped onto the hood of his car.

As Schulte raced off, the guard rolled off his hood. Panicked, Schulte drove to the nearby Ottawa Hills Police Department. There he was given a police escort back to the Toledo city line, where he was met by a Toledo police officer, who accompanied Schulte to the Frankel house. The officer went to the house, spoke with Frankel and his mother, and returned to Schulte with the news that his children were not there.

Schulte left without further incident, but the commotion Sonia's ex-husband had created further convinced Frankel that his life was in serious danger. Upon returning to Greenwich, Frankel demanded that he be protected by armed guards twenty-four hours a day. It was immediately arranged by Rosse, tapping into his network of New York police officers.

It was also in 1998 that Frankel made a move that would prove to be a fatal mistake. He relocated First National Life Insurance Company's headquarters from Alabama to Mississippi, which he knew to be a state that allowed wire transfers of insurance company reserves, subject to approval of the state Department of Insurance. But what he didn't know was that the man he needed to have sign off on such transactions was insurance commissioner George Dale, a fifty-eight-year-old former high school principal with a commonsense approach to problem solving, who would ultimately bring Frankel's house of cards crashing down.

Before he would give his approval to the wire transfers, Dale wanted to learn more about where the money would be going. What was this Liberty National Securities brokerage that would be handling the investing of the wired funds? Looking at the brokerage firm's track records, as the Tennessee regulators had done before him, the insurance commissioner became especially concerned about how this no-name brokerage firm from up north reported a 1998 trading volume of about $14 billion, from which the brokerage earned a paltry sum of only $40,000 in commissions.

"The method that they [First National] used was to put all of their investments through this one investment firm, and no one on our staff knew what this firm was, so our examiner contacted the insurance company and asked why are you using this investment firm, which is so small," Dale said. "Well, the answer he got back was that the insurance company was able to get a quicker and better rate of return on their investments by using Liberty National."

The Mississippi insurance examiner naturally wanted to know more about this high-performing investment firm, and so he shot a call to the New York Department of Insurance and made inquiries about Liberty National Securities. To his astonishment, the brokerage was not at 82 Wall Street, Department 1105, as it claimed. The address was nothing but a private mailbox.

Regulators did locate the legitimate Liberty National Securities, operating out of a house in Dundee, Michigan, but was told by owner Robert Guyer that while he was familiar with Frankel, he had not had any significant contact with him for several years. Guyer further told them that Frankel had approached him about buying Liberty National Securities in late 1998 but never acted on it.

Guyer had apparently lied to the Mississippi insurance officials. Far from being an acquaintance of Frankel's, the sixty-year-old stockbroker had in fact been another of Frankel's business partners. Guyer was working with Frankel and Sonia in 1991 when Liberty National Securities and Creative Partners were being run out of the same address in Toledo. After Guyer relocated Liberty National Securities to his modest home in rural Michigan in 1993, Frankel and Guyer shared a key for the same post office box in Dundee, from which Frankel's Greenwich office assistants made regular pickups. After leaving originals of documents they retrieved from the mailbox, the assistants would return to Connecticut with copies. Additionally, a Liberty National Securities telephone line in Guyer's house was call-forwarded to Frankel's Greenwich compound.

At the same time the Mississippi regulators were asking around about Liberty National Securities, they were also beginning to take a hard look at both the St. Francis of Assisi Foundation and Father Jacobs. And they were giving close scrutiny to documentation that purported to show a $600 million "contribution" the Vatican had made to Thunor-controlled insurance companies through St. Francis of Assisi, which now was identified as the owner of Thunor Trust.

This sounded the loudest alarm bell of all. Ownership transfers of insurance companies require Form A hearings to be held. The Mississippi Insurance Department had not been notified of this apparent change in ownership, which meant a possible violation of state law had occurred.

"After it was evident that the investment firm was not what it said it was, then we began to say, 'Well maybe there are other things about all of this, that they may not be who they say they are,'" Dale said.

The Baptist commissioner had a connection with the Catholic Church in his good friend Eddie Brunini, a Jackson attorney whose uncle, the late Joseph Brunini, had been archbishop of the local diocese. Dale instructed one of his deputies, Ron Hanna, to get in touch with Brunini. "I told Ron to give Eddie a call, because Eddie's the best Catholic I know, and if anyone can determine the authenticity of a Catholic priest, he can," Dale said.

Brunini's inquiries were referred by the Mississippi diocese to the Vatican's embassy in Washington, D.C., which only gave the insurance officials the runaround. "They called the consulate there in Washington, and what they got was somewhat of a cold reception," Dale said. "They said, 'Yes, we know about Father Jacobs, but he does not have his papers with any Catholic diocese in the U.S. at this time.' They made it clear they did not want to give out any more information, that they did not want to be involved. They basically said, 'Thank you very much for calling, but don't call us again.'"

The insurance commissioner had heard enough. "So now we'd discovered that Liberty National didn't exist at the location it said it does, and we discovered Jacobs was supposedly a bogus priest," Dale said. "That's when I told my staff I wanted them to round up all of the parties concerned— David Rosse, St. Francis of Assisi, Thunor Trust, and the insurance companies—and I want them all here in my office." An emergency hearing was scheduled for April 29 at the Mississippi Department of Insurance offices in Jackson.

Just as things were starting to look bleak for Frankel, another harbinger of things to come arrived in the guise of a Greenwich building inspector, who came knocking on Frankel's door in March 1999.

The unwelcome visitor had come as a result of action taken by Frankel's neighbors, who were suspicious and nervous by the drastic increase in limousine traffic and activity at the Frankel compound. They had hired Sutton Associates, a prominent private investigation firm owned and staffed by retired FBI agents, to look into the problem.

On February 24, 1999, Sutton Associates presented Frankel's neighbors with a forty-page report of its investigation. It began with a brief and blunt recitation of "The Problem":

> The problem lies in having mysterious if not unsavory, neighbors, illegally engaged in a large and growing commercial enterprise, creating vehicular and traffic hazards and a general atmosphere inconsistent with, and threatening to, an environment where children can freely roam and play near their houses and adults can fully enjoy the benefits of a pleasant suburban lifestyle. This problem is now further exacerbated in that Frankel and his cult, by virtue of their acquisition of the Davidson property and their placement of

sentries near the road, have established a psychological, if not physical, stronghold on the cul-de-sac.

As the result of extensive surveillance and records checks, the private eyes had learned of Frankel's previous run-in with the SEC and his banishment from the securities industry. Through their investigation, the private detectives learned the identities of three Frankel associates:

Rosse is a native New Yorker who, at age eighteen, had his first scrape with the law involving possession of a dangerous weapon. At age twenty-eight he was again arrested for carrying a prohibited weapon in New Jersey. . . . As far as our inquiries can tell, he is not licensed to carry a weapon in the state of Connecticut. While it appears that Rosse acts as Frankel's chief-of-staff, with responsibilities such as utilities, phones, the fleet of automobiles, etc., he greatly downplayed his role when he was being interviewed by Detective Zack subsequent to the 1997 suicide of one of Frankel's groupies, Frances Burge.

Miriam Fischer used to work for Frankel at the Lake Avenue compound and was apparently a key employee. Whether or not she continues to work for Frankel from her office/apartment in Manhattan is not known. She is being considered as a potential source in the IRS approach to Frankel. She will also be evaluated and considered as a potential source when we discuss the zoning approach to Frankel. . . . It is suspected she would probably be loyal to Frankel.

Sonia, who was married to John Schulte, apparently ran off with Frankel . . . she then moved to Jupiter, Florida. It was during this time that Frankel told people he was sending large amounts of money on a monthly basis to Sonia in Florida. . . . IRS in Ohio apparently has an interest in her along with Frankel. Sonia is also considered a potential source in the IRS approach to Frankel.

As for the various women at the Frankel estate, the private detectives reported that the 1997 suicide investigation "indicated that the principal resident placed ads in the *Village Voice* to hire young girls to work in his residence, because [Mike King] 'needed their social security numbers for buying and selling.'"

Frankel's neighbors provided the investigators with eyewitness testimony that since the beginning of the year there had been substantial electrical system upgrades to 889 Lake Avenue, and they noted the presence of general contractors and heavy construction equipment, which indicated that substantial renovations were under way there.

The investigators also developed a list of Frankel-controlled organizations, noting that "Frankel's former modus operandi often includes the formation of numerous companies, their eventual dissolution or lapse, and then their continued disuse for pretext reasons." The companies they identified included Sundew International, Gates Investments, W.A.B.S.T, AWV, RMI Investments, and Ala Carte.

From speaking with the Greenwich police detectives who had investigated Frances Burge's death, the Sutton agents further learned that Frankel had described himself as an investment manager for a Swiss bank. Checking with the New York Stock Exchange, they found that forty-one MDS devices—market quote machines—were being leased by Mike King and Gates Investments.

The private detectives then took all of their information to the feds. They met with assistant U.S. attorney Kerry Peterson, who expressed "a sincere interest in Frankel." Peterson asked that full disclosure of Sutton's findings be made to her investigator, IRS special agent Larry Marini of the Criminal Investigations Division (CID). The private detectives met with Marini and provided him with an outline of their report. They learned that Marini had been unaware that his own agency had previously investigated Frankel in Ohio "because Marini did not have King's [Frankel's] true identity or social security number." The space for Frankel's social security number in the 1997 Greenwich police suicide report had been left blank.

Sutton Associates also notified the SEC of its findings. However, the detective agency noted in its report, "The SEC seems overburdened, slow to react and not overly enthusiastic. Prospect for decisive and effective action in this matter: Unlikely. Most optimistic view: They would fully cooperate with and assist CID/IRS in an IRS investigation. We have linked the IRS to the appropriate SEC representative."

Then a meeting was held with two officers of the New York Stock Exchange—James Esposito, vice president in charge of security, and Simon Swidler, director of enforcement. "While they were understanding and sympathetic, no effective action will be forthcoming on their part," the report read.

The means by which the neighbors would be more likely to see immediate action taken against Frankel, the private detectives concluded, would be through the Town of Greenwich Planning and Zoning Commission. Such an approach, they advised their clients, "would be to constantly report, on an anonymous basis, to Zoning Enforcement Officer Maloney the presence of workmen or work being done at 889 Lake Avenue or now at the former Davidson property. Maloney has promised to respond and inspect work permits and get a foot in the door.

"This approach, while not designed to result in a cease-and-desist order, is likely to result in frustrating expansion efforts with a possibility of opening up new possibilities for Maloney. This approach also brings . . . the risk of incurring Frankel's wrath. It would probably be evident to Frankel that, if we seek testimonial zoning evidence from a worker [still loyal to Frankel] or if we launch a 'report the unauthorized construction' campaign, these efforts were generated in the interest of the immediate neighbors."

As a result of Sutton Associates' involvement, Greenwich zoning enforcement officer James Maloney did make several attempts to inspect 889 Lake Avenue, but each time he was turned away at the guard shack that had recently been built at the bottom of the driveway. A note was posted inside the shack that ordered guards to "immediately notify the main house" when and if any strangers came calling, specifically town building officials.

Maloney didn't have to enter the property to notice violations, however, as the guard shack itself, as well as the perimeter fencing around the main house, had been erected without obtaining the necessary permits. The zoning enforcement officer mailed notifications of the two violations to Frankel in April and again in early May, both of which were ignored.

The pesky neighbors were only a minor distraction for Frankel. More pressing business needed the boss's attention in Mississippi, where the investigation into Frankel's insurance empire began in earnest. When notified that Dale, the insurance commissioner, had scheduled the emergency hearing at the Mississippi Department of Insurance headquarters in Jackson, Frankel decided it was time to fight back. He noticed that the most skeptical of the Mississippi bunch appeared to be special assistant attorney general Lee Harrell, and so Frankel instructed his assistants to find out everything they could about him—who Harrell's friends were, and what skeletons might be in his closet.

He ordered his minions to begin assembling a "dream team" of lawyers, accountants, and others who could fend off the pesky, meddlesome southerners. Among those they were able to recruit was Nicholas Monaco, a former insurance regulator with a law practice in Jefferson City, Missouri. Monaco's job would be to prep Frankel's representatives for the grilling they could expect from George Dale and other Mississippi insurance regulators.

When Frankel's assistants found out that one of George Dale's close friends was Mississippi businessman Thurston Little, Frankel immediately hired Little as a consultant. Dale, a former high school principal and football coach, had been insurance commissioner since 1976, a year after having served as administrative aide to Mississippi governor Bill Waller. The governor was a good buddy of one of Mississippi's U.S. senators, James O. Eastland, who in turn was a close friend of Thurston Little. Little came from a prominent northeastern Mississippi political family, and his brother was serving as a Mississippi state senator at the time he was hired by Frankel. Dale became acquainted with Little during his three years with Waller, and the two men went on to become the best of friends.

What Frankel expected in return for the more than $6 million he gave to Little depends on whom you are talking to. Little's lawyer, Joey Langston, said his client had planned to enter into a real estate development venture with his new friend up north. He said that in either March or April 1999 Frankel wired $5 million to Little so that Little could retire personal and business debts before the partnership got down to business. Langston said the venture never got off the ground, however, because Frankel's alleged investment fraud scheme was found out soon afterward and he fled the country.

In addition to that money, the lawyer said, Frankel sent Little another $1.325 million, all but $25,000 of which Little used to buy a new Piper Cheyenne III to replace the older airplane Little already owned. "Frankel told Thurston that his plane was too dangerous, and that if he was going to be involved in real estate development, Thurston needed to be able to get around in a reliable plane," Langston said.

A former Frankel associate suggested that the airplane was the only actual payment Little received for his services, and that the rest of the money Frankel sent him was to have been used to "bribe" Mississippi insurance officials. No evidence has surfaced to show that actual or attempted bribes were ever made.

If they are to be believed, rumors that nearly a year later still circulated in Little's hometown of Corinth suggested that the real estate development partnership with Frankel had begun in earnest. According to some Corinth residents, the buzz about town in the spring of 1999 was that the local Trustmark National Bank branch had been the recipient of a wire transfer in the unheard of amount of $21 million. The local gossip was that the money had been sent by Frankel to Little, who then went on a binge buying up downtown Corinth's most valuable pieces of real estate. Whatever the case may be, employees at Frankel's Greenwich estate remembered that Frankel had emphasized to them how Little was someone special and should be treated with the greatest respect when he came to visit. "He told us that Thurston Little would be the most important guest we've ever had," recalled one employee.

One thing that is known for sure is that Little tried his damnedest to get Dale to sign off on Frankel's attempt to get permission to make out-of-state wire transfers of insurance assets. According to Dale, in a telephone call he had placed to the insurance commissioner's office he said, "Listen, George, this here is a good program that they are trying to do, and if you'll let them make these wire transfers, the company's going to make a lot of money in Mississippi. This David Rosse is going to buy a lot more insurance companies," Little said, "and he's going to headquarter them all right here. This is a tremendous economic opportunity for Mississippi, and if you help make this happen, it will be the biggest thing you've ever done."

Another of Frankel's objectives was to persuade regulators to allow him to combine the investments of the three Mississippi-based insurance companies so that he could wire them between accounts. Little explained to Dale that such a commingling of assets would give "David Rosse" flexibility that would allow the insurers to reap even larger returns. In response to his friend's urgings, Dale had said, "Thurston, this sounds just fine, and when my staff evaluates this thing and puts it in front of me on my desk and says this is a good thing for the state of Mississippi, and it's all legal and above-board, then I'll approve it."

Another weapon in Frankel's arsenal was former U.S. senator Harlan Mathews, an influential Nashville lawyer. He represented Frankel's interests after the Tennessee Department of Commerce and Insurance—upon finding out that Franklin American Corporation's $60 million in bonds were being held by Liberty National Securities—demanded that the bonds be placed with a bank in accordance with state law. Frankel complied in December 1998, but soon he whisked the bonds back out to the New York account of his bogus brokerage firm.

When the Tennessee officials discovered what had been done with the bonds, the regulators demanded that they be returned to the bank. After Mathews was brought aboard Team Frankel, however, the regulators gave Liberty National Securities a two-month extension, buying Frankel precious time.

It was at about this time that Frankel began spending thousands of dollars buying new luggage—just in case. When some of the lower-level employees at the Greenwich compound began inquiring about the suitcases and trunks they saw piling up in the garage security office, they were summarily fired.

"I saw Bob Biddle unwrapping all this new luggage, so I asked him, 'Is the boss going somewhere?' " Bryan Rodriguez, one of Frankel's chefs, recalled asking the compound's maintenance foreman. "This got Bob really pissed off, and he began yelling at me about how I wasn't doing my job, because at the time I had no meals to prepare and I was just sitting at a terminal in the kitchen surfing the Internet. The next week Cindy Allison called and said that my services were no longer required. When I asked her why, she said it was because the boss was no longer eating my food. That's bullshit. They just didn't like that I was asking questions."

As the meeting with Mississippi insurance regulators approached, Frankel put his staff into overdrive, cranking out packages of information explaining the mission of the St. Francis of Assisi Foundation, which were then shipped to regulators not only in Mississippi but in all states where Thunor companies were doing business.

"He had us pulling all-nighters toward the end," Mona Kim recalled. "The girls were staying up all night putting the packages together—photocopying, binding, hole punching, editing—they had to produce a certain number of packages every other day. They were St. Francis packages, and they were for prospective investors and insurance companies that we wanted to buy—also, for the regulators and anyone else who had doubts about St. Francis."

Frankel pulled his own all-nighters, going days without sleep as he worried whether his scheme would hold up under scrutiny. And it showed in his demeanor, as he snapped at his aides for the slightest of reasons. He spent more time alone locked in his trading room than usual, consulting astrology charts and going over doctored financial records with a fine-tooth comb.

While Frankel and his crew were scurrying around in Greenwich, the Mississippi insurance regulators were getting busy themselves as they prepared for the big showdown in Jackson.

On April 2 Mississippi Department of Insurance senior examiner Julie Dempsey wrote to John Hackney asking him for a detailed explanation as to how the St. Francis of Assisi Foundation had come to own Thunor Trust without the required Form A hearing. Showing an attempt at some deft footwork, Frankel had Hackney respond to Dempsey in an April 23 letter, in which he stated, "A subsequent event has taken place. The original grantors have decided to remain as grantors of the Thunor Trust. In doing so, the St. Francis Foundation will be an additional grantor to Thunor Trust. All grantors realize that the structure of Thunor Trust shall and will remain in place."

The same day, Hackney wrote to Commissioner Dale, declaring, "As a confirmation to clarify my relationship and responsibilities as Trustee of Thunor Trust, the Trustee has the sole and absolute responsibility to manage, invest, and control all funds that are contributed into the Trust. The Trustee will accept and consider request(s) and recommendations made from the grantors, however the Trustee will consider all alternatives and solely make the most qualified decisions as it relates to all investments which are under his authority."

To add emphasis to claims that Thunor Trust had not undergone a change in control, Father Jacobs also wrote a letter to Commissioner Dale. In the letter, also dated April 23, the priest identified himself as the "Chairman of the Board of Trustees" for the St. Francis of Assisi Foundation. "This is to advise you that the undersigned . . . disclaims having the power, directly or indirectly, to control Thunor Trust, Franklin American Corporation, or International Financial Corporation and their respective life insurance subsidiaries (i.e., the power to direct or cause the direction of the management and policies of the life insurance company subsidiaries)," Jacobs wrote.

All the efforts to allay regulators' concerns were for naught, and the meeting with Commissioner Dale was to go forward as scheduled.

On April 27, two days before the meeting in Jackson, Frankel's accounting firm provided a statement that seemed to show the Thunor-owned insurance companies were more than solvent, vouching for $600 million that had been "donated" by the Vatican. The accountants, from Baton Rouge–based Leuty and Heath, were careful to qualify the statement, however, saying that they had relied on financial statements that were provided by Frankel's organization. And despite the accountants' warning that the intent of their report was "solely to assist you with certain meetings and discussions with the Mississippi Department of Insurance," the statement wound up in regulators' hands nevertheless. It read:

> We have confirmed with the Monitor Ecclesiasticus Foundation, a Vatican foundation, that it is the source of certain contributions to the Saint Francis of Assisi Foundation to Serve and Help the Poor and Alleviate Suffering. . . . The board of trustees of Saint Francis placed its funds into Saint Francis Investment Fund, a wholly owned subsidiary of Saint Francis as of April 1999. Saint Francis Investment Fund conducts its business through several brokerage firms.
>
> In April 1999, we have confirmed that a total of $600,000,000 in two transactions were transferred from Saint Francis directly from its Saint Francis Investment Fund Account to the separate investment accounts of the Thunor Trust. . . . On the same dates in April, Thunor Trust transferred these amounts to its wholly owned insurance holding company, International Financial Corporation.
>
> Likewise, on the same dates in April, IFC transferred these funds to one of its wholly owned life insurance companies, First National Life Insurance Company of America (The Company). As of the date of this report, we have confirmed the Company possesses in excess of $758,900,000 in its investment portfolio.

Leuty and Heath also stated that as a result of donations totaling more than $1 billion, the St. Francis of Assisi Foundation's total assets rose from less than $1 billion at the end of 1998 to nearly $2 billion—$1,983,160,600, to be exact—as of March 31, 1999.

Frankel arrived in Mississippi the day before the hearing. Along with an entourage that included two former girlfriends and two IT guys toting boxes of files and computer equipment, he checked into the Hilton in Jackson, across the street from the Insurance Department's offices in the Walter Sillers Building. Checking into adjoining suites were Hackney, Atnip, Bolan,

Jacobs, Colagiovanni, and Eugene Wilkinson, a local Jackson attorney who was representing Thunor Trusts' Mississippi insurance firms. Frankel had signed the hotel register as David Rosse, the name by which he was known to most of those who had come for the meeting. The real Rosse joined the group the morning of the hearing, leading to some confusing moments when he and Frankel would be in the same room, both responding to questions posed to "David."

Later, when they were driving to the airport for the return flight home, Rosse confronted Frankel about having used his name. "If you ever tell someone you're David Rosse again, I swear, I'll hunt you down and kill you," the bodyguard said.

When Team Frankel assembled in one of their hotel's conference suites, security guards patrolled the hallway outside as Nicholas Monaco played the part of coach, trying to get Team Frankel psyched up for the big game. "Tomorrow is a critical day for Monitor Ecclesiasticus and St. Francis of Assisi Foundation," Monaco said. "The commissioner and his staff are very, very concerned."

Monaco then went through a litany of questions that Frankel's representatives could expect to be asked the next day: "Where did you get this kind of money? Is it a tax gimmick? Is it a dodge? How did this money get from here to there?" He also told them, "Commissioner Dale will want a paper trail—bank deposit slips."

At one point Monaco used role playing in his preparations, assuming the role of Dale as he questioned Bolan about his role as a St. Francis trustee. That prompted Frankel, who had been quietly working on a laptop computer in a corner of the room, to look up and register a loud objection. "Don't use Bolan as a witness," he cried out. "If you use him as a witness, we're lost."

Monaco turned toward Frankel and gave him a stern look. "You don't have any part here, David," the lawyer said. "Just shut up." Monaco made it clear to Frankel that he intended to do what he had been hired for without any interference, and then finished his witness preparation without further interruptions.

The next afternoon, Team Frankel—minus Frankel, who was already on his way back to Connecticut—marched across the street to the Sillers Building and rode the elevator to the Insurance Department's offices on the eighteenth floor. They were greeted by a receptionist, who ushered them into a conference room. They were soon joined by a few of the state's lawyers, who made small talk with their counterparts, Monaco and Wilkinson.

As the time for the 2 P.M. meeting approached, one of the state's lawyers left the group and went down the hall to alert Dale that it appeared as though Frankel would not show up. "Well, everybody else is here, so we might as well get going," the commissioner said.

By then the conference room was packed, and chairs had been lined up around the wall to accommodate the twenty or so participants. Dale took his position at the head of the table, and Colagiovanni and Jacobs sat to his immediate right. Filling out the rest of the table for Team Frankel were Hackney, Monaco, Wilkinson, and Bolan, and supporting Dale were Harrell and another assistant attorney general, Dave Scott, along with deputy insurance commissioner Ron Hanna, Harlan Dire, the insurance department's contractual actuary, and several Finance Examination Division members.

"As we were getting prepared to start the meeting and everyone else was still engaged in small talk, Father Jacobs had a picture of him standing next to a fire truck," Dale recalled. "He said to me, 'This is a New York City fire truck,' and so forth, and then the monsignor wanted to participate in the conversation. So he begins saying how he had flown in from the Vatican there, and that it was a long flight, and I said to him that I was glad he was able to make it. At that point in time he reached over and held up this ring that was on his hand and he said, 'This ring was given to me as a gift from Pope John Paul,' and then he asked me if I'd like to touch the ring. I said, 'No, not particularly.'" The fact that Dale was a Baptist had nothing to do with not wanting to touch the monsignor's ring. "I just got the impression that they wanted to show me how important they all were, and that I had bothered them by making them fly all the way from the Vatican," Dale said.

The commissioner opened the meeting and before too long got to the heart of the matter.

"I began to ask some questions about the Vatican's contribution of $600 million to the insurance companies—through St. Francis of Assisi, through Thunor Trust, and down to the insurance companies—and the answers that I would get would just kind of be rambling," Dale said. "They would just answer that, 'We want to do good for people. We get good returns on our investments. We want to help the poor people and sick children, and we want to build hospitals,' and those type things.

"The monsignor's English was terrible, and in fact a couple of times he slipped off into some other type of language, which I gather was Italian. Either myself or Lee Harrell asked the monsignor if he would just repeat that because we just didn't understand, so that's when he repeated it in broken English.

"Gary Atnip, who sat in a corner behind the two priests, remained silent. Bolan, who was supposed to be representing the monsignor, said practically nothing."

After Dale made several attempts at getting straight answers concerning the Vatican's purported involvement, he announced a recess and retired to a side office with Harrell, Hanna, and Scott. "I said to our lawyers, 'I don't like what I'm hearing one bit. I'm not getting straight answers to anything I'm asking. I don't like any of this at all.' And then I remember one of the attorney generals made the statement that 'You know, this is fraud. This is absolutely fraud.'"

After the brief side meeting, Hackney and Monaco were asked to join Dale in the commissioner's office. "It was at that point in time I said, 'Nick, I don't like any of these answers I'm getting. Something just doesn't smell right,'" Dale recalled.

The commissioner then accepted a suggestion by Harrell and Hanna that the Thunor insurance companies should be placed under the administrative supervision of the Insurance Department until things could be sorted out.

Monaco initially objected, saying, "You can't do that because it would do irreparable harm to their ability to do business in other states." But he relented when Dale assured him that the administrative supervision would be handled discreetly.

"We told him all of this would be done under confidential cover, and that once we're notified that the money is in a Mississippi bank of their choosing, we would remove the administrative supervision," Dale recalled. "But we also said to him that until we see the money, you're not even going to be able to write a check to pay your electricity bill unless it's approved by my examiner on-site at the company."

When the meeting resumed, Dale announced that allowing business as usual at the Thunor-owned insurance firms "would render the continuance of its business hazardous to the public or to its insurers." Hackney agreed to allow the three Mississippi-domiciled companies—First National, Family Guarantee, and Franklin Protective—to be placed under administrative supervision by regulatory officials, and he assured Dale that the companies' reserves would be safely back in a Mississippi bank by the following Monday.

Monaco called Frankel in Greenwich and assured him that everything was under control, and the worst that could happen was that he would have to pay a $100,000 fine.

By the end of the day on the Monday after the meeting with the regulators, the insurance reserves hadn't been sent back to Mississippi. "And then Tuesday came and it still wasn't done," Dale said. "Well, then it was on Friday—a week and one day from the date of our meeting—that John Hackney calls us back and says, 'I can't get anyone at Liberty National to take my calls. I can't get in touch with anybody. I'm not able to transfer the money to a Mississippi bank.'"

Hackney's call left the commissioner fuming mad. He immediately got on the phone to Harrell and directed him and one of the department's examiners to go the next day to First National Life's headquarters to make sure no more money left the state and fell into Liberty National Securities' hands.

The following week, Harrell went into court with a petition to have the three Mississippi-domiciled insurance companies placed under the direct administration of the insurance department in order to protect its remaining assets.

"On Friday, May 7, 1999, Mr. Hackney informed the Commissioner's representatives that he had been unable to locate any officers or employees of Liberty National Securities Inc.," Harrell stated in the petition he submitted on May 19 to Hinds County court in Mississippi. He further stated, "Mr. Hackney and Mr. Gary Atnip advised that they could not locate representatives of Saint Francis."

By that time, Frankel was long gone and it would take several more months of searching the globe before anyone could find the fugitive financier.

Chapter Nine

With the insurance regulators now hot on his heels, Frankel knew the game was finally over. He had always figured that things might end up this way, just as they had for Robert Vesco. And, just like Vesco, the best course of action for Frankel to take was to leave the country.

Yet despite his recognition that such an eventuality might occur, Frankel remarkably had made no contingency plans for life as a fugitive, and his final days in Greenwich were marked by anxiety, confusion, depression, and fear.

His mind raced. "Where am I going to go? How will I survive? If they find me, what then? Will I spend the rest of my life in jail?" These and similar thoughts played inside his head on a continuous loop. FBI agents could come crashing through his front door at any moment, but Frankel needed more time to think. He went days without sleep, playing different escape scenarios over and over in his mind. No matter where he ran to, he was going to need money and allies. But who among the cast of characters he now regretted having become involved with was plotting against him, and who could still be trusted?

In his trusty astrology journal, a copy of the spiral-bound *1999 Daily Planetary Guide*, Frankel jotted down some of his innermost thoughts and paranoid fears.

"Tom Q. goes crazy and threatens to kill me," he wrote. "K. threatens me. Alfredo will kill me." And he constructed horoscope wheels, placing in their hubs the questions that troubled him the most: "Will Tom turn me in? Will I go to prison? Will I be safe?"

Frankel was teetering on the edge of delirium. Wild-eyed from lack of sleep and sheer terror, he marched about the mansion throwing his arms up in despair while asking no one in particular, "What the hell am I going to do now?"

He logged on to the Internet and began researching the extradition laws of various countries and their treaties with the U.S. government. He looked into Brazil and other South American nations but discarded the notion of going to a place where a very white and unusual-looking person such as he would be so conspicuous. He also thought about going to Switzerland, where Marc Rich openly enjoyed his freedom despite being wanted by the FBI for evading $50 million in taxes. He ditched that idea because while tax crimes were not grounds for extradition in Switzerland, federal wire fraud and racketeering crimes were.

The immediate solution that came to mind was to flee to Italy, where he could call on associates to help hide him in order to buy time to decide where his ultimate destination would be.

"If I go there, it might take the feds weeks and even months before they find out that I went there," Frankel thought. "And the Faustis, they'll help me. They'll know what to do."

He called the Faustis to tell them what his plans were, and sent them $40,000 with which to lease him an apartment. More money followed, with $2 million being sent to Alfredo in one of several last-minute wire transfers.

But before leaving for Italy, Frankel needed a passport with a new identity. With Tom Corbally's help, he was able to obtain eight different passports, of both British and Greek origin, each bearing a different alias next to Frankel's photograph. Once again using his underworld connections, Corbally got the fake passports from a man who would identify himself only as Mikey. Corbally accompanied Mikey to Geneva, where Mikey gave the passports to Kaethe in exchange for $800,000 that was withdrawn from Frankel's Banque SCS Alliance account.

Corbally's assistance, as usual, came with a high price. Frankel gave him $5 million so that he could move out of the Delmonico and buy his own apartment in Manhattan. "Blackmail!" Frankel noted in his daily astrology planner, directing his anger at the associate who had just threatened "to take away all the good times."

Frankel decided he would need to have with him a large cache of gold and diamonds that he would be able to convert to cash as needed. He told Mona Kim to find a gold dealer that could fill large orders on short notice. She came up with a list that included the Monex international commodities dealer in Newport Beach, California. On April 6 Frankel had his Swiss bank wire $16 million to a Monex account at Farmers and Merchants Bank in California as payment for Vienna Philharmonic gold coins. The coins were then shipped to Frankel's safe-deposit box in Switzerland.

David Rosse told Frankel he could help him out with the diamonds, as he would check with Robert Teel, owner of Teel's Jewelry in Los Gatos, California, from whom Rosse had bought an $8,000 diamond engagement ring in December. Rosse called Teel and explained that his boss, whom he described as an extremely wealthy and eccentric industrialist, had been advised by his accountant to convert 2 to 3 percent of his assets into precious gems and metals before the new year as a hedge against any Y2K-related banking problems.

Teel agreed to broker a diamond deal, and Frankel had $2 million wired to an account at Bank Leumi in Beverly Hills, California, belonging to the diamond dealer World Wide Diamonds. Rosse flew to California to pick up the diamonds, which were to be just the first installment of more jewels should his boss like what he saw. The diamonds, nearly two hundred in all, had been handpicked by Teel. Each was a "round brilliant," ranging in size from one to three carats—the most desirable diamonds with the highest demand.

Frankel approved of the diamonds, knowing that they could be easily resold because of their high quality and accompanying Gemological Institute of America certificates. Three weeks later Frankel personally called Teel, informing him that he wanted to buy another $40 million worth of diamonds immediately. Teel conferred with World Wide Diamonds owner Robert Weiner, who advised against such a large transaction of high-quality diamonds because it could destabilize the market by artificially inflating diamond prices.

The dealers sought a compromise and offered to provide the $40 million in diamonds over a period of time, in amounts of $5 million a shot, but Frankel declined.

"How much can you deliver now?" he asked.

The diamond dealers told Frankel they could get together $10 million in high-quality diamonds in one day. Within twenty-four hours, the $10 million was wired from the Swiss bank account of another of Frankel's dummy corporations, Devonshire Technologies, to World Wide Diamonds' Bank Leumi account in Beverly Hills. Arrangements were made to have the diamonds shipped to the East Coast.

To satisfy his immediate demands for cash, Frankel ordered Mona to clean out his local bank accounts, which contained a total of about a quarter of a million dollars.

There were a few other details that Frankel had to attend to before leaving. He had an assistant cut a check for $10,000 so that one of the IT guys could buy new laptop computers, which Frankel could take with him. Then ex-girlfriends and selected employees were summoned to the main house, where an assistant handed out titles to some of the cars in Frankel's fleet of thirty-three vehicles. The vehicles had been registered under the names of Frankel's dummy corporations—Sundew International, Good Luck Corp. and Bunnies Inc.—and the proud new owners were instructed to reregister them under their own names.

No one outside the inner circle had been told that Frankel would be leaving. When Adriana asked what was going on, Frankel told her that he was leaving just for a few weeks, until things cooled down.

"Don't worry, we'll be back when things die down a little," he said.

On the morning of May 4 more than two dozen pieces of luggage plus the new computer equipment were crammed into two SUVs. Shortly before 1 P.M. the SUVs formed a caravan behind the limousines carrying Frankel, Mona Kim, and Jackie Ju as they left the Greenwich compound for the final time and headed for nearby Westchester County Airport. Three of Frankel's assistants left the country as well. Adriana went back home to Brazil, Kaethe returned to Germany, and Karen Timmins went somewhere in Europe, presumably Ireland.

Later on during the day of the "great escape," some of the lower-level employees who arrived for work at the Greenwich compound were given no explanation as to what was going on, other than that they no longer had a job. "When I got there the only thing they told me was, 'It's over. He's gone,'" recalled one of the chauffeurs, Patrick Vecchio.

The following evening, Frankel's maintenance foreman, Bob Biddle, arranged to meet with some of the chauffeurs so that they could be paid back wages. "He told me I could get the $1,300 they owed me, but that I'd better come alone," Vecchio said. As the now-unemployed driver waited at the designated meeting place, a Mobil station on the Sprain Brook Parkway in Yonkers, New York, he saw Biddle and Karen Timmins' brother, Jimmy, pull up in Biddle's black Chevy Tahoe. Jimmy went through a stack of envelopes he was holding until he found one with Vecchio's name on it.

"Here you go," Biddle said as he took the envelope from Jimmy and passed it out the window to Vecchio. "We're all square now."

Some of the assistants who remained behind, including Alicia Walters, had been instructed by Frankel to move the boxed documents into storage. But when the moving vans arrived to take the papers away, it apparently was decided by Frankel's assistants that the trucks would be best put to work hauling away the more valuable property Frankel had left behind, including computers, television sets, and stereos. And instead of just leaving the documents there, it was decided that they should be destroyed.

With the possibility looming that authorities would show up at any time, they knew the job had to be completed as quickly as possible. A paper shredder was placed into action, but it soon became clear that that method of destruction would take too long. Two of the house's fireplaces were put into use, one in the study and the other in the kitchen. They were both filled with documents and set ablaze.

With the destruction appearing to be going smoothly, and with the hour growing late, Frankel's minions decided to take a dinner break. The oven was turned on and a frozen dinner was taken out of the refrigerator and placed on a counter. A bottle of white wine was uncorked, and macaroni and cheese was simmering in a saucepan on the stove.

Suddenly the fire alarm sounded. Flames from the kitchen fireplace had licked out beyond the hearth and set a nearby couch on fire. The fire was in the process of being put out with fire extinguishers when the phone rang. It was the security company that monitors the residence calling to verify the alarm. Walters answered and told the security company operator that there was no fire, that everything was under control. But the security arrangement had required that someone inside the house provide a code in order to cancel the alarm. Walters didn't know it.

Panic set in. Realizing that it would be only minutes before fire engines and police cars roared into the driveway, it was hastily decided to heap as many of the remaining documents as they could into the fireplace. The rest would be torched where they sat in their file cabinet drawers. Walters and at least one other companion then fled the house, with the macaroni and cheese now starting to burn on the stovetop.

When the firefighters arrived, they didn't know what to make of the scene. All the doors appeared to be locked, but as one firefighter began climbing through a kitchen window, another found a sliding glass door at the rear from which the lock had been removed. The first thing the firefighters did when they got inside was to quickly douse the file cabinet that was burning in the kitchen. Because the entire first floor was filled with smoke, and a woman had answered the security firm's earlier call, the first concern was to look for possible victims. The rescuers couldn't believe the number of locked offices they encountered, and doorjambs needed to be pried off to gain entry into each one.

While the house was being ventilated and the smoke began to clear, the firefighters saw that the interior of the house had been trashed. Furniture was upended, and file cabinets lay on their sides. One file cabinet had been tipped over into a miniature waterfall inside the mansion's front entrance. Computer keyboards that had been disconnected from their missing terminals were strewn about. On one side of each of the roaring fireplaces were boxes brimming with documents, and on the other side of each were empty boxes.

Also found inside the dwelling were many pieces of new luggage, some of which had not been removed from their original boxes and wrapping.

While at first it appeared as though the house might have been broken into and ransacked by a burglar, it was becoming apparent that the systematic destruction of documents had taken place, and that whoever was responsible had fled. It was also becoming evident to the Greenwich police officers who began arriving that they had on their hands something that went way beyond a routine arson investigation. They secured the house for the night, not wanting to further disturb the scene until they could obtain a search warrant for the arson probe.

The next morning, as the local police waited for a Superior Court judge to sign the search warrant, Detective McConnell, who had investigated Frances Burge's death just two years before, phoned the FBI to tell them about what had happened at the Frankel compound. He was taken aback by the lukewarm reception his call received.

"I told them that we were in the process of getting a warrant, and that it should be signed by the afternoon, and the agent I spoke with was, like,

'Well, I really don't think I have to come down there, but when you get stuff out of the house let me know what you've got and we'll go from there,' " McConnell recalled.

The next morning, at about 7 A.M., the phone at the front desk of Greenwich police headquarters rang.

"Greenwich Police Department, Lieutenant Ridberg."

"Yeah, I heard there might have been a fire at my house yesterday," the voice on the line said.

"What is your name, sir?"

"It's Marty Frankel. I own the house at 889 Lake Avenue. Listen, I heard about the fire alarm going off there yesterday and, really, there's no problem. There's no need for the police to be involved."

Lieutenant David Ridberg asked for a callback number, to try to verify that he was actually speaking with the property owner, but in a somewhat garbled response Frankel declined to provide one.

"Then what's your attorney's number, sir?"

"Attorney? What do you mean, an attorney? What do I need an attorney for?"

The conversation ended with Frankel abruptly hanging up.

Before too long the police department received a call from Mark Durkin, a Greenwich attorney who had represented Frankel in housing court when the landlord of the house where Frances Burge had died instituted eviction proceedings. "My client doesn't want an investigation," Durkin insisted. "If there was a fire, it probably had been an accident." Durkin was advised that the search of the Frankel compound was going forward as planned, and it was suggested to him that his client might want to consider retaining a criminal defense lawyer.

That led to another call to police from Mickey Sherman, the Stamford defense attorney who had successfully shut down detectives when they were questioning Frankel about Burge's death. "Yeah, I know you're going to do what you've gotta do," Sherman said. "It's just that my client wanted me to inform you that he didn't want a search."

A few hours later, with a signed search warrant in hand, Greenwich police began going over the Frankel property with a fine-tooth comb. Durkin showed up in a final bid to thwart the inevitable. He was clearly upset, demanding to see the warrant as he handed a police supervisor a letter in opposition to the search.

"Sorry, but this court order supersedes your wishes, Counselor," said Sergeant Timothy Duff as he showed Durkin the search warrant.

The attorney then took up position in front of the main entrance to 889 Lake Avenue, where he began to scribble furiously on a yellow legal pad. Some of the officers laughed to themselves, thinking that if Durkin's intent was to block their way into the house, then he was apparently oblivious to the boxes of documents and evidence already being carried away through a rear door and loaded onto dump trucks that the police had borrowed from the Highway Department.

Inside the house, some detectives sifted through the papers that had been salvaged from the fireplaces, while others made a room-by-room search, finding that each of the second-floor offices had been ransacked, with their floor safes wide open and the locks on their emptied file cabinets having been broken off. Inside one of the garage offices they found a handwritten list headed "Things To Do." The number one thing to do was "Launder money," followed by "Get $ to Israel, get it back in." They also turned up a fax in which Frankel, as David Rosse, on behalf of the First National Life Insurance Company, stated, "I need to buy 15 of each of the Notes and Bonds [U.S. Treasury] listed on the following 2 pages. Then I need to sell twelve of each and then buy twelve back."

Then there were what appeared to be astrological charts, to which the following questions had been posed: "Will I go to prison? Will Tom turn me in? Should I leave? Should I wire money back from overseas? Will I be safe?"

The detectives also came across documentation of the research that had been done on the extradition laws of various countries.

"So many people were going, 'Holy shit,' each time they found something, it was hard to keep track," one detective recalled. "Someone would find one thing and say, 'Holy shit, would you look at this,' and another would yell out, 'You're not going to believe what I found.'"

Spreading out from the main house, detectives came across a locked storage shed on the side. Inside they found about thirty more boxes stuffed with documents. Then they came across mounds of freshly dug earth. Because of the compound's mysterious history, and especially in light of Frances Burge's death, a state police K-9 unit trained in body recovery was summoned, only to find out that the mounds had resulted from recent landscaping activity and not the interment of bodies.

By this time the Frankel compound was swarming with Greenwich's top police brass, including Chief Peter Robbins. Robbins wanted to know why the FBI wasn't there, and McConnell told him that he had called the agency's Connecticut offices several times. When the FBI still had not been heard from by May 7—two days after the fire—Robbins personally called the agency, plainly laying out the situation for an FBI supervisor, Robert Marston.

"Peter," the agent said, "I'll have eight agents down there by noon."

Meanwhile, as the search of the compound continued, telephones rang incessantly inside the main house. Most of the time the phones rang only once, as the calls were automatically forwarded to another line. But when one of the phones continued to ring, Sergeant Duff picked up the receiver and found Alicia Walters on the other end. Walters identified herself as an employee of Frankel, and declined when Duff asked her to come to the compound. She suggested that the officer contact David Rosse or Bob Biddle.

When police called Rosse's cell phone, the bodyguard also refused to come to the crime scene, as did Biddle when he returned a police officer's page. "How the hell did you get my pager number?" Biddle demanded to know.

Then two of Frankel's chauffeurs arrived, bewildered at the intense level of police activity they had driven into, and explaining that they had come to pick up paychecks. One of the drivers, John Jordan, told the police of the incredible amount of document shredding that had gone on during the week, and about Frankel's assistants removing computers from the main house and bringing them to the other house at 895 Lake Avenue.

Then a moving van pulled up at 895 Lake Avenue, and the driver explained he was making his second trip after having been hired to remove all of the contents from the house.

At about 5 P.M. on May 7, Greenwich police spoke with assistant U.S. attorney Kari Dooley, senior litigation counsel for the District of Connecticut. She ordered the local police to limit their search to looking for typical arson-related evidence, such as insurance policies and records of financial debt. Dooley further instructed the police to leave the computers as they found them until a federal search warrant could be obtained.

With the telephones continuing to constantly ring, it was decided that they had to be disconnected in case the computers were being remotely accessed in order to delete files.

Soon after, the feds finally committed themselves to the case. A team of computer experts from FBI in Quantico, Virginia, was dispatched to the Greenwich compound. Upon seeing the size of the computer systems there, they first thought of moving them to a warehouse the FBI had seized in Bridgeport, but opted to download the data on-site, a process that took over two weeks.

A team of prosecutors was assigned to the case, including Dooley and assistant U.S. attorney Mark Califano, son of former U.S. Secretary of Health Education and Welfare Joseph Califano. Although relatively young, Dooley and Califano were both experienced in prosecuting white-collar criminals. One of Dooley's highest-profile cases ended in victory when she sent supermarket chain owner Stew Leonard Jr. to prison on tax-evasion charges. Califano was well grounded in the area of fraud; when he was just out of law school, he had clerked for U.S. District Judge Stanley Sporkin, the former director of the U.S. Securities and Exchange Commission's Enforcement Division, known as the king of SEC enforcement actions. Califano had successfully prosecuted the elderly parents of south Florida drug pirate Jimmy Monaco, who had been sentenced to a thirty-five-year federal prison term. Five of Monaco's family members, including his parents, were sentenced to prison terms of their own in 1998 after Califano made a case that they had helped to launder Monaco's drug profits in Connecticut.

In the Frankel matter, the federal prosecution team quickly amassed a mountain of evidence that went way beyond the probable-cause threshold for an arrest.

One example they were able to document clearly showed how Frankel used a complicated web of transactions to conceal his illegally obtained fortune: On April 9, 1999, $44 million was transferred from Settlers Life in Virginia to a First National Life account at the First National Bank of Tennessee, and then the money was immediately wired to a Dreyfus Cash Management Plus account in New York. Three days later the $44 million was wired to a Bloomfield Investments account at the Stamford, Connecticut, branch of United Bank of Switzerland, and then wired again to Geneva. The final stop for the money was Banque SCS Alliance account number 70026, in the name of Bloomfield Investments.

Then there were the research on extradition laws and the questions in Frankel's handwriting about getting caught and going to prison.

It was enough for U.S. magistrate Holly B. Simmons, who on May 16, 1999, issued a warrant for Frankel's arrest on unspecified wire fraud and money-laundering charges.

Nine days later, on May 25, an affidavit prepared by FBI special agent Joseph Dooley was presented to U.S. magistrate William I. Garfinkel in support of an application for a search-and-seizure warrant for fourteen separate bank accounts in six states containing a total of more than $13.8 million in laundered funds. In the affidavit, Dooley stated:

> I have probable cause to believe, and do believe, that since at least 1991 Martin R. Frankel, operating under several different aliases and corporate entities . . . has devised and executed a scheme to defraud by wire several insurance companies across the country.
>
> Frankel, through fraudulent pretenses, representations and promises, obtained control of the liquid assets and insurance policy premium proceeds of these companies through acquisition, reinsurance or other agreements, and ostensibly invested these assets in government securities through a fraudulent brokerage company known as Liberty National Securities Inc.
>
> Frankel systematically drained these assets through various financial accounts and transferred them into accounts in and outside this country under his control and for his own use. Frankel then laundered these funds, purchasing untraceable assets and paying for the expenses of his operation inside this country and otherwise. Indeed, the contents of the account(s) identified are assets purchased with the proceeds of the wire fraud described herein and are instrumentalities of money laundering.

Garfinkel signed the warrant, and the largest chunk of money to be seized was the $10 million Frankel paid to World Wide Diamonds. Another $950,000 had been held in an account belonging to Park Avenue Travel Services in Manhattan. The company, run by Corbally associate Philip Roam, had booked many of Team Frankel's commercial airline flights. Other seized bank accounts included the $75,000 that was held in the name of Thomas Bolan by the Bank of New York and $50,000 at the National Bank of Virginia in an account for a private investigation firm called Decision

Strategies, which had performed a security assessment for Frankel's Greenwich compound after the November 1998 incident with John Schulte following Leon Frankel's death. Decision Strategies was headed by Bart Schwartz, who went to work for Jules Kroll after having led the Criminal Investigations Division for the Southern District of New York under then–U.S. attorney Rudolph Giuliani.

FBI and CID/IRS field agents were now fanning out across the country, speaking with as many Frankel associates as they could find. They were very much relieved that the story of the massive investment fraud had yet to spread beyond the pages of *Greenwich Time,* giving them the chance to catch witnesses and suspected co-conspirators off guard. But this window of opportunity soon closed. By late May and early June, as other media realized the significance of what had occurred in Connecticut, those of Frankel's former associates who remained in the United States retained defense lawyers to fend off reporters and run interference with the government.

But the media frenzy that ensued after the Lake Avenue fire and reached a fevered pitch by early July was actually a blessing for the investigators. Frankel's face was appearing on the front pages of major newspapers and on television news broadcasts across the country and around the globe, severely limiting the places the now-infamous fugitive could hide. Frankel's days as king of his own financial empire were quickly numbered.

Chapter Ten

Frankel's flight from justice got off to a shaky start.

As pressure leading up to the decision to take off had mounted, Frankel began to believe that his once trusted bodyguard, David Rosse, had somehow betrayed him and was behind all of his woes. So he decided that in addition to taking Mona and Jackie with him, he would leave Rosse behind and bring along Biddle as his security aide instead.

The only problem was that Frankel had not foreseen this break with Rosse and so had not arranged for Biddle to have a passport in time. On May 4, the day of the flight from the country, Biddle spent nearly the entire day in New York scrambling to find a passport. By the time Frankel and his assistants had arrived at Westchester County Airport a passport still hadn't been found, so Frankel ordered him to remain and accept delivery of the incoming diamonds from World Wide later that evening.

Frankel felt as though he needed still more diamonds for insurance, and so he spent part of his last day in Greenwich looking to buy another large cache of the stones—$30 million worth. On May 4 the Lipworth Diamond Corporation in Manhattan received a fax in which Frankel stated, "My desire to purchase the cut diamonds I described is very strong. I know that my purchase will push the market up, but I do not care as much as most people about what to me are relatively small sums."

Frankel indicated in the fax that his Swiss bank accounts had "ample funds" to cover the transaction, and that the money could be wired to New

York the next day. "I need to purchase these diamonds no later than Friday May 7 if possible," the fax stated. "I know this must seem eccentric, and I know others do not operate the way I do, but I know of no one else who routinely sends his assistants around the world on Gulfstreams when regular commercial airlines would be sufficient. Everyone who works for me receives the car and house or apartment of their choice." Lipworth decided against selling the diamonds because the dealer sensed that it might involve a money-laundering scheme.

The next glitch in Frankel's hasty escape plan occurred that afternoon, when the private jet that was supposed to pick him up at Westchester County Airport never came, sending Frankel and Mona scrambling to find a replacement. When the plane finally arrived, Frankel spent hours haggling with the pilots over a flight plan. They eventually settled on stopping over in Spain en route to Rome's Ciampino Airport.

Frankel was extremely fidgety during the flight. He chatted nervously with the pilots as Mona and Jackie watched videos in the cabin. While the plane was refueling in Spain, he hopped out to make some telephone calls. Frankel returned to the plane with his usual pasty complexion whiter than ever. The diamonds he had counted on to finance his life in exile were missing.

While Frankel and his traveling companions were flying over the Atlantic, members of his staff had clashed over who would take possession of the gems, which had been delivered by a chartered Gulfstream IV jet to Teterboro Airport in New Jersey. When the jet carrying Robert Weiner and Robert Teel touched down in New Jersey at about 1:30 A.M. on May 5, the two diamond dealers looked out the Gulfstream's windows and saw a group of men standing on the tarmac near a limousine and three SUVs. They were supposed to have been met by Bob Biddle, but when Biddle did not come forward Weiner and Teel began to panic. They relaxed a bit when Rosse bounded up the stairs and into the jet. Weiner and another colleague who had come along remained on board to complete some paperwork, and Rosse helped Teel off the plane with three duffel bags and a locked metal suitcase that contained nearly five hundred diamonds.

Then, suddenly, Rosse hopped into his Tahoe with one of the duffel bags and drove off, leaving the rest of the cache on the tarmac. The members of the security detail that remained became clearly upset and all at once dialed their respective cell phones. Biddle then identified himself to Teel, and the two men were both at a loss as to what Rosse had done.

By then it was after 2 A.M., and the limousine, which the diamond dealers assumed was there to pick them up, drove off with the Gulfstream's flight crew. Biddle and the security guards began peppering the increasingly nervous dealers with questions.

"Why did you give Rosse the diamonds?" they demanded.

Teel explained that Biddle had not identified himself earlier, and he was comfortable with Rosse because he had personally dealt with him in the past. Besides, Teel added, "If Rosse wasn't supposed to take the diamonds, then why did you let him drive away?"

As the two men remaining inside the jet looked on with disbelief, Weiner's colleague observed, "Someone's getting scammed."

The security guards ushered Teel into their SUV, telling him he was going to have to accompany them as they looked for Rosse. Weiner and his colleague got into a taxicab that had arrived, and Biddle followed the other vehicles in his Tahoe as the three cars filed out of the airport. Then suddenly the caravan stopped at the exit, and Teel was allowed to rejoin Weiner in the taxi. The guards had decided to take what remained of the diamonds to a motel in Newark, where they would await further instructions from Frankel.

The diamond dealers arrived at their hotel in Manhattan about an hour later. The following morning they received a call from Rosse. "Listen, I'm very sorry about the confusion last night," Rosse said. "But while you guys were still in the air I stopped up at the boss's house and all of the security guards were gone. And I could hear the sound of paper being shredded coming from inside the house. All I could think was that my boss was in some kind of trouble, so I decided to come to the airport and grab as many diamonds as I could so I could take them somewhere safe until I could sort out what was going on."

Now the diamond dealers didn't know whom to trust, and this was just the beginning—there still remained $2 million in diamonds that had already been shipped to a Brinks office in Manhattan. Teel paged Frankel, and when Frankel called he was surprisingly unruffled by the fumbled airport handoff. He told Teel that had he been in Rosse's position he might have done the same thing.

Frankel said he would send a list of names of people who were authorized to pick up the remaining diamonds from Brinks, and a fax with those names was awaiting the men upon their return to California. The diamonds were picked up at Brinks a couple of days later and hand-delivered to

Frankel in Italy on June 12. Frankel put the diamonds in a black suitcase, which would never leave his side for the duration of his sojourn.

When the jet touched down at Ciampino Airport in Rome, Frankel went through customs using a British passport, which listed his identity as Roger John Ellis. He, Mona, and Jackie were then met by Fausto and Alfredo Fausti.

Once in Italy, the women began wondering whether they had done the right thing in accompanying Frankel, as one of the first things the Faustis said to Frankel on arrival was, "Do you want David Rosse's ear before we kill him?" Apparently Frankel had told the Faustis about his perceived betrayal by his longtime bodyguard.

The Faustis loaded Frankel's cargo into their van and drove the fugitive and his two assistants to a two-room apartment in an older, working-class neighborhood of Rome. After what he was used to back in Greenwich, Frankel despised his new accommodations. He called the apartment "a dump." There was no telephone or television. He decided the Faustis had again taken advantage of him by renting the cheapest place they could find and pocketing the bulk of the money.

When the Faustis weren't around, the Americans were virtually stranded because none of them spoke Italian. Mona and Jackie gave themselves a crash course in rudimentary Italian, learning enough to be able to give directions to cabdrivers and figure out the lire-to-dollar exchange rate.

Without a telephone, Frankel had the two women buy dozens of prepaid phone cards. On the morning of May 6 he went to a public telephone and called Tom Corbally in London. Corbally told him that he had been in touch with some of the underlings Frankel had left behind, and that they informed him that there had been a fire at 889 Lake Avenue the day before. Frankel then placed his calls to the Greenwich Police Department and attorney Durkin.

Although federal agents managed to identify and freeze a good chunk of Frankel's ill-gotten assets fairly quickly, including $26 million in Switzerland, and insurance regulators had recovered more than $57 million in Thunor assets, Frankel had been able to scatter millions among various bank accounts of associates, including Tom Corbally and Fausto Fausti. And he received a timely cash infusion when World Wide Diamonds gave him a $454,000 sales tax refund, which was transferred into an account Mona had opened at Banca Popolare in the nearby Piazza Giuseppe Verdi. This sum was in addition to the $2 million in diamonds that was delivered to Frankel in Rome.

During their three-week stay at the apartment, Frankel and the women scoured English-language guidebooks in search of better digs. They relocated to a small hotel in a more fashionable part of the city, near the elegant Villa Borghese park and museum. It would seem many of Frankel's peccadilloes were surviving the stress of life on the lam. Upon renting the hotel suite, Frankel promptly demanded the benches in his room be replaced with hard-backed chairs. And even though he was in the heart of what would be paradise to many food lovers, Frankel sent Mona and Jackie out searching for take-out Chinese food.

The choice of the new location for a fugitive in hiding was highly questionable, as it was next to the Israeli embassy, which had "surveillance up the yin-yang," as Mona put it. But Frankel thought the location could prove to be beneficial, because if he were to find out that authorities were closing in on him, he could merely run over to the embassy and declare his Israeli citizenship, as is the right of all Jews no matter where they were born.

At about midnight on May 25, the silence was shattered by a knock at the door. It was the hotel owner demanding to see the guests' passports. It would appear that because of heightened concerns about terrorism, Israeli security officials regularly checked the hotel's register. The hotel's proprietor explained that because they had not presented passports when checking in, the embassy contacted the local police chief, who in turn notified him about the breach of security.

The flustered trio left the proprietor in the hallway while they conferred. They came up with the story that because they had been unable to figure out how to open the safe in their room, they had decided to place the passports in a safe-deposit box at a nearby bank, and that they would get the passports when the bank reopened the next morning. Then Frankel lashed out at the hotel owner, yelling, "Do you have any idea what time it is? I paid good money for this villa. You have no right to come here at this hour."

The embarrassed proprietor profusely apologized for the intrusion, invited all three Americans to lunch the next day, and spent nearly a half hour demonstrating how the room's safe worked. As soon as the hotel owner left, Frankel, Mona, and Jackie began packing their bags, and at dawn they loaded their luggage into several cabs that whisked them to the Faustis. With the help of their Italian friends, they found new lodgings at a villa on Via Asmara in Trieste, an upper-middle-class section of Rome.

Knowing that he was the FBI's most wanted white-collar criminal, Frankel had a strong need to see what was being written about him. He dispatched Mona and Jackie to scour the Roman cafés that provided computers with Internet connections so they could download all the news articles about him they could find.

The women came across stories in *Greenwich Time* about how the insurance companies blamed Frankel for looting nearly $1 billion from their reserves, and about Tom Bolan hiring a lawyer to look for another $1.9 billion that was thought to be missing from the St. Francis of Assisi foundation. They confronted Frankel about the astronomical figures, at which time Frankel confessed to having inflated the numbers through creative bookkeeping and outright deception. "He said, 'Well, it's not $3 billion, it's just $300 million,'" Mona recounted in a later interview.

That his scam was being laid bare in the Greenwich newspaper did not seem to bother Frankel, but when stories began appearing in the *The Blade* in Toledo several weeks later, he began to fret about the impact they would have on his family, especially Tillie Frankel. According to Mona, Frankel curled up on a couch and cried, "My poor mother."

But when Frankel saw that on June 25 *The New York Times* had gotten into the act with its story "Phantom Insurance Empire Yields Puzzles (and $335 Million Gone)," the fugitive was beside himself, his mood suddenly and strangely buoyed. "Do you see this?" he shouted to his companions. "I'm on the front page of the *Times*—above the fold on the front page of the goddamn *New York Times!* I am the most important news item in the whole fucking world!"

It was clear that the hunt was now on in earnest, and Frankel began exploring the options that were available to an American expatriate in need of safe exile. He first sought the advice of a Rome-based attorney, and then went to Naples, where he consulted with an extradition law expert. Then he met with a friend of the son of Libyan dictator Muammar el-Qaddafi, seeking the protection of the American-hating dictator, but they never reached any kind of agreement.

In what may have been an attempt to throw a red herring on the European trail being followed by the FBI, Adriana reportedly called her ex-husband, Carlos, in Brooklyn to tell him she had recently been with Frankel in Brazil. Gustavo passed on the tip to Mike McIntyre, who had been reporting on the hunt for Frankel for the *Hartford Courant*, the largest-circulation newspaper in Connecticut. "Adriana said she and Marty were in São Paulo for a while, and that she left him there and went to visit her parents in Goiania," the woman's ex-husband told the reporter. The following day, McIntyre's story, "Frankel Might Be In Brazil," was picked up by the Associated Press and appeared in newspapers across the country.

Back in Rome, Frankel continued to closely monitor press accounts of the search, as well as the rapidly unraveling saga of life at the Greenwich compound. He briefly considered finding an Italian woman to marry, so that he could settle down and blend in with the local population, and even drafted some personal ads, which were never placed. But on the whole, the pervasive mood was morose. When drawing an astrological chart about his flight from justice, Frankel divined that his fate was to meet a violent end.

His life as a fugitive might have been cut short in Rome had Italian authorities acted on the FBI's information that the Faustis might be able to lead them to Frankel. Explaining that they were swamped with other cases, however, the local police waited weeks to obtain a judicial order allowing them to question Frankel's Italian associates. By then Frankel had left the country.

As they grew weary of both their lives on the run and being confined with an increasingly neurotic boss, Mona and Jackie began talking about possibly returning to the United States. Frankel panicked at the thought of being left on his own in a strange land. A master of manipulation to the very end, he resorted to trickery that seemed to convince the women to stay with him. "The Italian police have your names, and you'll be arrested the minute you set foot on the plane," he told them.

But Jackie—the most thoughtful and likable of Frankel's girlfriends—had had enough of the constant bickering with her stir-crazy pals, and in early June packed her bags and hopped a plane for home. Frankel sensed that Mona would soon follow Jackie's lead, and so got on his cell phone and tried convincing those of his formerly loyal female followers who had not fled or disconnected their telephones to join him in Italy.

The only one he could get to agree to go was Cindy Allison, a plump thirty-five-year-old from a small town in Illinois who had been the last to join the Frankel flock. In fact, she had been Frankel's last choice as a new traveling companion, for when he was back in Greenwich, he considered Cindy to be emotionally unstable and felt threatened by her. Cindy had a huge crush on her boss and desperately wanted to be his girlfriend. She would have her hair done two or three times a week, and clamored to be Oksana's nanny just so she could be close to Frankel.

Frankel had set Cindy up at a rented home in Greenwich, at what he believed to be a safe distance, and he assigned her tasks that could be done off the compound. Cindy, who was prone to unexpected and violent outbursts, continued to pursue Frankel in telephone calls that he refused to take. At one point he barred her from setting foot on his estate and distributed photographs of Cindy to the security guards with orders not to allow her into the compound.

Nevertheless, when Frankel called for Cindy to join him, she didn't need to think twice about saying yes. She later recounted, "He sounded really depressed, like he really needed me there. . . . I didn't want him to be alone."

Mona said good-bye to Frankel on June 26, a week after Cindy had joined them in Rome. But before Mona stepped onto the airplane that would take her back to the United States, Frankel told her that he "would never go to Germany. It's the worst place. People would rat." Frankel was in fact considering going to Germany, but he also knew that Mona would likely be detained by authorities after setting foot on American soil, and he hoped that if she repeated Frankel's parting words during questioning, the authorities would rule out Germany in their search.

With Mona gone, Frankel tried setting up another checking account in Rome under Cindy's name in which to store the large diamond sales tax refund. But by then FBI agents had already been speaking with the California diamond brokers, and they were able to trace the movement of the $454,000 refund to Italy, where they had the money frozen with the cooperation of Italian authorities.

With his options being whittled away, Frankel became more despondent than ever. "Do you think they're going to catch me?" he asked Cindy over and over again. He again called on the Faustis for help but was told that the money he had previously left in their keeping had been "stolen." In the *1999 Daily Planetary Guide* he still carried with him, Frankel noted that on June 27, "Alf[redo] abandons me—tells me to go."

On the evening of June 28 Frankel left Cindy alone in the apartment in order to hash out his difficulties with his Italian friends. But when he returned several hours later, he announced to his companion, "We're leaving."

At dawn the next morning Frankel and Cindy loaded up a chauffeured blue Mercedes-Benz and drove north for fourteen straight hours, through Tuscany, Milan, the Austrian Alps, and finally Munich. The timing of the departure couldn't have been better, as Italian police were stepping up their search for Frankel. Only four days after Frankel and Cindy left the country, a tourist from Philadelphia who was spotted trying to rent a van near Villa Borghese in Rome was mistaken for Frankel and detained by local police for seven hours. He was released after an FBI agent and a U.S. embassy official confirmed that fifty-year-old John Zuchero was not the fugitive financier.

Once in Munich, Frankel called upon his sister's former fiancé, an American stationed with the U.S. military in Germany. With the help of Amy Frankel's ex, the fugitive and Cindy Allison checked into the Astron Hotel. Their stay there didn't last very long, as a result of a frantic call Frankel had placed to Corbally in London.

"Tom, you've got to help me," Frankel pleaded. "The newspapers said they almost found me when I was in Rome, and if I stay in Europe much longer they're going to catch up with me. I still have money—gold and diamonds too—I'll give you whatever it takes to get me out of here."

But by this time Corbally was in no mood to help his former business partner. In fact, Corbally was in the process of accusing Frankel in the press of having duped and publicly embarrassed him, and ruining friendships Corbally had enjoyed for thirty years.

"Look, Marty, you just sit tight—stay where you are and I'll figure something out," Corbally reassuringly told Frankel. "I know some people who might be able to get your money for you, and you know I can get you a new passport. So look, just calm down, stay right there, and I'll handle everything."

What Corbally did next was to call a longtime acquaintance of his at the *Daily Express* of London, investigative reporter Michael Gillard. Gillard then became point man for a team of four *Express* reporters in organizing a sting in which the *Express* would get an exclusive interview with the infamous fugitive and then claim credit for his capture when Frankel was arrested by German police, who would be standing by.

Through Corbally, the *Express* received a recent photograph of Frankel that was supposed to be affixed to the new passport. A meeting was scheduled at a location near the Munich hotel where Frankel and Cindy were staying.

"The deal was we would supply him with passports and a jet and fly him to Cyprus, which doesn't have an extradition treaty with the U.S., and in return Frankel would pay us 500 pounds," recalled Jonathan Calvert, the *Express* editor who helped supervise the sting.

With Corbally acting as intermediary, Frankel negotiated plans for his escape with the *Express* over the course of two weeks. Meanwhile, the newspaper's team argued among themselves as to what they should do once Frankel was on the plane. Should they hold him there for German authorities, or fly him back to London and let Scotland Yard have the honor of making the arrest, with *Express* reporters and photographers on hand to document the fugitive's capture? It was finally decided that capturing criminals was not their job as journalists. The newspaper's final plan was to have Gillard meet with Frankel in Hamburg, ostensibly offer him the passport in exchange for an interview, and then tip off the German police that Frankel was in town.

The morning of the planned meeting, the *Express* arranged for a private Lear jet to be standing by just in case Frankel called the airport to find out if Corbally's contacts were holding up their end of the bargain. But also that morning, Frankel correctly sensed that Corbally was setting him up.

"On the morning of the meeting he rang up to say, 'I'm sorry, I can't quite make it, we'll have to have the meeting on another day,'" Calvert recalled. "He said, 'I've been looking at my stars and they say this is a bad day for me,' which of course it would have been."

A month or so later, Corbally expressed disappointment that the sting didn't go off as planned. Still proclaiming his innocence in any of Frankel's schemes—"I don't have a fucking thing to hide," he said—Corbally explained his reasons for wanting to see Frankel behind bars. "As much as I wanted to see him caught, I was also concerned because I heard organized crime was after him and was going to kill him or steal whatever he had with him," he said. "Now, I didn't want that to happen because I wanted the truth to come out, you know. Because I was embarrassed by the people who I'd introduced him to. I didn't want to see him dead. I wanted to see him in custody, and answering for what he did."

Fearing it was only a matter of time before he would be caught, Frankel had been trying to initiate a dialogue with the U.S. authorities. Before the end of June, he had contacted them through a Connecticut criminal defense attorney he had hired over the phone, Hugh Keefe. Disputing a published news report, Keefe said he was not negotiating a surrender for his new client. In one of his conversations with Keefe, however, Frankel did say surrender was something he had been contemplating, but when the lawyer told him he faced between forty and sixty years in prison, Frankel decided to continue taking his chances on the run.

Because of the bad vibes he had gotten from Corbally, Frankel thought it best to immediately check out of the Astron Hotel. He and Cindy packed their bags and slipped away at midnight the day the sting was supposed to have gone down. Frankel asked his chauffeur, "Should we go to Amsterdam?" The driver said no, that it would probably be too risky going there.

Frankel remained unusually quiet as the car sped north into the Bavarian night. The silence was broken when he turned to Cindy and asked, "Do you still believe in God?"

The woman replied that she did.

"How can you believe?" asked the man who not long before had professed a deep admiration for the Catholic Church along with a desire to "assist the poor and alleviate suffering."

The chauffeured blue Mercedes rolled into Hamburg, Germany, on July 2. Frankel decided he would remain in the bustling cosmopolitan city for only a few days while he thought up a new plan, and he rented a two-room $300-a-day suite at the Hotel Prem on the banks of Lake Alster. But the plan never materialized. The little boy who was afraid to take tests in school, who grew up to be a man who was afraid to execute trades, was again paralyzed with fear.

"He didn't know where to go, what to do," Cindy later recalled.

The days turned into months. Frankel passed the time with an occasional stroll through the garden that the balcony connecting the suite's rooms overlooked. He and Cindy ventured into the city several times, once eating at the world-class Atlantic Hotel dining room, which had been featured in the James Bond movie *Tomorrow Never Dies*. They spent a few evenings in Hamburg's red-light district, where they strolled the Reeperbahn, or "street of ropes"—a surreal thoroughfare famed for shops and merchants catering to every conceivable sexual fantasy, and lined with young men and women in various gaudy and splendid states of dress and undress.

But Frankel's routine consisted largely of poring over his astrological charts several times a day and reading the *Sun* and *Mirror*, British tabloid newspapers, for their entertainment value. He would send Cindy on daily reconnaissance missions to hunt down the latest stories being reported about him. But mostly they remained inside the Prem, where they either ate in the hotel's La Mer seafood restaurant or ordered room service, and watched a lot of television. They felt relatively secure in the hotel, which was rated as one of the world's finest lodgings. Hotel Prem regularly caters to diplomats and rich businessmen, and its discreet staff is used to protecting the privacy of its guests.

Most of Frankel's nights were restless ones, however, and sometimes Cindy would be awakened by his screams for help as he was gripped by nightmares of being chased by bogeymen. Watching her boss fall apart was too much for the former office assistant to bear, but whenever she thought of returning to the States Frankel managed to talk her out of it.

"Please, don't you go betraying me too," he whined.

By the end of July the FBI had begun focusing its hunt on Germany, based on information they received from disgruntled former associates with whom Frankel had been staying in touch. When that information was matched up with the trail of bank account and credit card charges the FBI agents were following, the search was further narrowed in scope to Hamburg. By September 2 an agent from the FBI's legal attaché office in Berlin, along with German police, had begun staking out Hotel Prem.

Shortly after 11 P.M. on September 4, Frankel and Cindy had just finished eating halibut steaks for dinner, and had settled onto their separate beds to begin watching the movie *Patch Adams* for the fifth time when Marty heard the doorknob being jiggled.

"What's that?" he asked. "Do you think they're coming to get me?"

"Don't be ridiculous," Cindy reassured him.

Then the door burst open. Two men with guns drawn behind Plexiglas bulletproof shields came storming in, and in broken English they shouted that they were looking for two Americans. Identifying themselves as police detectives, the men then hovered over Cindy as they bombarded her with questions about her use of a fraudulent passport.

Looking up at the detectives, Frankel calmly said, "I'm the one you're looking for."

Epilogue

I had just finished eating dinner early in the evening of September 4, 1999, when the telephone rang. It was *Greenwich Time* calling to let me know the FBI had just phoned the office looking for me.

"They said for you to be at the New Haven federal courthouse at 8:30," assistant city editor Katie Mulvaney said. "That's all they would say."

As I drove Interstate 95 north into Connecticut, I heard it said on the radio that the Associated Press was reporting Frankel had been captured, but details were not yet available. I began to wonder whether I would soon be coming face-to-face with the man I had been so preoccupied with for the past four months.

As it turned out, there would be no courtroom drama this day. Upon arriving in New Haven I learned I was one of a number of reporters who had been summoned to a hastily arranged press conference in which Justice Department officials would make a formal announcement of Frankel's capture.

Gathered in a conference room on the fifth floor of the Robert N. Giaimo Federal Building was FBI Special Agent in Charge for Connecticut Michael Wolf, flanked on one side by Special Agent Robert Marston, the FBI supervisor for the Frankel case, and Assistant U.S. Attorneys Califano and Dooley on the other. Watching from the hallway outside the packed conference room with a satisfied look on his face was Special Agent Joseph

Dooley, who, along with IRS Special Agent Larry Marini, was one of the grunts of the operation.

Standing beside the agents was Deputy U.S. Attorney John H. Durham, who had assumed ultimate responsibility for the case from his boss, U.S. Attorney Stephen Robinson, who removed himself because of a possible conflict of interest. Robinson had once been legal counsel for Kroll Associates at the same time Corbally was consulting for the firm.

Meanwhile in Germany, Frankel appeared before a local judge on an accusation that the passports recovered from his room at the Prem were fraudulent. He was then taken to a prison called Untersuchungshaften. Translated, the prison's name means "prison for those who are under investigation." Located on Holstenglacis Street in Hamburg, it was a 110-year-old pretrial holding facility that once had been used as a detention center for Jews during the Holocaust. Plaques on the prison's outside walls tell the story of the more than one thousand men and women—mostly Jews—who performed forced labor inside, and how inside "almost 500 death sentences were carried out, most by decapitation."

Cindy, who had been traveling with Frankel under the alias of Susan Kelly, was quickly released and returned to the United States within three days. Before departing for home, she collected from Hotel Prem Frankel's *1999 Daily Planetary Guide.* Although the journal—a potentially powerful piece of evidence that was filled with names, dates, and other details about Frankel's crimes—had been overlooked by German police, Cindy gave the journal to the FBI upon returning to the United States.

Now, for the first time in his life, Frankel truly was all alone, and more fearful for his life than ever. It was as if his darkest fears had come true: The milquetoast mama's boy from Toledo, Ohio, was trapped and surrounded by common criminals in a faraway land. He nervously winced at each guttural scream in a language he could not understand that echoed back to him in his tiny prison cell. He couldn't reach for a phone to page David Rosse to come running and protect him from the bogeymen. He didn't have the security blanket that his computers and quote machines had always provided.

The closest thing to a friend Frankel would have for some time was his court-assigned legal counsel, Hamburg attorney Thomas Piplak. In an interview a few days after Frankel's arrest, Piplak described his American client as a virtual basket case. "Marty is very frightened, very panicked. Physically he is quite weak," the lawyer said. "He is trembling and his motions are very slow. He walks very slow and he says over and over, 'My life is at an end. For the rest of my life I will stay in prison.'"

Making matters worse was that Piplak learned from his American counterpart that a contract on his client's life might have been taken out. "Hugh Keefe told me there was some information from the FBI that Mr. Frankel was being followed by two groups of people, but they didn't tell him which groups they were and they didn't have any information about their interests or why they were after him," Piplak said. "Mr. Frankel fears being attacked because he knows a lot of things." The Hamburg attorney added, "He has some idea how it works [in prison] and he says it is no problem for someone to hire a person to hurt you or kill you."

Piplak noted that Frankel was aware of his reputation as a pathological liar and did not hold out great hopes that his safety would be ensured. "He is doubtful whether anybody will believe him," the German lawyer said.

As someone who had always been a control freak, finding himself behind bars and subject to the ironfisted control of corrections officials was Frankel's worst nightmare come true. He tried to reassert a small element of self-determination by demanding he be served kosher food—something the atheist had never before requested of his private chefs—but he was rebuffed by the officials in charge of the prison.

On September 21 Piplak notified Frankel that he was dropping him as a client because he had yet to be paid for his services. With most, if not nearly all, of Frankel's assets seized or frozen, Piplak said the likelihood of getting paid was too uncertain. Frankel's family was unable to afford to help out, because Tillie Frankel's health was failing and what little money they had was being used to pay for mounting medical bills. Frankel had given his German lawyer the names of a few friends who might be willing to send money, but Piplak never contacted them because he noted that all of those names were listed in court documents as possible co-conspirators in Frankel's fraudulent scheme.

Three days after Piplak bowed out of the case, Hugh Keefe announced that he too was withdrawing. Keefe also cited his former client's inability to pay for the costly legal battle to come. In addition to Keefe's own steep hourly rate, a competent defense for Frankel would involve an array of forensic accountants and other expert witnesses. The New Haven attorney then formally requested a federal public defender be assigned to the case, noting in the application that Martin Frankel was destitute.

Frankel found a new lawyer in Germany, Dirk Meinicke, who apparently thought he could be paid for his services by selling his client's story.
"Frankel believes his story is worth a lot of money," Meinicke said the week
he took over the case.

On October 7, 1999, a grand jury sitting in U.S. District Court in New
Haven, Connecticut, returned a thirty-six-count indictment charging Martin Frankel with massive wire and mail fraud, embezzlement, money laundering, conspiracy, and racketeering. According to the indictment, Frankel
had gained control of embezzled funds between 1991 and April 1999.

"After the liquid assets of the insurance companies were received by
Frankel, Frankel converted, stole, and embezzled the majority of the funds
for the personal use and benefit of himself and others known and unknown
to the grand jury," the indictment stated. "In total, in excess of $200 million
was converted, stolen, and embezzled by Frankel through the scheme and
artifice to defraud, all to the detriment of the victim insurance companies,
their policyholders and, where applicable, their shareholders." If convicted
of all charges, he could be sentenced to a maximum of 410 years in prison.

But as of February 1, 2000, Frankel was still awaiting extradition.
Knowing full well that they would be allowed by law to prosecute Frankel
only on those charges on which he was extradited, members of the U.S. Justice Department decided to allow Frankel to remain on ice while they went
after his American co-conspirators and perhaps build a stronger case
against him.

On December 3, 1999, Frankel's right-hand man, David Rosse, pleaded
guilty to a single count of conspiracy for his participation in Frankel's illegal operation. He did so as part of a plea agreement in which he would
cooperate with the ongoing investigation of Frankel's criminal enterprise,
in return for the prosecutors requesting that the judge suspend sentencing
guidelines and require only that Rosse serve several years of probation. It
was a bit of a crapshoot, as the sentencing judge could in the end ignore the
prosecution's request for leniency and sentence Rosse to the maximum
twenty years in prison.

Califano told Judge Ellen Bree Burns that if Rosse's case were to go to
trial, he would present evidence proving that Rosse had received shipments
of traveler's checks worth tens of thousands of dollars from Frankel's Swiss
bank and that Rosse had facilitated the purchase of $2 million worth of dia-
monds with stolen insurance funds.

Additionally, Califano told the judge:

The government would present evidence that Mr. Rosse, in the course of working, traveled between Connecticut and Tennessee couriering materials between Mr. Frankel and individuals associated with SCS trust. The government would also present evidence that Mr. Rosse opened several mailboxes for various shell entities to be run at 889 Lake Avenue in Greenwich, Connecticut, for Mr. Frankel, where Mr. Frankel's illegal operations were based.

The government would present evidence that Mr. Rosse opened certain mailboxes in New York City and in the New York subsections which were used for Liberty National Securities Incorporated. And the government would present evidence that Mr. Rosse established a number of phone lines for various shell companies that were part of the enterprise, phone lines that were based in New York City and elsewhere outside of Connecticut, and with the assistance of Mr. Rosse, forwarded to ring at 889 Lake Avenue, one of the bases of operation.

After mentioning the security arrangements Rosse implemented on his employer's behalf, as well as the airplane Frankel bought for Rosse for use in furthering the racketeering enterprise, Califano said he had proof that "Mr. Rosse allowed Mr. Frankel to use his name as an alias in the operation of a number of the shell entities involved in the enterprise."

In conclusion, the prosecutor said, "The government would produce additional evidence, Your Honor, but believes that should cover the bases for the plea in this case."

When asked by Judge Burns for an allocution of his crime, Rosse read from a prepared statement:

At a point in time, in approximately 1990, I learned that Mr. Frankel and others had maintained control of certain insurance companies. We were unlawfully obtaining cash from the insurance companies by way of wire transfers, and proceeds of these traveler's checks were used to fund Mr. Frankel's business operations to maintain his lifestyle and pay other members of my group, including me.

Among other things, I received a number of shipments from [UBS] in Switzerland and later learned that they contained traveler's checks. Upon receipt, I delivered the same to Mr. Frankel, which was used by Mr. Frankel to fund his operation, including me.

I also introduced Mr. Frankel to a diamond dealer and personally picked up a number of diamonds from this dealer and delivered them to Mr. Frankel. The source of these funds from these transactions were from the [UBS] account in Switzerland, the account where Mr. Frankel maintained the funds he fraudulently obtained from various insurance companies.

Rosse was released on $100,000 bond but within a month was jailed for an undisclosed violation of his cooperation agreement.

On December 23 thirty-four-year-old Karen Timmins pleaded guilty to one count of misprision of felony, that is, her concealment of Frankel's fraudulent scheme by knowing about it but failing to report it to authorities.

Taking her turn before Judge Burns, Timmins said, "In 1996 I began working for Martin Frankel, and sometime later on in my employment there, I became aware that he was using moneys that he obtained from insurance companies and putting the money in Switzerland and then bringing it back into the United States. At various points I did assist him in restoring—returning—some of the money to the United States."

As Rosse had done before her, Timmins waived indictment by entering her plea. Kari Dooley, the senior federal litigation counsel, told the judge:

Your Honor, the government's evidence would consist of the testimony of numerous law enforcement officers, to include forensic financial analysts and other special agents. It would include the testimony of lay witnesses from the various insurance companies in Tennessee as well as individuals who were employed at 889 Lake Avenue, Greenwich, Connecticut, and it would include a large volume of documents from various financial institutions as well as a volume of documents seized from 889 Lake Avenue in May of this year.

That evidence, Your Honor, when presented, would establish beyond a reasonable doubt that in approximately 1991, Martin Frankel and others formed an entity known as the Thunor Trust in

Tennessee. That trust was formed using nominee guarantors so as to conceal Mr. Frankel's role as the true controller of that trust. The trust was established to purchase the majority shares of a company known as Franklin American Corporation, which in turn owned Franklin American Life Insurance Company.

Franklin American Life Insurance Company, as an insurance company, is subject to the regulations to which insurance companies must adhere, and kept a certain amount of required liquid reserves, approximately $18 million. Those funds were required to be invested in safe and secure investments so that they're available as needed should policyholders make claims to the insurance company.

Around the same time, Martin Frankel also anonymously, through the use of nominees and aliases, controlled an entity known as Liberty National Securities, Inc. . . . Following the acquisition of Franklin American Life Insurance Company, Mr. Frankel caused the liquid assets and reserves of that company to be sent to Liberty National Securities for safe and secure investments. So he was essentially anonymously controlling the entity that owned the money and the entity that was supposed to be investing the money.

After those funds were received by Mr. Frankel and brought under his control, they were immediately liquidated and siphoned off and sent out of the country, where they were used to pay his personal debts as well as to pay for the costs of his ongoing operation. For the next seven and a half years, Your Honor, essentially the same procedure was followed:

Through Franklin American Corporation and another holding company that was acquired or established, additional insurance companies were purchased, additional liquid proceeds or reserves were brought under Mr. Frankel's control. He caused those liquid reserves to be sent, again, to Liberty National Securities, where they were converted, stolen. I should note that the funds were invariably sent to Liberty National Securities via interstate wire transfer.

After the funds were received from the various insurance companies, they were almost without exception sent to bank accounts in Switzerland. After the money was received in Switzerland, a large portion of it—not the majority of it, but a large amount—was converted into traveler's checks. Those traveler's checks were then sent back from Switzerland to Connecticut to 889 Lake Avenue. That is the address out of which Mr. Frankel operated all of these entities, where he had a number of employees and vendors that allowed him to do that, including employees to include the defendant.

Karen Timmins was hired by Mr. Frankel in 1996, approximately mid-1996, as an office assistant. It was among her job responsibilities to distribute the traveler's checks received from Switzerland to the various employees and vendors who provided services at 889 Lake Avenue. At some point in time after she became employed by Mr. Frankel, she learned that the insurance company moneys were being taken out of the country and into Switzerland and that it was these moneys that were being used to purchase the traveler's checks that were then coming back into the country.

After she learned this, Your Honor, she did not at that point go to law enforcement or a judge or any other authority recognized by this court as appropriate under the misprision of felony statute, and, indeed, she continued to perform her job responsibilities, which included handing out these traveler's checks, which were the proceeds of the money laundering, to the various employees and vendors. The government believes that that act assisted in the concealment of the money-laundering activities engaged in by Martin Frankel and others.

As of February 1, 2000, Rosse and Timmins were the only ones of Frankel's associates to have been charged in the conspiracy.

As for the other associates, with the boss in jail and his assets seized or frozen, what had once seemed to be an eternal money spigot had been abruptly shut off. This sent several of Frankel's former compatriots scrambling for ways to continue getting money without really working for it. Some of the women received thousands of dollars from newspapers and television programs for their stories. The news organizations got around the ethical issue of paying sources by telling the women the money was to buy rights to photographs, and that any interviews they gave would strictly be incidental.

Upon her return from Italy, Mona Kim filed a $4 million lawsuit against a doctor in Rockland County, New York, whom she had met through a personal ad in May 1997 while still working for Frankel. She alleged that the doctor had tortured her emotionally and physically by making her his sex slave during their two-year liaison.

Of Frankel's ex-girlfriends, Sonia Howe Radencovici and Kaethe Schuchter may have had the most to fear from prosecutors because they had known Frankel the longest and had been privy to his innermost secrets. Neither woman would speak publicly about their association with Frankel, referring all questions to their lawyers.

All of Frankel's remaining ex-girlfriends, assistants, and associates similarly retained legal counsel, as they continued to be questioned by federal investigators. Bob Biddle became engaged in a finger-pointing match with Rosse, with each man blaming the other for diamonds the U.S. government could not account for.

Some of Frankel's most important associates who had once granted limited and guarded interviews, including Tom Corbally and Father Jacobs, suddenly stopped making public comments right after Rosse and Timmins entered guilty pleas. Others who had never allowed themselves to be interviewed, such as attorneys Larry Martin and Tom Bolan, continued adhering to that legally safe policy.

Also facing massive legal bills and possible indictment was Frankel's Tennessee business partner, John Hackney. Unable to afford their upscale Franklin home anymore, the Hackneys moved to another house they had bought in 1998 with earnings from Frankel in Ann's hometown of Guntersville, Alabama. On February 2, 2000, the FBI seized the vacated Franklin house, alleging that the $515,000 Hackney used to buy the dwelling "was the proceeds of Martin R. Frankel's illegal activity," making the purchase a violation of the federal money-laundering statute.

Then the insurance commissioners in Mississippi, Oklahoma, and Arkansas filed suit to seize the Hackneys' Alabama house, alleging that the nearly $600,000 that had been used to buy and remodel it came from embezzled insurance assets.

Meanwhile in Franklin, six local couples and two preachers banded together to form the Hackney Family Fund. "We know that every dollar we can raise will mean a dollar they will have to take care of their family," the group said in a December 21, 1999, letter. Michael Saint, a public relations executive and one of three trustees in charge of the Hackney fund account at a local bank, said he and others stood firm behind their friend. He described

Hackney as a humble pillar of the community who served on a variety of boards and had manned phones for a suicide hotline. "I don't believe he would take a dime that he didn't believe belonged to him," Saint said.

Back in Greenwich, a land grab was on for Frankel's vacated estates. The FBI had already seized 889 Lake Avenue in May, based on its allegation that the property had served as headquarters for the criminal enterprise. Then liens were placed on Frankel's other property, at 895 Lake Avenue, as the result of $1 million and $2 million lawsuits filed by Rosse and Frankel's original Greenwich landlord, respectively. Rosse's claim, that his reputation was damaged because Frankel had misappropriated his name for his fraud schemes, became all but moot when he pled guilty to conspiracy.

The other lawsuit, by Cheryl Lacoff, alleged that she had been unable to rent her house at 881 Lake Avenue after Frankel moved out of it because he had trashed the inside. Lacoff won a $2 million judgment on her complaint that Frankel had caused hundreds of thousands of dollars' worth of damage through unauthorized alterations he made when converting the leased residence into office space. She then filed a motion to institute foreclosure proceedings so that the judgment in her favor could be satisfied.

The neighbors on the Lake Avenue cul-de-sac also sued, complaining that their multimillion-dollar property values had depreciated as a result of their former neighbor's notoriety and the hordes of reporters and television camera crews it attracted. One aggrieved neighbor had an assessment done that alleged the value of his $3.1 million estate had decreased to $2.5 million.

All claims on Frankel's property at 895 Lake Avenue were superseded by the IRS when, on September 10, it seized the property on charges it had been bought by Frankel with laundered money. Shortly thereafter the IRS recovered more than an additional $1 million when it seized thirty of the thirty-three vehicles in Frankel's fleet, including eleven Mercedes-Benzes, five BMWs, six SUVs, two Volvos, a Lexus, and a 1999 Cadillac limousine.

It had been expected that some heads among insurance regulators would roll for having allowed Frankel's criminal enterprise to flourish for years. One of the first casualties may have been Douglas Sizemore, who had been appointed as Tennessee insurance commissioner in 1994 and resigned from the post in October 1999. Although state insurance officials denied his resignation was linked to the Frankel fiasco, Sizemore stepped down amid intense criticism that he'd been slow to act on irregularities others within his department had noted concerning the investment practices of Thunor-controlled companies. Tennessee has an unusual law that requires insurance companies to put investments such as bonds in the physical custody of a bank, yet the Sizemore-led regulatory agency failed to act against Franklin American Life even though it had admitted in each of its annual statements from 1994 to 1997 that the bonds were being held not by a bank but by Liberty National Securities.

Meanwhile, lawsuits and accusations were flying all over the place down south as attempts were made to clean up the financial disaster Frankel had caused.

In one such action, Mississippi insurance commissioner George Dale was sued by his Virginia counterpart, Alfred Gross, in connection with the reinsurance deal between First National Life Insurance Company and Settlers Life Insurance Company in Virginia that had fattened Frankel's Swiss bank account by $44.8 million. Gross's suit stated that Settlers was left insolvent by $20 million as a result of the reinsurance deal, which should be invalidated because it had been made under fraudulent pretenses.

One positive outcome of the Frankel imbroglio might be insurance regulatory reforms. High on that list should be a system providing for the sharing of information among state insurance officials. For example, had regulators in Mississippi and Virginia known about the failed Capitol Life deal in Colorado—resulting from official scrutiny of the St. Francis of Assisi Foundation and its purported Vatican ties—they probably would not have signed off on the Settlers Life reinsurance deal.

Reforms should probably also include more stringent reporting requirements regarding the investment firms to whom insurance companies entrust their assets. When Commissioner Dale wanted to find out about Frankel's Liberty National Securities, it took him only a few phone calls to learn that the brokerage was a fraud.

With the likelihood that Frankel-related matters will tie up the civil and criminal courts for years to come, one cannot help but be amazed at how much havoc was wreaked by one insecure man from Toledo, Ohio. Whether or not Frankel was an actual genius, one thing is certainly clear: It was awfully easy for someone with above-average intelligence and a working knowledge of electronic financial transactions to steal hundreds of millions of dollars.

As George Dale said, "We used to have people come in with guns and rob banks. This may be the new sophisticated way to rob."

Perhaps Martin Frankel's undoing sounded a wake-up call. But more likely than not, another breed of white-collar criminals will come along selling the same snake oil and using yet other variations of the same primitive pyramid scheme to hoodwink hundreds of people around the globe. Robert Vesco did it. Twenty years after him, Martin Frankel did it too. The shortcomings of regulatory measures at the highest levels of the financial world continue to mean only one thing: A cunning thief will live to steal another day.

Index